D0546768

Witnessing and Testifying

Witnessing and Testifying

Black Women, Religion, and Civil Rights

Rosetta E. Ross

Fortress Press
Minneapolis

HOUSTON PUBLIC LIBRARY

R01284 79951

WITNESSING AND TESTIFYING
Black Women, Religion, and Civil Rights
Copyright © 2003 Augsburg Fortress. All rights reserved. Except for brief quotations in critical articles or reviews, no part of this book may be reproduced in any manner without prior written permission from the publisher. Write: Permissions, Augsburg Fortress, Box 1209, Minneapolis, MN 55440.

Cover photograph (1962) is copyright © Bruce Davidson, Magnum Photos, Inc. Used by permission.
Book design: Beth Wright

Scripture quotations are from the New Revised Standard Version Bible, copyright © 1989 by the Division of Christian Education of the National Council of the Churches of Christ in the USA, and are used by permission.

Library of Congress Cataloging-in-Publication Data

Ross, Rosetta E., date–
Witnessing and testifying : Black women, religion, and civil rights / Rosetta E. Ross.
p. cm.
Includes bibliographical references (p.) and index.
ISBN 0-8006-3603-1
1. African Americans—Religion. 2. African American women civil rights workers—Religious life—History—20th century. 3. Civil rights—Religious aspects—Christianity—History—20th century. 4. Civil rights—Religious aspects—Islam—History—20th century. 5. Civil rights—United States—History—20th century. 6. Womanist theology—History—20th century. I. Title.
BR563.N4R67 2003
323'.092'396073—dc21
2002155091

The paper used in this publication meets the minimum requirements of American National Standard for Information Sciences — Permanence of Paper for Printed Library Materials, ANSI Z329.48-1984.

Manufactured in the U.S.A.
07 06 05 04 03 1 2 3 4 5 6 7 8 9 10

In memory of
Bertha Lee Thomas Ross
and
Shawurn Lorenzo Ross

Contents

Photography Credits

A gallery of photographs can be found after page 162.

1. Ella Baker at a news conference on January 3, 1968. Photo copyright © AP/Wide World Photos. Used by permission.

2. Septima Poinsette Clark (right) with Rosa Parks at the Highlander Center (date unknown). Photo courtesy Highlander Center. Used by permission.

3. Fannie Lou Hamer (front row, left) and Ella Baker (front row, right), along with other Mississippi Freedom Democratic Party delegates, sing at a rally on the Boardwalk in Atlantic City, New Jersey (August 10, 1964). Photo copyright © 1976 George Ballis/Take Stock (San Rafael, California). Used by permission.

4. Fannie Lou Hamer marches in a voter registration demonstration outside Forest County Courthouse, Hattiesburg, Mississippi; the hand-lettered sign reads: "Freedom Now, SNCC" (January 22, 1964). Photo copyright © 1976 Matt Herron/Take Stock (San Rafael, California). Used by permission.

5. Victoria Way DeLee (circa 1971). Photo courtesy *The State* newspaper of Columbia, South Carolina. Used by permission.

6. Clara Muhammad with her husband, Elijah (center), at a Nation of Islam conference (date unknown). Photo copyright © AP/Wide World Photos. Used by permission.

7. Ruby Doris Smith (center), Mary Ann Smith (second from right), and Diane Nash (far right) with two other students, sing together at the Atlanta airport after their return from serving thirty-day jail sentences in South Carolina (clipping from *The Atlanta Inquirer,* March 18, 1961). Photo and original caption courtesy *The Atlanta Inquirer*. Used by permission.

Acknowledgments

I was introduced to the Civil Rights Movement as a little girl. Some memories of the time are vivid: the uncertainty that was palpable one morning as my parents, Thomas and Bertha Ross, prepared to go into voting booths for the first time; the pride and trepidation of my father when he was elected one of the first Black local Democratic Party precinct officers; the night Daddy came home telling us he drove through our town into another one because he was certain someone followed him as he left a civil rights meeting; the energy, excitement, and hope in the meetings at Bethel African Methodist Episcopal Church in Ridgeville or "the old school" in St. George, South Carolina; the charisma and enthusiasm with which Mrs. Victoria DeLee—"our" Civil Rights leader—participated in, and often led, the meetings. My parents, Mrs. DeLee, and other adult participants in civil rights activities across rural Dorchester County helped me understand that something important was happening. At the same time, by their examples, they taught me the meaning of what I now call living their faith. In addition to being Civil Rights Movement workers, they all were active church members and concerned community participants.

Although other men like my father were prominent in civil rights activities of our area, it was women who sustained the Dorchester County movement in significant ways. Mrs. Victoria DeLee led the movement, and neighbors and friends like Mrs. Geneva Tracy, Mrs. Cora Lee DeLee, my mother, and others supported her. I am grateful to these women and men in Dorchester County, South Carolina, and those like them across the South and the country, who tried to help our nation live up to its creeds. Seeing their work in my own community helped prompt my interest in religious ethics.

Other persons and institutions helped make completion of this project possible. I am thankful for opportunities to teach courses on Black women in the Civil Rights Movement at the Interdenominational Theological Center (ITC) in Atlanta and United Theological Seminary (UTS) of Minnesota as I worked through some ideas and materials for this book. I am also thankful for support from the ITC faculty during my first semester of teaching, when I received a reduced load and was permitted to develop a course from my dissertation. A sabbatical from teaching at UTS, a Small Faculty Grant from the Association of Theological Schools, and a residency at the Institute for Ecumenical and Cultural Research of St. John's University in Collegeville, Minnesota, all supported travel, research, and writing for this project.

I am grateful to the staff of the South Caroliniana Collection at the University of South Carolina; Special Collections at the College of Charleston Libraries, Charleston, South Carolina; the Robert W. Woodruff Library of the Atlanta University Center, particularly Special Collections, and Ms. Budhwanti Masih and Ms. Stephanie Bernard of the Cataloging Department; the Southern Oral History Program, the University of North Carolina at Chapel Hill; Ms. Ida E. Jones and the Moorland Spingarn Research Center at Howard University; the Schomberg Center for Research in Black Culture; the University of Southern Mississippi Center for Oral History and Cultural Heritage; and the Microfilm Archives, Wilson Library, the University of Minnesota. Finally, I am especially thankful to my husband, Ronald Bonner, whose patience, encouragement, and support witness to me in so many ways.

Preface

Religion and religious institutions have pervaded the lives of Black people as long as they have lived in the United States. This is particularly true for Black women. Moreover, the predominant need to focus on physical and emotional survival for well over 250 years was a most powerful component in the matrix of circumstances out of which Black religion in the United States evolved. A full exploration of African American women's civil rights activism, therefore, should include analysis of their religious consciousness (particularly, *but not only,* their Black Christian consciousness) and its relationship to motivations that foster ordinary and superlative practices by many Black women activists. In addition, we must note the role of racial oppression in shaping various expressions of Black religion as well as the experience of Black people in America.

Because of the racism historically inherent in American society, many scholars argue that there never was nor ever could have been a Black religion of the pre-Civil Rights Era that focused solely on other-worldly ends. Theological and, by consequence, religious knowing among African Americans has pragmatic origins, embedded in a predecessor African spirituality but related directly to this prominent need to attend to survival concerns related to racial oppression. Moreover, the primary need to focus on racial advancement always developed alongside the collateral need to address formal and informal social policies and conventions that engendered racial oppression.

As an exploration of religious moral practice, this book argues that Black women's civil rights activism is their female enactment of Black religious values that reflected an internal concern for the Black community's survival and flourishing and a related external concern to address society's formal and conventional sources of inequality.

The core of the book focuses on the lives of seven Black religious women who were civil rights activists—Ella Baker, Septima Clark, Fannie Lou Hamer, Victoria DeLee, Clara Muhammad, Diane Nash, and Ruby Doris Smith Robinson. Six were Christian, and one was Muslim. Although they came from different life circumstances and contributed in different ways, these women had several things in common. They were all deeply influenced by some elder or elders and by traditions of faith in their early lives. They all maintained deep connections to their communities through community work motivated by religious traditions. Each of these women sought to make our society better. Because they became leaders in their communities and the nation, these seven women were exemplary. At the same time, however, narratives of their early lives, norms and values motivating their activism, and their desire to improve life for both African Americans and the larger society demonstrate similarities not only to one another but also to tens of thousands of other women whose civil rights or other community activism emerged from comparable life contexts, were motivated by related values, or sought comparable ends.

Sometimes the absence of lively engagement by faithful people in public life results from the absence of moral exemplars. It may be that the accounts included here will remind us of, encourage, and even inspire responsible moral practice for the common good and based in faith.

1

Religion and Public Life

Early Traditions of Black Religious Women's Activism

> In stories about the civil rights movement you hear mostly about the black ministers. But if you talk to the women who were there, you'll hear another story. I think the civil rights movement would never have taken off if some women hadn't started to speak up. A lot more are just getting to the place now where they can speak out.
>
> —Septima Poinsette Clark

Black religious women in the Civil Rights Movement embraced a worldview that held racial uplift and social responsibility as central to the value and meaning of religious life. Their practice within the Movement was continuous with this concept of religious duty that pervaded earlier traditions of Black women's religious activism.

Clearly Black religious institutions and Black persons with religious self-understanding played central parts in the movement that sought to expand inclusion and participation of African Americans in U.S. social life. Since the United States segregated and excluded African Americans well into the twentieth century, the role of Black religious institutions as buffers against the cruelties of racism was particularly significant before and during the Civil Rights Era. At that time, Black religious structures continued their antebellum tradition of affirming humanity and providing opportunities to participate in society for descendants of former slaves, who held U.S. citizenship *de jure* but often were excluded from full exercise of that citizenship.[1]

Ironically, civil rights literature often recognizes the moral import of the Civil Rights Movement's achievements but neglects to explore substantial relationships among religious motivations, civil rights participation, and the subsequent social and moral changes.[2] Major studies of the Civil Rights Era often discuss the function of Black religious institutions, especially churches, in the Civil Rights Movement, stressing religious institutions' roles in shaping Martin Luther King Jr.'s identity and self-understanding. Typically these studies focus predominantly or exclusively on male elites, especially Black ministers. Substantive studies of women's civil rights activism have only very recently begun to appear in representative numbers.[3] Studies of the Civil Rights Movement that *have* treated religious self-understanding do not examine the role of an African American religious worldview and gendered, particularly Black women's, interaction with Black religious traditions and institutions and with U.S. social life.[4]

Working for Survival and Liberation: Racial Uplift and Social Responsibility

Perhaps the most potent aspect of an African American religious worldview is the understanding that religious duty includes racial uplift and social responsibility, two foci that derive from, respectively, survival and liberation themes of Black religion.[5] The earliest independent religious movements among Africans in America reflect survival themes. Emanating from traditional African religious affirmation of life as God's gift, survival themes assert that religion and religious practice should help sustain and enhance life. Liberation themes in Black religion derive from the context of the slave society in which African American Christianity originated and from the necessity to emphasize life as God's gift that includes freedom to flourish fully as human beings. Generally, a major theological emphasis of slave religion opposed both enslavement and the view of slaveholding religion that God ordained human bondage.[6] Developing from and alongside survival themes, liberation themes—often called *freedom concerns*—reflect the consequence of affirming God's gift of life, and entail discourse and practices for social change. Liberation themes in Black religion have implications for the entire society, since discourses and practices opposing slavery focused on a public realm that formally and conventionally prevented flourishing of Black persons as human beings.[7]

While racial uplift and social responsibility are distinguishable categories of an African American religious worldview, they also are an interdependent aspect of this worldview, one often permeating the other. The concept of *racial uplift* names the perspectives and practices of African Americans that primarily attend to survival and have implications for liberation. One version of racial uplift is the post-Reconstruction ideology of an aspiring Black middle class, which believed that to convince white America of its respectability, it must encourage Victorian morality and middle-class values among the Black masses through social and moral work to uplift themselves and the race. Since this ideology originated to refute and oppose racism, the concept of racial uplift was not simple capitulation to judgments of white American racism. Moreover, it yielded significant progress for African Americans as the small Black middle class regularly engaged in activities to improve the lives of the Black masses. In the ideology of uplift, however, based on arguments about behaviors of African Americans to the exclusion of social structural analysis, as Kevin Gaines writes, "the Black intelligentsia replicated the dehumanizing logic of racism."[8]

Another, more democratic version of uplift refers to activities by legions of parents, educators, businesspersons, ministers, artists, and other professionals and nonprofessionals "as community builders" seeking to realize a more inclusive vision of group advancement. This more popular conception of uplift (reflecting practices of many persons across social locations to ameliorate all features of Black life) contrasts with the nineteenth-century middle-class ideology and is "rooted in public education, economic rights, group resistance and struggle, and democracy."[9] Practices of racial uplift pervaded the earliest development of independent Black churches[10] and, reflecting the continuing concern of the majority of Black communities for survival and forward progress, persisted and remain vital in many ordinary religious structures of African American life today.[11] In this account of popular practices, racial uplift includes the desire and striving of African Americans to survive slavery, gain independence, develop self-sufficiency and well-being, and engage as full participants in the body politic. Its specific historic manifestations represent throughout Black religious traditions practices for survival and racial progress, or what Fannie Lou Hamer called "keeping on down the freedom road."

Throughout Black religious life, racial uplift practices, including survival concerns, were not ends in themselves, as progress and "keeping on" suggest. Uplift activity is part of the continuum of African Americans' living out the movement toward freedom. Because complete freedom for African Americans always has implications for moral, social, and political life of the entire society, conventional racial uplift practices relate directly to social responsibility motifs in Black religion.

While the norm of racial uplift attends to ensuring life and human flourishing, the norm of social responsibility, always alongside and continuous with racial uplift, seeks to ensure that African Americans, as full members of society, are able to realize God's gift of life. Sociologist and former Student Nonviolent Coordinating Committee (SNCC) worker Joyce Ladner identifies Black women's social responsibility as originating in practices of Black forebears to sustain and improve African American life. Citing Black women activists from Harriet Tubman and Sojourner Truth to Ella Baker, Ruby Doris Smith Robinson, and Mother Clara Hale, Ladner writes that Black women's social responsibility derives from "the generations of our foremothers and forefathers" who participated in and passed on this "sense of mission and sense of history." Ladner continues:

> All around us the idea was hammered into our heads that social responsibility was a normal part of life—it was not something that was tucked off to the side as a special volunteer activity. It was part of the way you defined your identity, your sense of purpose, your values, your reason for being. Our religious upbringing reinforced this concept of obligation, this sense of helping the needy, giving something back to the community, or in the words of my mother, "earning your space in the world."

The "obligation" to contribute to improving social life as "earning your space in the world" originated in response to the particular circumstances of African Americans. Black women understand this value as responsibility, Ladner writes, to "assure progress for the race . . . through the dint of their own efforts." The obligation does not stop with the needs of Black communities, however. As a moral value, the social responsibility of Black women, she writes, is "the idea and value that it is our duty to help those in need." Fulfilling this responsibility means determining the appropriate and necessary response to social needs. "They were taught that they had to learn to be flexible," Ladner writes; "they had to learn to wash, cook, sew, get an education, raise children, work in their churches and clubs, establish orphanages, relief societies, become presidents of colleges, start colleges, and everything else that needed to be done" to improve human life.[12] This means, of course, that religious duty includes responsibility for social structures, since social context significantly influences the meaning and experience of being human. An obvious relationship of social responsibility to racial uplift is the obligation to attend to racial justice, the absence of which hinders or completely obstructs progress toward African American freedom. The more full conception of social responsibility in an African American religious worldview is what Peter Paris calls the "quest for human freedom and justice, that is, the equality of all persons under God."[13] Social responsibility motifs in Black religion assert that moral goodness includes racial justice, but ultimately relates to universal human flourishing.

Womanist Theology and "Keeping on Down the Freedom Road"

From the period of slavery through modern times, many Black religious women in the United States practiced racial uplift and social responsibility as a means of fulfilling what they understood as their duty to God. In the mid-nineteenth century, Sojourner Truth felt called by God to escape bondage, speak against slavery, agitate for women's rights, and variously support emancipated slaves. Immediately after emancipation, many educated Black women felt "a strong conviction of duty" to go South to teach newly freed persons. Around the turn of the century, Nannie Helen Burroughs and the National Baptist Convention's Women's Convention felt it was their duty to link racial advancement with spiritual and social regeneration. During the U.S. Civil Rights Era, religious Black women were leaders and followers in various crusades to increase racial justice in society.[14]

Recently, Black women scholars have begun to theorize Black women's religious perspectives and practices. Teaching and writing in the fields of theology, religious ethics, Bible, sociology of religion, and ministry practice, these scholars use the term *womanist* (coined by novelist, poet, and essayist Alice Walker)[15] to identify their work of retrieving, interpreting, and theorizing. Womanist theology engages Black women's religiosity with other theological discourse and religious interpretation. "Through the work of womanist theologians and ethicists," Delores Williams writes, "the Christian community is discovering the theological import of liberation activity of some leading nineteenth-century African American women."[16] In their work, four first-generation womanist scholars—Katie Geneva Cannon, Delores S. Williams, Jacquelyn Grant, and Cheryl Townsend Gilkes—explore ordinary Black women's activities for survival and community progress as practices that coincide primarily with the generalized racial uplift stream in Black religion. These scholars argue that Black women's activities, attending especially to overcoming racial impediments to African American well-being, reflect virtues attendant to survival and well-being, practices to ensure survival and general well-being, attention to "the least" in their communities, and community-building/community-sustaining activities.

Beginning with the social context of Black people as oppressed persons in the United States, these womanist theologians explore how survival themes or racial uplift practices dominate Black religious women's thought and activities. While they establish that survival themes and racial uplift practices predominate in Christian Black women's historic activism, womanist theologians also demonstrate the relationship of survival and racial uplift to liberation themes and social responsibility. According to womanist theologians, Black religious women's traditions of combating and overcoming devastations of chattel slavery and its legacies provide the foundation and means of moving from survival to full social participation and social responsibility (or moving fully toward freedom).

Virtues Attendant to Survival and Well-Being

Social ethicist Katie Geneva Cannon identifies concern for physical and emotional well-being as central to Black women's moral reasoning. Cannon explains that African American women's determinations about right or wrong and good or bad derive from "various coping mechanisms related to their own cultural circumstances."

Because their reality includes a struggle against white supremacy in an exploited and oppressed world, Black women have "regarded survival against tyrannical systems of oppression as the true sphere of moral life."[17] Cannon explores the ways Black women have determined the actions that sustain life in their contexts and how they have developed practices accordingly. The result of Black women's historical efforts is the cultivation of three virtues—invisible dignity, quiet grace, and unshouted courage—that, Cannon says, characterize activities through which Black women determine the means to survive. Invisible dignity includes "functional prudence," discerning how and to what extent to confront threats to survival, and "unctuousness," maintaining a "feistiness about life" in face of such pervasive threats. The former attends to preserving life, while the latter relates to living and participating fully in what life offers. Cannon identifies *functional prudence* as early twentieth-century Black elders' attempts to induce compliance and docility in strong-willed children. These elders, she says, sought to inculcate character traits necessary to determine appropriate responses to threats of physical and emotional violence in retaliation for having "too much spirit" or expressing too much familiarity toward whites.[18] At the same time, elders also encouraged self-affirmation and self-assertion through *unctuousness,* exhorting children to "jump at de sun," to "strive continually for individuality and self-expression," and to avoid having a "squinched spirit" by the time of adulthood.[19] Unlike functional prudence, Cannon says, unctuousness expresses knowledge of "how to grasp the positive side of life amidst a system of brutalization."[20]

The other two virtues that Cannon explicates, *quiet grace* and *unshouted courage,* identify Black women's expression of what traditionally are designated as *fidelity* and *fortitude.* Quiet grace is the persistent struggle for human dignity in defiance of degrading oppression.[21] In the context of racial oppression—contrasted with the normative expectation of unbridled individual freedom—faithfulness means persevering in efforts to ensure physical and emotional well-being while encountering incessant practices specifically opposed to that well-being. Unshouted courage is the capacity to constantly confront threats to survival in the face of reprisals for one's determination to survive.[22] In the context of the struggle against white supremacy, fortitude for Black women includes confronting first-order racial violence that opposes Black life and second-order racial violence as retribution for opposing first-order violence. Coincident with identifying this practice of and passing on virtues for survival, Cannon also analyzes and challenges prevailing traditions of patriarchy in Black churches, especially in preaching. While Black preaching opposes power relations of the larger society, it also marginalizes and oppresses women, Cannon says. She argues that the task of womanist theology includes "unmasking" the patriarchy of Black religious traditions while "disentangling" affirmation for Black women found there.[23]

Practice to Ensure "Survival/Quality of Life"

Delores Williams explicates survival themes in Black religion by construing Hagar, a character in the Old Testament, as a paradigm of Black women's commonplace use of practical wisdom to live. Comparing circumstances of African Americans to those of the servant Hagar, whose masters sent her with her child into the wilderness to make a way for herself,[24] Williams calls the normal life conditions of African Americans a wilderness context. Privileging practices of everyday Black folk culture, Williams asserts, the Black community's faith emerges amid experiences of oppressed men and women in the wilderness. "'Wilderness' or 'wilderness-experience,'" she says, "is a symbolic term used to represent a near-destruction situation in which God gives personal directions to the believer and thereby helps her make a way out of what she thought was no way."[25] Through practice of folk culture in the "wilderness," traditions arise that reflect hope based in divine promise[26] and that determine life-affirming practices wherein God works through the community "in behalf of the survival, liberation and positive quality of life of suffering people."[27] Williams calls these traditions survival/quality-of-life practices.

For Black women, she says, the wilderness context includes surrogacy or loss of control over their bodies in the larger society,[28] and oppression within Black denominational churches. Like Hagar, many Black women served as sexual and labor surrogates for others. This included coerced surrogacy during slavery and voluntary (though pressured) surrogacy during the postbellum period. And just as Cannon calls attention to the duality of Black preaching, Williams claims that while Black churches "sustain Black women emotionally and provide 'theological space'" for their expressions of faith, Black churches also "suppress and help make invisible Black women's thought and culture."[29] With other African Americans, Black women exercise survival/quality-of-life practice for African American communities, but Black women also attend to their female experience of the wilderness context. While survival/quality-of-life practices focus on survival and quality-of-life concerns, Williams identifies liberation as their final goal. For Williams, the priority of liberation practice is mediated by survival considerations. Although the servant Hagar is "free" once slavemaster and slavemistress Abraham and Sarah expel her, the meaning and value of her freedom is severely attenuated by the immediacy of survival concerns and the absence of recognition and participation in social community for which existence is basic. "Liberation is an ultimate," Williams writes, "but in the meantime survival and prosperity must be the experience of our people."[30]

Attending to "the Least" in the Community

Jacquelyn Grant presents theological hope as a basis for survival strategies by interpreting the biblical category "the least" as a metaphor for Black women's social situation. Including racial, gender, and economic oppression, she says Black women's social condition in far too many instances involves relegation to the class of servants in society and churches. Grant says the broad context of Black women's experience of race oppression is the continuing dominant and subordinate social relationship of white and Black persons.[31] Black women experience gender oppression through the larger society's subordination of women and through sexism in Black communities, particularly within Black churches, which often intensify women's diminished social status by relegating Black women to the background through celebration of their "backbone" service.[32] For Black women, racial and gender discrimination intersect to produce economic oppression and situate Black women disproportionately within poor and working classes. Taken together, racial, gender, and economic oppression interrelate to place many Black women among the least advantaged groups in society. "The notion of 'the least,'" Grant says, "descriptively locates the conditions of Black women."[33]

Situated as the least, Black women derive hope from the focus in Black Christianity on the life of Jesus, who, though born in a stable and died on a cross, overcame through resurrection. Relating their circumstances to those of Jesus, Grant says, Black women reinterpret their situation not as the end but as the context in which they struggle to experience hope and liberation. Through hope, Black women develop "survival strategies in spite of race and class oppression"[34] and affirm themselves in spite of gender oppression.[35] Since Jesus identified with and gave special regard to the least, Grant says, Black religious institutions are called to attend particularly to Black women, and in the wider Christian community attention to the least is a primary measure of authenticity in theological formulations and religious practices.

Community-Building/Community-Sustaining Practice

Cheryl Townsend Gilkes, a sociologist of religion, explores Black women's work for the least through formal and informal vocations as community workers. "Community work," Gilkes writes, is "a wide range of diverse tasks performed to confront and challenge racism as a total system" and is executed as "women's activities to combat racism and empower their communities to survive, grow, and advance in a hostile society." Asserting that Black women's community work arises not only in response to racism but also as ordinary practice of persons within the context of segregated communities, Gilkes says, like other communities, Black communities develop norms, cultures, and social structures of their own. "Community work is focused on internal growth and external challenge and creates ideas enabling people to think about change."[36] In everyday life of Black communities and in response to racism, Black women determine and maintain traditions integral to survival and enhancing the welfare of African Americans. Community workers perform a range of activities that derive their character from the specific nature of problems confronting African Americans. Community work includes "arguing, obstructing, organizing, teaching, lecturing, demonstrating, suing, writing letters," and other activities, often concluding as organized actions or programs.

Within Black communities, community workers often organize and coordinate work of religious institutions crucial to building and sustaining Black community life. In religious institutions they develop education programs that support general literacy, biblical literacy, and post-secondary achievements, and coordinate outreach programs that attend to family and social concerns of Black communities.[37] Alongside religious institutions community workers found para-religious organizations that attend to poverty, homelessness, education, political participation, and other community interests.[38] Although they wield moral authority and have social prestige because of their tenure, accomplishments, and status, Gilkes says, community workers have less access to power in Black religious institutions than in broader Black communities or the larger society. In Black religious institutions their work often is identified with or overshadowed by male leaders, and in spite of their functions in religious institutions, community workers encounter "unyielding male authority" and "ideological and theological ambivalence" about women's roles.

In the larger society, community workers identify with African Americans, to whom they relate as peers, friends, and relatives, and view problems of Black communities as issues of group survival caused by systems hostile to their lives. Formal community workers with institutional roles and responsibilities often "move up in the opportunity structure primarily to change the society and the quality of life for Black people."[39] Sometimes they are at odds with professional patterns and create ruptures to act in behalf of African Americans.[40] At times, because of their influence within Black communities, political actors in the larger society seek them out for counsel or other assistance.[41] In Black communities and in the larger society, they focus especially on conditions of the most marginalized. Correlating with Grant's focus on attention to the least, Gilkes says community workers presume that in being "responsive to the most oppressed and deprived, they [are] responsive to everyone."[42] Their work, she says, "is the effort to make things better and to eliminate the problems and structures that make life difficult."[43]

Through their focus on Black religious women's practices in the everyday world of African Americans, these womanist theologians assert mundane existence as the place of encountering and responding to God. They present four themes of responsibility among Black religious women: (1) responsibility to practice and pass on particular virtues that attend to surviving and thriving as persons, (2) responsibility to work in partnership with God for community survival and positive quality of life, (3) responsibility to attend needs of the least, and (4) responsibility to participate in community-building and community-sustaining practices. In conjunction with these themes of responsibility, womanist theology identifies and interrogates traditions within Black communities and especially Black religious institutions that impede Black women's well-being. Womanist racial uplift practices, then, respond to the needs of Black communities, including attending to what Williams calls "woman-inclusive wilderness experience,"[44] challenging what Cannon calls "the givens of patriarchal consensus"[45] of Black religious institutions, and overcoming what Gilkes calls "unyielding male authority"[46] and what Grant identifies as "treat[ment] of Black women as . . . invisible creatures . . . outside . . . the Black experience."[47]

Departing from sharp distinctions between survival and liberation, womanist theologians advance a broader meaning for survival as both preserving life and determining ways for living life fully. Cannon, for example, explicates womanist virtues as attending both to survival and to "grasp[ing] the positive side of life." Williams insists that Black women's practices include "survival" *and* "quality-of-life" concerns. Likewise, Grant and Gilkes call attention to self-affirmation and social change in addition to survival considerations. In the tradition of Black religion that affirms God's intention for life as living (not merely existing, but always moving toward the "more" that God offers), religious duty means surviving, opposing, and overcoming realities that impede living fully. In this regard, womanist theology asserts that in the ordinary processes of living and moving on down the freedom road, practices for social change and liberation emerge. This does not mean Black religious women capitulate to gradualism, especially since their ordinary practices often depart radically from prevailing norms. But this radical departure occurs within the tradition of ordinary response to God by giving regular attention to surviving and enhancing the quality of life.

The assertion of continuity of survival and liberation (of racial uplift and social responsibility practices) is an important contribution of womanist theorizing to continuing exploration of Black religion. By exploring Black women's religious practices in everyday life, womanist theologians identify aesthetic and preconceptual religious values and ideas commonly communicated through routine activities (like singing, dancing, and working). In this way Black women respond to God in their ordinary activity, which involves attending to community members' physical and emotional well-being. By calling attention to survival concerns and identifying ordinary virtues and values, womanist theology helps to give a more complete picture of the meaning of religion in African American life, providing a contrast to the general tendency to characterize Black religion as contributing either to social justice or to conservation of oppressive traditions. In its identification of specific indigenous practices for survival and liberation as religious activity, womanist theology opens the way for evaluating a host of other functions of religion in Black communities, including, but certainly not limited to, its role in ordering and legitimating ordinary social interaction. This enhances opportunities for future studies to explore Black religion's dynamic and often ambiguous nature, characteristics all religions share.

Witnessing and Testifying

Womanist scholars present what may be called a "ritualized" understanding of Black religious women's persistent work to preserve and enhance Black life every day. This assertion of the "ritualized mundane" coincides with traditions of scholarship asserting the everyday world as sacred in an African worldview.[48] Moreover, the "ritualized mundane" concurs with two practices in African American religious life, "testifying" and "witnessing," which also cast everyday life as sacred by asserting divine intervention in ordinary circumstances. Rooted in accounts of slaves and ex-slaves after conversion experiences, testimonies in African American religion are verbal affirmations of belief and narratives of divine interaction with ordinary life. "In testimony, people speak truthfully about what they have experienced and seen, offering it to the community for edification of all," theologian Thomas Hoyt writes. "In testimony, a believer describes what God has done in her life, in words both biblical and personal, and the hands of her friends clap in affirmation. Her individual speech thus becomes part of an affirmation that is shared."[49] Most slave testimonies told of God's work in creating a new self, affirming the humanity of and even superseding the condition of the physically enslaved testifier.[50] As affirmation of the testifier's humanity, in opposition to the social status of a slave and in opposition to the institution of slavery, slave testimonies also were refutations of the state of the testifier and arguments against the institution. For slaves, to testify was both an acknowledgment of God's work and the act of refuting the circumstance of bondage. Concurring with this, Hoyt says, testimony is "public speech that is honest and empowering." Testimonies "keep alive the truth—a truth that society often does not honor."[51] As the practice evolved in Black religious traditions, *testimony* grew to mean articulating some account of God's interaction with one's life. Continuing in some contemporary Black American religious traditions, *testifying* occurs both as interpersonal narration of divine interaction with everyday life and as a formal portion of worship wherein believers share in community what God has done in their lives. This includes expressions of praise and descriptions of deliverance. "The testimony of ordinary persons in Sunday morning worship and weeknight prayer meetings," Hoyt writes,

> is characteristic of worship in the "free church" tradition, where services are relatively informal and expressive. One classic praise testimony, popular in the contemporary Black Church, goes something like this: "Thank you, God, for waking me up this morning; for putting shoes on my feet, clothes on my back, and food on my table. Thank you, God, for health and strength and the activities of my limbs. Thank you that I awoke this morning clothed in my right mind."[52]

In addition to the praise testimony, the evolved form of testimony often continues the pattern of slave testimonies, including two parts. The first part identifies a deficit, problem, or difficult situation. The second part tells of God's work in overcoming it.

Testimonies require the presence of witnesses, persons who also have seen or experienced God's work and who are able to certify or attest to the truth of it in the testimonies they hear. By identifying oneself as a witness, a believer asserts that she has personally experienced God's provision or other intervention. Moreover, emerging from some traditions in early Christianity and developing along with the Black religious practice of testifying, the term *witnessing* has arisen as a complementary way of naming the believer's ordinary moral practice—way of living—as religious practice. In Black religious traditions, testifying is telling stories of divine intervention (often in a worship service) through speech, while witnessing is attesting to faith in the divine by living in expectation of divine intervention and experiencing God in everyday life. To say "I am a witness" may indicate at once God's fulfillment of an expectation and one's encounter with God in daily life. In general, witnessing occurs in everyday life as believers assert through everyday practices interaction with the divine and an expectation of divine presence, including, as Delores Williams writes, anticipation of God's making a way.

Witnessing and testifying both anticipate a response from persons, frequently functioning to encourage others to act or to persevere. In Black religious communities, witnessing and testifying often are equally as important as canonized texts and inherited rituals and doctrines, and in some cases they supersede these formal traditions in bearing religious value and meaning and in mediating interaction with the holy. Although distinctions between witnessing and testifying remain, sometimes the two terms are used interchangeably, especially when applied to everyday life. "A quiet act of compassion can sometimes testify . . . powerfully to God's presence," Hoyt writes, as "persons reach out to others in trust and care," bearing "witness to God's presence before the world."[53] As moral practice, the significance of witnessing and testifying (like other resources from religious communities) lies in the possibility and hope these practices bring to common civic life. Witness and testimony are means of embodying and practicing particular virtues. Witness and testimony carry religious values and practices into the public square, and identify and pass on values that help form other individuals as religious persons. To the extent that Black religious women activists affirm and talk with others about divine interaction with their racial uplift and social responsibility activities, including the assertion that God requires or enables their activism, they are participating in the Black religious practices of witnessing and testifying.

Sojourner Truth:
A Black Religious Woman's Antebellum Activism

The extent to which race interacts with religious self-understanding of African American women is, perhaps, nowhere more evident than in the life of Sojourner Truth (a.k.a. Isabella Baumfree and Isabella Van Wagener). Born in bondage in Ulster County, New York, where she remained enslaved well into adulthood, Truth spent few of her formative years among large Black populations, where many African American religious traditions emerged. Yet when Truth herself told the story of her life, she included interpretations of divine intervention related to ameliorating or completely overcoming her status as a slave. In this regard Truth is one of the earliest, and perhaps a paradigmatic example of, religious Black women activists.

Escaping slavery around 1826, then changing her name and setting out as an itinerant preacher in 1843, Sojourner Truth is likely the most well known Black religious woman activist of the antebellum period. Her social and political analysis reflected religious perspectives she articulated throughout her life. Truth was an abolitionist and an advocate for women's rights and frequented the lecture circuit in support of these causes. After the Civil War, Truth spent time in Washington and Northern Virginia assisting newly freed persons in determining how to survive and establish normal lives. Truth persisted as an influential advocate for African Americans and for all women's suffrage throughout her life.

Social and Religious Influences in Truth's Early Life

Born to slave parents James and Elizabeth in Ulster County, New York, around 1797, Truth was named Isabella and took the family name of the last persons to whom she was legally bound, Isaac and Maria Van Wagener.[54] Isabella was separated from her parents through her (and her brother Peter's) sale at age nine when the family's owner, Dutch slaver Charles Ardinburg, died. Approximately ten siblings had preceded her in this fate. Her earliest memories of religious instruction are of her mother crying about children who had been sold and telling Isabella and Peter of a God who could protect them from the same future. In addition to this teaching of God's providence, Truth said her mother taught her to pray, including the Lord's Prayer, and to be honest.[55] Shortly after Isabella's sale, her mother died. Still, Isabella's beliefs about God's providence persisted throughout her life. For example, she looked for divine provision through her father (whom she only saw twice after Elizabeth's death) when abusive owners, the Nealys, repeatedly whipped her because she could only speak Dutch. Reflecting her belief in divine interaction with everyday life, "she began to beg God most earnestly to send her father to her, and as soon as she commenced to pray, she began as confidently to look for his coming, and, ere it was long, to her great joy, he came. . . . [She] unburdened her heart to him, inquiring if he could not do something to get her a new and better place." In her narrative told years later, Truth declared God as the provider of relief when her father James arranged for her to be sold to a man named Scrivner.[56] About a year later Scrivner sold Isabella to the John J. Dumont family, where she stayed for approximately sixteen years. In the course of that time, she married fellow slave Thomas and bore five children, all of whom were also enslaved and taken away from her.[57]

Isabella decided to escape to freedom in late 1826 (six months before the state of New York emancipated enslaved persons), assuming God would direct her. She prayed for guidance and left one morning before daybreak. Although she had no legal standing to do so, Isabella took her infant daughter, who was also a slave. She found shelter in the home of the Van Wageners, who paid twenty-five dollars for Isabella and her daughter and treated her as a near equal.[58] Isabella's reliance on divine rescue persisted, and a short time later, she said she expected God's help when her son (also named Peter) was sold to slavers in Alabama. After learning of Peter's sale, Isabella went to the home of the persons who held him. Although they discouraged her, she responded in "tones of deep determination—'*I'll have my child again*.' 'Have *your child* again!' repeated her mistress [*sic*]. . . . 'How can you get him? And what have you to support him with, if you could? Have you any money?' 'No,' answered [Isabella], 'I have no money, but God has enough, or what's better! And I'll have my child again.'" Literally expecting God to make a way in spite of her lack of resources and influence, Truth said later, "I was sure God would help me to get him." After some maneuvering, which included entering a complaint with the grand jury, seeking assistance from Quakers, raising funds, and hiring an attorney, Isabella prevailed, and Peter was returned to her custody.[59]

While living with the Van Wageners, Isabella, whose religious sensibility was syncretic, moved toward Methodism. With the Methodists she practiced "holiness," including simple living, abstaining from alcohol, and avoiding anger. During this period, she had a conversion experience in which she said she became aware of God's presence everywhere. In her *Narrative*, Truth wrote: "God revealed himself to her, with all the suddenness of a flash of lightning, showing her 'in the twinkling of an eye that he was *all over*'—that he pervaded the universe—'and that there was no place where God was not.'" Moreover, she said she felt the need for an intercessor and in a vision came to know Jesus, of whom she had heard.[60] As in the testimonies of other slaves, this conversion seems to mark a significant turning point in Isabella's feeling empowered through faith.[61] Shortly thereafter she left the Van Wageners and the area of New York in which she had spent her life up to that point and moved with son Peter to New York City, where they stayed for several years. While in New York City her son engaged its temptations, in spite of his mother's efforts during his and his siblings' childhoods, when she "took them to religious meetings; . . . talked to, and prayed for and with them." Peter never fell into deep trouble, however, and eventually, Isabella was relieved to see him leave New York for a career at sea on a whaling vessel.[62]

In New York City, Isabella continued association with Methodists, becoming a member of the John Street Methodist Church (where she belonged to an all-Black class, a small group within the congregation). Later she joined the all-Black Zion Church. After some time she affiliated with the extremist religious sect of Robert Matthias, a commune that practiced a more intense form of holiness, including separation from society, fasting, and other efforts toward extreme perfectionism. Matthias's group fell apart after financial and moral decline, including the suspicious death of one community member.[63]

Truth's Practice of Living Out Religious Belief

On June 1, 1843, Isabella changed her name to Sojourner and left New York City, which she came to see as a kind of "second Sodom."[64] When Sojourner left the city, she identified herself as following divine direction to go east, "'testifying of the hope that was in her'—exhorting the people to embrace Jesus, and refrain from sin. . . ."[65] She traveled to Long Island, New York, where she joined the Millerites, a millennialist sect, with whom she associated in Connecticut and Massachusetts throughout the summer and fall of 1843. In addition to attending their meetings, Sojourner sometimes called meetings of her own. Her religious and emotional boldness continued to evolve. When a gang of young men opposed to the millennialist doctrine disrupted a camp meeting, Sojourner overcame fear by reciting scriptures and declaring to herself "the Lord will protect and go with me." After she calmed herself, she stood up, started singing and then preaching, and subdued the attackers.[66]

During this period Sojourner began to develop a reputation for powerful preaching, remarkable praying and singing, and cogent, inspiring speaking.[67] By the late fall of 1843, she joined the cooperative community Northampton Association for Education and Industry in Northampton, Massachusetts. A nondenominational religious society, the Northampton Association began as an egalitarian community of free expression, supporting various issues, including women's rights, abolition of slavery, temperance, and vegetarianism. During her affiliation with the Northampton community, Sojourner encountered abolitionist and women's rights perspectives through frequent lectures by reformers. It was also during this time that she took the surname Truth.[68] When the Association dissolved in 1846, Truth was without permanent residence and subsistence. Following the example of Frederick Douglass, whom she had met there, Truth published the narrative of her life for income, which enabled her to purchase her first home from among Association properties being sold.[69]

Clearly influenced by abolitionist sentiments she encountered at Northampton, Truth began giving antislavery speeches in 1844 and 1845, first in Northampton and subsequently in New York. Later, at the invitation of William Lloyd Garrison, she joined the antislavery lecture circuit to sell her narrative.[70] During the course of these lectures, her reputation as a powerful and entertaining speaker grew. By 1846 Truth regularly addressed antislavery and women's rights gatherings, presenting arguments advocating equal rights for women and abolition of slavery from a religious perspective.[71] In her most well known speech (one of only two recorded), given at the 1851 Akron, Ohio, women's rights meeting, Truth made frequent use of Scripture to argue for women's rights and abolition of slavery.[72] Perhaps the most intricate record of her use of Scripture is the talk at a New York women's rights meeting in September 1853, in which she used the story of Esther, an outsider because of her gender and her race as a Jew, to argue for the full citizenship of white women and all Black people.[73]

With outbreak of the Civil War, Truth supported the Union cause and persisted in agitating against slavery. Before one speech in Indiana, where she encountered serious hostility, Truth refused counsel that she arm herself against threats, saying, "I carry no weapon: the Lord will reserve [preserve] . . . me without weapons." Describing the incident later, Truth compared herself to the biblical character David: "I felt as I was going against the Philistines and I prayed the Lord to reliver [deliver] me out of their hands."[74] In addition to speaking against slavery and for women's rights, Truth moved to Washington, D.C., in 1863 to assist Blacks fleeing war in Virginia. She taught domestic skills, organized charitable aid, and in 1867 "initiated a job-placement effort that matched refugee workers with employers in Rochester, New York, and Battle Creek, Michigan." After some time she drew up a petition, collecting signatures throughout New England and the Midwest calling Congress to settle freed people on western lands.[75] Congress never acted on the petition. Truth died at her home in Battle Creek, Michigan, in 1883.

Truth's Moral Vision

Throughout her life, Sojourner Truth participated in traditional religious practices. She prayed for relief from harshness of mistreatment while enslaved, for direction when she escaped slavery, for help to secure her son from slavers, and for his safety in the city. When she began to itinerate, she routinely prayed for her work and for protection when she was threatened. As a free person, she regularly attended worship meetings when she had liberty to do so. Even while she was enslaved, she created a sanctuary for herself, selecting "a small island in a small stream, covered with willow shrubbery, beneath which the sheep had made their pleasant winding paths. . . . She improved it by pulling away the branches of the shrubs from the center, and weaving them together for a wall on the outside, forming a circular arched alcove," where she went for daily communing with God.[76] Throughout her life she practiced holy living. While she could not read, she had Scriptures read to her, preferring the service of children in this regard because they did not seek to interpret to her what they read.[77] The most poignant of Truth's religious practices coincides with Black religious traditions of witnessing and testifying. She identified her work after leaving New York City as telling of divine participation in her life, calling her to share this with others, to go "testifying of the hope that was in her." As Truth said, "The Lord made me a sign unto this nation, an' I go round a-testifyin', an' showin' on 'em their sins agin my people."[78]

Truth said she experienced God's provision and guidance for her life beginning in her youth. She expressed expectation of divine intervention in her behalf. She felt "that the Lord was her director; and she doubted not [God] would provide for and protect her."[79] Her knowledge of the Bible is evidenced through her frequent references to it and paraphrases of it in her speaking. Through her own study of Scripture, she made determinations about its truthfulness by comparing "teachings of the Bible with the witness within her."[80]

The legacy of racial uplift in Truth's life reflected, first of all, survival and quality-of-life concerns for herself and her family. Throughout her life in bondage, her religious practices related directly to surviving and overcoming her own and her children's situation as enslaved persons. Because of her status as a slave, Truth's earliest racial uplift practices entailed less community work and more personal and family survival and quality-of-life work through which she sought to improve conditions for herself and her children. Once she was free, Truth became an active abolitionist, and after emancipation she personally assisted and organized help for newly freed persons to reach levels of subsistence. In addition to abolitionist and postbellum survival and quality-of-life work in behalf of African Americans, Truth also advocated for women's rights.

Perhaps most important in Truth's moral vision is affirmation of her own human identity. She expected divine intervention in behalf of her own life and her children's lives. Her religious perspective sustained her emotionally and guided her social activism. In addition, her use of Scripture to support her arguments and her expectation of divine protection as she lectured about the rights of all women and Black persons reflects a perspective that divine intent included full life for all human beings.

Nannie Helen Burroughs: A Turn-of-the-Century Activist

Like Truth, Nannie Helen Burroughs overtly articulated a religious perspective throughout her life. But unlike Truth, Burroughs practiced a particularly sectarian religiosity, exercising her life of public activism in one way or another connected to the National Baptist Convention (NBC).[81] For most of her career this meant leading efforts of the NBC's Women's Convention, which she helped found and for which she shaped and led racial uplift and social responsibility activities in concert with other Black club women. Like other Black women's clubs of the late nineteenth and early twentieth centuries, the Women's Convention supported education, resettlement of Black persons moving to cities, and social and moral reform.

Social and Religious Influences in Burroughs's Early Life

Born May 2, 1879, to John and Jennie (Poindexter) Burroughs in Culpepper, Virginia, Nannie Helen Burroughs was the daughter of an itinerant Baptist minister. She determined early to dedicate her life to the "work of the Lord." At age five, Burroughs moved with her mother to the District of Columbia because Mrs. Burroughs saw better educational opportunities for her daughter there. Nannie's only sibling, an infant sister, died shortly before the move. Her father, who apparently did not go with the family to Washington, died a few years later. While her family was not wealthy and she was not able to attend college like many of her peers, who also were Black women race leaders,[82] Nannie Helen Burroughs's social circumstances reflected changes of the post-emancipation era that were quite improbable one or two generations earlier. Unlike Truth, whose material well-being depended solely on her own ingenuity, Burroughs's maternal and paternal grandfathers both acquired land before the end of the 1860s. In addition, her maternal grandfather "earned a comfortable living for his wife and children as a skilled craftsman." Her father farmed in addition to preaching. Burroughs's mother was a domestic.[83]

In Washington, Burroughs maintained her religious roots at the Nineteenth Street Baptist Church, where she worked actively in church school and with the young people's group. She finished the prestigious M Street Preparatory School in 1896 but could not find work teaching domestic science, for which she had trained. Consequently, she moved to Philadelphia and secured a position, perhaps with the help of her pastor, as associate editor of *The Christian Banner,* an NBC newspaper. A year later she returned to Washington, where she planned to live with her mother. Burroughs never married.

When, upon return to Washington, she was denied anticipated

employment as a civil service clerk, Burroughs worked briefly as a "janitress" before taking a position as bookkeeper and editorial assistant to the Reverend L. G. Jordan, corresponding secretary for the National Baptist Convention's Foreign Mission Board. She moved with the Board to Louisville, Kentucky, to continue her position. This post proved to be a significant segue to Burroughs's lifelong vocation. Jordan, already a powerful figure in the NBC, officially made the motion recommending formation of the NBC's Women's Convention in 1900. Through the Women's Convention, Burroughs launched her life's work.[84]

Burroughs's Practice of Community Work as a Moral Value

Although there were several persons during the 1880s and 1890s who preceded her in agitating for a women's convention distinct from the NBC,[85] Burroughs made a speech at the 1900 Richmond NBC Convention, titled "How the Sisters Are Hindered from Helping," that significantly advanced the women's cause. Though she was only twenty-one years old, Burroughs already had developed a reputation as a powerful speaker.[86] With Jordan's recommendation and the support of several other influential Baptist clergy, the NBC's 1900 convention approved that year's recommendation for a separate women's group. Notwithstanding this separation and the continual opposition to women's leadership, through the Women's Convention Burroughs fulfilled what she most probably understood as a religious calling to practice racial uplift and quite explicit religious social responsibility, attending especially to Black women and girls.

Burroughs initiated racial uplift work at the beginning of her career. Prefiguring activities she later led in the Women's Convention, during early 1900 in Kentucky, alongside her work for Jordan, she organized the Woman's Industrial Club to address the needs of Black working women. Supported by boxed lunches sold to Black workers and dues of ten cents per woman, the club offered women day and evening classes in clerical skills, homemaking, and handicrafts. The group increased its income by selling pies and cakes and purchased a building for classes and to provide transitional shelter for women moving to Louisville for work.[87]

Elected corresponding secretary of the Women's Convention at its inception, Burroughs immediately set about organizing and leading activities of thousands of Baptist women who belonged to the Women's Convention nationwide. Reports of her first year in office record that she "traveled 22,125 miles, delivered 215 speeches, organized a dozen societies, wrote 9,235 letters, and received 4,820."[88] In 1901 she presented the idea, later approved by the Women's Convention, to develop a national school to train women for missionary work, teaching Scripture, homemaking, domestic service, and general industrial work. Perhaps one of Burroughs's most significant accomplishments was opening the National Training School for Women and Girls in Washington, D.C., in 1909 with the support of the Women's Convention. Burroughs eventually moved from Kentucky to Washington to serve as full-time president of the school, while continuing her organizing work as corresponding secretary of the Women's Convention.

As the school's focus evolved to include training women for a range of industrial opportunities, the Women's Convention also renamed the institution the National Trade and Professional School for Women and Girls. Responding to the context of most employed Black women of the era, the school focused especially on domestic service, where over 80 percent of nonagricultural Black women worked. Saying "first-class help must have first-class treatment," Burroughs asserted an intention to improve domestics' status to that of skilled workers by redefining and professionalizing domestic work. Concentrating on efficiency as well as quality of work and on respect and comfort in the workplace, Burroughs focused "upon the economic and moral status of the great mass of laboring people—especially Black women."[89] Yet the school did not center exclusively on preparing women for domestic service. Modeled after her Kentucky organization, courses at the school covered sewing, home economics, practical nursing, bookkeeping, shorthand, interior design, shoe repair, gardening, and barbering. The curriculum also included courses in Latin, English literature, and history, and required that each student take at least one course in Black history.[90]

Along with other Black female leaders of the era, Burroughs explicitly identified her activism as racial uplift work. Her publicity brochure for the National Training School described it as an institution that would provide "'uplift' of thousands of women and young girls throughout the entire country."[91] The language of racial uplift was prevalent among late nineteenth- and early twentieth-century Black race leaders, and especially Black club women who stressed education as a means of achieving racial advancement. At that time, Black churchwomen and club women collaborated to foster reform work. Their goals and activities intersected across boundaries of region, social status, and organizational affiliation.[92] Through various clubs Burroughs participated with other Black women in an array of social justice activities, including advocacy for women's suffrage and education and labor reform, and organizing for political participation.[93] To complete this work, Burroughs organized or participated in several Black women's clubs. In addition to the Women's Convention, she was active with the National Association of Colored Women (NACW), the Washington and Vicinity Federation of Women's Clubs, and the International Council of Darker Women, which she helped found. The International Council of Darker Women identified itself as devoted "in general to uplifting the race and to the advancement of Negro womanhood in particular."

During 1920 and 1921, Burroughs led the way in connecting middle-class professional club women with women industrial workers (including housekeepers and laborers in shops, factories, laundries, and hotels). In the Women's Convention Burroughs urged and received support for organizing domestic workers. "The only possible way for the Domestic Workers to get what others will demand and finally get," she said, "is to organize their own unions." She sent out a letter soliciting participation from domestic and industrial women workers across the country. With the support of the Women's Convention and the NACW, in 1921 Burroughs helped found the National Association of Wage Earners, which elected her president and set as their objectives ensuring efficiency, just wages, and legislative change, and addressing mutual grievances and better living conditions for working women.[94] Attentive to immediate survival and quality-of-life issues arising from the Depression, Burroughs also organized a Washington, D.C., community cooperative, which provided facilities for and access to medical care, a variety store, farming, canning, and hairdressing, among other things.[95]

In 1934 Burroughs founded *The Worker,* a quarterly leadership devotional and informational publication for women's missionary societies. In her editorial in the first issue—launched during the

Depression—Burroughs wrote, "We realize that financial conditions are not altogether favorable to launch a magazine, but *our church women need it. God will, therefore, make it possible* for us to meet this definite need." Through *The Worker* she sought to systematize women's activities and influence their perspectives. Addressing topics as varied as domestic work, social issues in Black communities, and parenting, Burroughs "selected and prepared the Scripture reading, wrote the devotions, and selected and wrote the information on the discussion topics" for each issue.[96]

Although she championed the cause of Black working and lower classes and participated in various practices of racial uplift, Burroughs's perspective coincided with that of racial uplift ideology. Like other proponents of the ideology of racial uplift, Burroughs asserted the need for African Americans to justify themselves. She envisioned that the National Training School would win friends and foster "positive images of Blacks in the minds of white employers." She argued "that Black domestic servants could vindicate their race by 'proving themselves industrious, upright, and honest.'"[97] At the same time, like many other proponents of racial uplift ideology, Burroughs also strongly advocated for racial justice.

While she advanced varied causes and achieved major accomplishments through the Women's Convention, throughout her lifetime Burroughs contended with male leaders of the National Baptist Convention who contested women's leadership, power, and recognition. In her first talk before the NBC, Burroughs "denounced impediments to women's equal participation in the church," presenting in her speech a position corresponding with that of other women who worked to develop an independent convention over the previous two decades.[98] Although the 1900 recommendation to develop a separate women's group passed, efforts to rescind the action recurred several times in the years immediately following.[99] In 1900, after the NBC vote that formally sanctioned formation of the Women's Convention, NBC President Elias Camp Morris attempted to have the vote rescinded. In 1901, Morris tried to take away the women's autonomy by making the Women's Convention a board of the NBC. Women's Convention President S. Willie Layten gave an address acquiescing to Morris, but Burroughs and others opposed the move and prevailed, as women of the Convention voted to maintain their independence.[100] In 1903, I. W. D. Isaac, editor of the *National Baptist Union,* supported efforts to place the Women's Convention under NBC control by exploiting tensions between Burroughs and an older Women's Convention leader through negative press coverage of their political differences. By late summer, however, the women overcame the controversy and showed such unity that during the fall Isaac printed a statement of support for the women's work.[101]

In addition to organizing and advocating on behalf of Black women, Burroughs worked for racial justice. Her integration of religion and social practice is most evident in her assertions about race relations. Throughout her life Burroughs called racial justice an expression of God's will. "God is on the side of men who live and fight for justice," she wrote in a short essay, "The Hope of the World." Opposing war and faith in the atomic bomb as a securer of peace, Burroughs wrote, "Peace is made out of respect for human personality." "Think of a nation," she continued, "talking about enduring peace when it spends Five Dollars on the education of a white child and Fifty Cents on the education of a Negro child! Think of a nation talking about enduring peace when it sends Black men to fight for world freedom and denies these same men a semblance of it when they return to 'the land of promise.'"[102] Burroughs said peace reflected the divine intention that all persons "enjoy the earth and be fully free."[103]

Burroughs asserted a responsibility of religious persons and institutions to make a difference in society, including, but not limited to, improving race relations. "Every church should attempt a definite program that projects itself into the community," she wrote.[104] Moreover, "no church should be allowed to stay in a community that does not positively influence community life."[105] Advocating a position of Christian chauvinism interrelated with democracy, Burroughs's perspective on divine intention and human responsibility ultimately asserts radical material democracy. Democracy "means that every human being born into the world has a right to equal opportunities with every other human being," she said. From Burroughs's perspective, there is a kind of inevitability to this divine intention, for, she held, the "ferment" and "leaven" of democracy "will eventually unloose the God-given wealth of the world to all men." She wrote, "wealth will never be secure until it is democratic."[106]

Burroughs's Moral Vision

Burroughs participated in traditional religious rituals like praying, reading Scripture, and attending worship. Her expectation that Christian living, generally, would make society more just reflects her participation in the Black religious traditions of witnessing and testifying. As Burroughs herself wrote:

> The Women's Convention calls . . . women and young people of the churches to give themselves as never before to that personal service that shall witness most truly of the power and glory of our Christian faith in a world that has sadly drifted from God. . . . Organized personal service is the united spirit and work of a group of Christians, directed toward solving problems, ministering to the needs, and abolishing evil conditions in their community.[107]

Burroughs asserted and sought divine guidance throughout her work. She maintained that there was divine interaction with her efforts and expected providential support in starting the National Training School, *The Worker* missionary magazine, and a Summer Institute to train women church leaders.[108] "I felt God wanted me to go ahead," Burroughs said, "and I knew if I did what I could and trusted Him, He would see it through. And He did."[109]

Burroughs frequently spoke of her own practice of Christian ritual traditions and sought to make them a regular practice in the lives of others. Shortly after formation of the Women's Convention, she advocated that it begin each meeting day with prayer and devotion.[110] She prayed about starting the National Training School for a long time because she "wanted to be sure God was leading" her.[111] In 1919, Burroughs led the Women's Convention executive board in calling for a day of prayer and fasting to protest lynching, racial mob violence, and "'the undemocratic and un-Christian spirit the United States has shown by its discriminating and barbarous treatment of its colored people.'"[112] Burroughs felt regular practice of studying Scripture resulted in changes in persons and society. "There is no hope for the world unless humanity as a whole is educated in the spirit and principles of the Bible," she wrote. "It offers an effectual remedy for all the evils that drag mankind down."[113]

Burroughs used Scripture throughout her speeches and writing to support and make arguments for racial uplift and social justice. She often related Scripture to the history and circumstances of African Americans. During a 1933 address to young people she quoted from the Bible to assert a democratized conception of racial uplift. Advocating individual participation and responsibility, as well as group consciousness, she told the youths, "Don't wait for a deliverer. . . . I like that quotation, 'Moses, my servant, is dead. Therefore, arise and go over Jordan.' There are no deliverers. They're all dead. We must arise and go over Jordan. We can take the promised land."[114] In 1934, when she issued a letter inviting women church workers to the first of regular summer leadership courses at the National Training School, Burroughs used Scripture to advocate invigorating church work and enriching lives by stirring "'up the gift [talent] of God which is in thee.'"[115] In her general admonition to Black people, "Twelve Things the Negro Must Do for Himself," Burroughs used the Bible story of Jesus interacting with a paralytic to urge persistence in work among African Americans, who must carry their "own load."[116]

Burroughs also used Scripture to argue for racial justice. In her companion admonition, "Twelve Things the White Man Must Stop Doing to the Negro," she quoted Scripture to affirm human equality, asserting "one blood of all races" and "all ye are brethren." Furthermore, she sought to debunk conventional perspectives about white supremacy. In this latter instance Burroughs offered her own interpretation of Scripture to argue against the so-called curse of Ham by God, saying Noah, who had been drinking, pronounced the curse. "God did not even appear on the scene while Noah was drunk," Burroughs wrote, and "Noah did the same kind of 'running off at the mouth' that drunks usually do. . . . God has never cursed any race."[117]

Once she determined God was directing her, Burroughs went energetically about work that witnessed to divine direction. Moreover, she judged clergy by the extent to which they promoted living as witness. Religion must be "an everyday practice and not just a Sunday-go-to-meeting performance," she wrote.[118] She "criticized ministers who preached 'too much Heaven and too little practical Christian living.'"[119] For Burroughs, such practical Christian living included persons, particularly African Americans, standing up and fighting for their rights. "It is no evidence of Christianity," she said, "to have people mock you and spit on you and defeat the future of your children."[120] While she persisted in activism and advocacy for women, in her later life Burroughs became more involved in racial justice practice connecting nineteenth- and early twentieth-century religious activism to the Civil Rights Era. After women's enfranchisement through passage of the Nineteenth Amendment to the U.S. Constitution, Burroughs sought to mobilize Black women politically. She helped found the now-defunct National League of Republican Colored Women and was an active member of the National Association for the Advancement of Colored People (NAACP).[121] Her other civil rights work preceding the Civil Rights Movement included advocacy for antilynching laws, calls for desegregation of public facilities, fair wage advocacy, and activity related to the status of African American home ownership. Burroughs died in 1961.

Although their lives differed significantly, both Sojourner Truth and Nannie Helen Burroughs sought transformation of social life in the United States. Truth focused on her own survival and liberation, abolishing slavery, women's enfranchisement and participation, and helping African Americans overcome difficulties arising immediately after emancipation. Burroughs sought to improve life for African Americans, especially Black women, as the nineteenth century and vestiges of Reconstruction ended. While they lived in different eras, the two women shared the view that their religious values and their practices as religious persons were important to social life. Many Black women civil rights participants followed Truth and Burroughs in what now frequently is called the tradition of social activism in African American religion. Furthermore, like Truth and Burroughs, Black women civil rights participants also sought to transform U.S. social life as they actively engaged moral possibilities of their own time.

2

Continuing the Traditions

Attention to the "Least" in Civil Rights Activism

Nannie Helen Burroughs and Black women of her generation may be seen as successors in religious activism to antebellum freedwomen and slavewomen like Sojourner Truth. Burroughs and other Black race women (especially, but not only, Black club women) born soon after emancipation and during the Reconstruction period attended to issues facing African Americans during emancipation and well into the twentieth century. Women born after Reconstruction, near the turn of the twentieth century, both helped carry on work of late nineteenth-century activists by attending to African American quality-of-life issues, and benefited from the work of those activists, often having more access to education, sometimes through schools Burroughs and her peers helped establish. As material circumstances of African Americans began to change, and as the social and political climate of the new century slowly yielded to African Americans' efforts toward full citizenship, some Black women activists born near the beginning of the twentieth century also initiated particular practices to improve life through full participation as citizens of the United States.

Ella Josephine Baker and Septima Poinsette Clark, college-educated professionals born around the turn of the century, were two women of this generation. They not only carried on the work of improving African Americans' immediate material conditions but also saw the bigger picture and more possibilities. They helped inaugurate and shape the Civil Rights Era. Their social status, defined largely by their having an advanced education and not having endured the Southern sharecropping system, significantly determined ways they entered, participated in, and experienced the Civil Rights

Movement. Both Baker and Clark understood themselves and their activism as religious work originating in moral perspectives they learned as children and developed more fully as adults.

Ella Baker: Passing on Values of Attending to the "Least"

In some sense, Ella Josephine Baker could be called a renaissance woman. If there are architects of the Civil Rights Movement, she is one of them. Baker helped found two major organizations through whose programs structure of the movement developed: the Southern Christian Leadership Conference (SCLC) and the Student Nonviolent Coordinating Committee (SNCC). In addition, Baker influenced SCLC and SNCC programs and completed invaluable legwork during an important period for the NAACP. Through this work Baker helped determine the evolution of the Civil Rights Movement by swaying the direction of its activities, which led to several of its distinct features, including the first major SCLC campaigns, the origin and work of SNCC in Mississippi, Freedom Summer, and more.

Having been involved in grassroots organizing campaigns for survival and fair treatment as early as the 1930s, Baker developed a perspective on human dignity and human rights that shaped the Civil Rights Movement as well as the character and direction of other New Left movements that originated in and evolved from the tumult during the 1960s. She is rightly called a mother and a midwife of the Civil Rights Movement.[1]

Baker's Moral Formation: Social and Religious Influences in Her Early Life

Born in 1903 in Norfolk, Virginia, Ella Baker came to know herself through religiously motivated practices of racial uplift and social responsibility.[2] Her parents, Blake and Georgianna (called Anna) Ross Baker, were educated descendants of former slaves. Blake Baker worked as a ferry waiter on a Norfolk–Washington line. Anna Ross (Baker) taught school until she married. After marriage, Mrs. Baker reared three children—Curtis, Ella, and Margaret—and quite persistently engaged in formal and informal Baptist "missionary work."

When Ella was eight, because of her mother's respiratory problems and her father's work, which took him away from his family for twenty-four-hour periods, the Bakers moved to the rural farming community of Littleton, North Carolina, for its fresh air and proximity to Anna's family.[3]

In Littleton, Mrs. Baker continued missionary activities. During early years as a mother and missionary she regularly participated in local and state Baptist Missionary Union meetings. She likely used resources prepared by Nannie Helen Burroughs for state and local women's Baptist societies. Mrs. Baker was a leader in the missionary unions, offering speeches for mission society gatherings, encouraging others to respond to people's needs, and offering suggestions on how to do so. At a 1924 Women's State Convention she spoke on "The Needs of the Hour and How to Meet Them."[4] She also encouraged women of the convention to reflect their faith in everyday practices. "Let Christ take the first place in your vocation and life. Inquire of the Lord what he would have us do," she charged them. "Let us stay on the job for Christ."[5] Informally, in her local community, Mrs. Baker's missionary work was general ministry to the poor. She shared from the family's relative prosperity, giving milk, fruit, eggs, and vegetables generously; she cared for the community's sick; and she gave special attention to poor women giving birth.[6] Ella Baker remembered frequently waking up at night to respond to knocks on the door from persons calling on "Miss Anna," who always attended to the sick.[7]

In addition to helping with planting and harvesting the family's farm, the Baker children worked with their mother "ministering to the needy." Ella recalled a regular assignment at about age twelve to care for children of a neighboring farmer whose wife had died. "The little ones would be very unkempt," she said, "and part of my weekend 'pleasures' was to go over with clean clothes and try to catch the young ones and give them a bath. . . . Mama would say, 'You must take the clothes to Mr. Powell's house, and give so-and-so a bath.' . . . The kids for the devilment would take off across the field. We'd chase them down, and bring them back, and put 'em in the tub, and wash 'em off, and change clothes, and carry the dirty ones home, and wash them. Those kinds of things were routine."[8] As she grew, Ella assimilated her mother's values and began to develop her own perspective about the dignity of people. She recalled another occasion when, passing the home of a mentally disabled neighbor, she noticed "unusual bleeding" as the woman stood on the porch. Assuming she needed medical attention, Ella reported the incident to her mother as in keeping with "what you do" for persons in need. She said,

> Mandy, I think we called her, was standing in the doorway on her little porch, and she was bleeding. I wasn't too aware then of the menstrual period. But I knew this was more blood than anybody *should* be having, just standing. So when I came back home I told mama, and so she went down, and the woman was having, I don't know whether it was a hemorrhage or just *what*. She needed medical attention. So what do you *do*? I mean, she was a *person*. You couldn't just pass her by and say, "Oh, that's just Mandy Bunk, you see, who also raised a pig in one room and herself in the other room." You don't do that. At least this is the way we happened to grow up.[9]

Young Ella's concern to attend to Ms. Bunk because "she was a person" reflects an early perspective about the dignity of humans that remained with Baker throughout her life.

Not only did Ella participate with her mother in informal "mission" work, she also joined Mrs. Baker's activities in Baptist mission societies. Anna Baker often took her children along on trips to local and state mission union meetings. By age seven Ella was a leader in the local church's missionary adjunct, the Sunshine Club. She became a frequent speaker at regular mission society meetings, and when she was twenty-one, she "gave the address at the first night's session" of the North Carolina Baptist Women's Union State Convention.[10] What she saw and participated in through her mother's missionary activities blended into Ella's identity. As she initially contemplated her life's work, Ella Baker sought to emulate her mother; she wanted to be a medical missionary. The cost of education, however, closed this option.[11] Throughout her life, Ella spoke of Anna Baker as a "force" whose "strict standards—of speech, decorum, religiosity, and neighborliness"—deeply influenced her.[12] She recognized the role her mother's example played not only in shaping her understanding of human relationship and human dignity, but also in determining the religious roots of her identity and life as an activist. "I became active in things largely because my mother was active in the field of religion," she said years later.[13]

But Mrs. Baker was not the only strong influence in Ella's self-understanding. Ella's grandfather also impressed her deeply. Founder and pastor of the family's congregation, Roanoke Chapel Baptist Church, Anna's father Mitchell Ross began the family's tradition of practicing community ministry. Intent on fostering a healthy local Black community after he came out of slavery, Ross took responsibility for the community's basic physical and emotional survival and quality of life. He purchased and parceled out to extended family portions of the land on which he had served while enslaved. "He believed in the old pattern of providing," Ella said. "He insisted on having plenty to eat, which meant that he always had milk by the gallons." In addition Ross had plenty of other foods that he shared with neighbors. Baker recalled:

> We had a big garden, much too big for the size of the family. I'd pick a bushel or more [of green peas], and we didn't need them, so you'd give them to the neighbors who didn't have them. That's the way you *did*. It was no hassle about it. I don't think it ever occurred to our immediate family to indoctrinate children against sharing. Because they had the privilege of growing up where they'd raised a lot of food. They were never hungry. They could share their food with people. And so you share your *lives* with people.

Having lived as a slave with less than sufficient food, Ross not only determined a means for much of the community's being well fed, but he also personally opposed certain foods that reminded him of bondage. "He did not believe in eating certain things that he had eaten during slavery," Ella reflected later. "He could not eat corn bread as such. . . . He wouldn't let his wife even force the children to eat the corn bread."[14] She saw her grandfather's concern for the community's well-being as both pragmatism deriving from experiences of hunger and deprivation during slavery and a religious principle.

As a pastor Ross made a circuit of four churches (to at least one of which he deeded land for the building), traveling across country roads in horse and buggy, often taking along his granddaughter Ella, whom he called "the grand lady."[15] As a child, Ella also sat in a chair beside her grandfather in the pulpit of Roanoke Chapel Baptist Church, over her mother's objection that the space was designated for the "visiting preacher."[16] Had she been a son, it does not seem unlikely that Mr. Ross would have groomed his grandchild for ministry. Traveling with her grandfather as circuit pastor, Baker saw his role as caring community leader and minister overlap. Ella also saw Ross's pragmatism come through in his conception of the role and meaning of preaching and worship. Baker remembered her grandfather's preaching and general religiosity as sober and reserved. She describes him in his pastoral role as concerned with instruction. Mitchell Ross, Baker said, "'was a minister, but he was a very unusual type of minister, especially for that period. He was the teacher-type to the extent that even when people began to shout in his church, he would call them by name and say "Sit down. Nothing but the devil makes you make so much noise." . . . He was a very unusual person, and to some people, a very taciturn type.'"[17] Ross admonished parishioners to "listen" and learn. "'He'd stop people and tell them to be quiet and listen. When a young minister came to preach at [Grandpa's] church and felt he had to act as some ministers acted, which was to put the "rousement" over you, Grandpa would catch him by the coattails and pull them and say, "Now you sit down and rest yourself while I sing this hymn and then get up and talk like you got some sense."'"[18]

In his role as a leader and "teaching" pastor (to use Baker's language) who cared for the community's spiritual lives, Ross also attended to their material well-being. In fact, as in much of traditional African American Christianity, for Ross the two were deeply connected. This certainly helps explain why Baptist minister Ross objected to "shouting" and "rousement" among his congregants and to the efforts by visiting ministers to arouse them. For Ross, who had survived slavery and stridently practiced overcoming the material deprivation caused by slavery, religiosity was quite pragmatic, demonstrated in what Baker describes as "a deep sense of community," where "if there were emergencies, the farmer next to you would share in something to meet that emergency. For instance, when you thresh wheat, if there was a thresher around, you didn't have each person having his own. So you came to my farm and threshed, and then you went to the next one. You joined in."

For Ross religious duty had a quite material function, related to survival and well-being, and he was a leader in this. Baker continued, "Part of the land was on a riverbank, the Roanoke River. . . . But the river would overflow at times and certain crops might be ruined. So if that took place, and it wrecked havoc with the food supply, I am told that my grandfather would take his horse and wagon and go up to the county seat, which was the only town at that point, and mortgage, if necessary, his land, to see that people ate."[19]

Alongside community ministry and missionary union activity, Ella Baker grew up participating in various traditional religious rituals. She regularly attended worship at her grandfather's church and read Scripture as a child and young adult. The practice of Scripture reading may have been more frequent when she was a child, since by the age of ten "she had read the Bible two or three times." Baker also participated in her denominational practice of baptism by immersion, deciding at age nine to follow the lead of cousins. In 1912, during a revival at a nearby church, Baker said,

> My brother and I . . . had heard that Joseph and Bertha . . . my cousins, had confessed and were therefore to be baptized in September. We had to do something about it. . . . We went to church, and I don't know whether we both got religion the same night or not. We weren't very dramatic about it, but we were ready for baptism, and all four of us were baptized at the same time in the old mill pond.[20]

Afterwards Baker sought to realize congruity of "getting religion" and being baptized in her everyday behavior. "I took the position that you were supposed to change after baptism," she said, and tried "to control my temper. I had a high temper. . . . And so this was my way of demonstrating my change, by trying to control my temper."[21] Baker's concern for agreement of her "being" religious and "practicing" religion by "demonstrating my change" reflected continuity with what she saw in her mother, grandfather, and other members of her childhood community, and signaled a lifelong concern to overcome "contradictions" between professed belief and practice. After Baker left home to attend Shaw University (a Baptist institution where she completed high school and college), she continued regular Scripture reading, since the Bible was the "proclaimed principal Shaw textbook."[22] Baker also attended worship daily and continued regular worship attendance throughout her adult life in New York.[23]

Baker's Early Community Work

As early as her undergraduate years at Shaw University, Baker organized and worked for liberty of others. Although she did not date frequently and could not afford silk stockings, Baker advocated free expression by leading protests in support of male and female students who wanted to walk across Shaw's campus together, and in support of the right for women students to wear silk stockings on campus. In asserting her own right to free expression Baker refused to participate when Shaw's president showcased the school choir to white visitors, because she found it demeaning.[24]

Whereas Nannie Helen Burroughs lamented not having opportunity to teach, Ella Baker disdained teaching as a profession for herself. Baker saw teaching as a safe occupation, especially for women whom she felt eventually ended up under some control of education authorities.[25] She did have high regard for teachers, however, and particularly emphasized the important role teachers could play in the lives of youth. "I believe it's important for children (especially poor children, who are the last to receive consideration) to feel a sort of communion and friendship with their teachers," she said. "I know it was important for my childhood. As I think back to my public school teachers in the South, they seem to have had a conviction that their major role was to provide an extra amount of support for a child in his growing up years."[26] Notwithstanding this regard for teachers, Baker shunned the employment expected of her and, when she graduated Shaw University in 1927, moved to stay with relatives in New York. Baker initially worked as a waitress, factory worker, and then for several newspapers as reporter and editorial assistant before becoming fully employed in the community work that evolved into her role in the Civil Rights Movement.

When Baker arrived in New York, the Harlem Renaissance was at its height. New York was at that time, she says, a "hotbed of . . . radical thinking."[27] Celebration of Black cultural and intellectual life was in high gear. Baker engaged fully Harlem's social, artistic, and cultural renaissance, and moved beyond Harlem to take in and encounter as fully as possible new ideas available to her. She considered Shaw conservative and inclined to offer a traditional liberal arts education: "I never heard any discussions about social revolution." Baker was intrigued by this new thinking and said she "went everywhere there was a discussion." Because there were discussions in so many places, she "had lots of opportunity to hear and evaluate whether or not this was the kind of thing you wanted to get into."[28] Notwithstanding her fervent integration of new ideas with her expanding worldview, during this period and throughout her life Baker maintained strong ties with Friendship Baptist Church in Harlem, where she regularly attended Sunday worship while living in New York and sent back contributions to cover Sundays she missed when she moved to Atlanta.[29]

In a 1930 newspaper post at the *Negro National News*, Baker met Black socialist intellectual George Schuyler. Deeply influenced by Schuyler's socialist perspectives, particularly his views on cooperative buying among African Americans, and moved by the tragedy of seeing so many people "actually waiting on the bread line, for coffee and handouts," Baker began what were likely her first national organizing efforts. That same year, based on Schuyler's assertions about Black participation in cooperative economics and radical social change, she joined other young African Americans in forming the Young Negroes' Cooperative League (YNCL). Espousing a pragmatism reminiscent of her grandfather and of Nannie Helen Burroughs, Baker said the YNCL's initial objective was to promote "buying together, as over against separately. To buy for your group. And therefore save." Through Schuyler's influence with the widely distributed Pittsburgh *Courier*, people from all over the country became founding YNCL members. By 1932, there were local councils in twelve communities. Their buying clubs and other cooperative ventures helped mitigate devastation of the Depression and increased social and political analysis within Black communities.

Through the YNCL Baker engaged new ideas she was assimilating with attempts to provide relief for persons suffering most intensely from the Depression. A year after its founding, and as the Depression moved into full swing, the YNCL elected Baker national director. From this post she traveled into various Black communities studying local problems, organizing cooperatives, and sharing insights.[30] Baker also participated with various efforts opposing lynching, seeking equal employment, and seeking to empower Black women.[31] In 1935, she was publicity director for the National Negro Congress, an attempt to unify Black organizations and various efforts combating discrimination and lynching. Baker had by this time cultivated a vocation for herself as a professional community organizer, work that complemented activities she enjoyed in her spare time. Beginning in 1934, she worked for the New York Public Library in Harlem, where she led parent education, continued antilynching advocacy, and participated with the Library Project of the Works Progress Administration (WPA). In the WPA Baker advocated quality and cooperative buying and continued to encounter "every spectrum of radical thinking."[32]

As she absorbed New York's political and social climate, Baker organized programs to help persons take charge of their lives. During the Depression she focused particularly on cooperative economics to help alleviate immediate material deprivation. But by the mid-1930s, she developed a growing critical leftist sensitivity that propelled her to explore the Depression's effects on human dignity. Along with colleague Marvel Cooke, Baker conducted participant-observer research on Black women forced to participate in "a street corner market for domestic servants." After visiting the market, Baker and Cooke published an article in *The Crisis* titled "The Bronx Slave Market." Owing to "economic necessity," they wrote, Black domestics were "forced to bargain for a day's work on street corners" of what Baker and Cooke called "slave marts." "In an effort to supplement the inadequate relief received," Black women, young and old, waited "expectantly for Bronx housewives to buy their strength and energy." While they disapproved of such a low level of public assistance, Baker and Cooke recognized it as helpful to many domestics and other women. With "its advent," they wrote, "actual starvation is no longer their ever-present slave driver and they have been able to demand twenty-five and even thirty cents an hour as against the old fifteen and twenty cent rate." Baker and Cooke's analysis of the "economic necessity" to sell "their strength and energy" betokens the discussion of "surrogacy" by scholars like womanist theologian Delores Williams. Williams says full surrogacy during slavery and voluntary (though pressured) surrogacy after emancipation were historic aspects of Black women's context in the United States. This concurs with Baker and Cooke's analysis that some women surrendered some control of their bodies because of material need.[33]

By this time, Baker began to espouse three perspectives that permeated her work, namely, that human dignity entails, among other things, liberty and control of one's body, that human liberty consists of opportunity and responsibility for its exercise, and that organizing is a powerful weapon against injustice. Through the study of women in the Bronx corner markets, Baker and Cooke commented on the relationship of opportunity, responsibility, and organizing to group progress. Reflecting the influence of socialist ideas critical of U.S. capitalism, they described domestics participating in the Bronx markets as willing participants in individualistic opportunities for advancement, apparently lacking consciousness about the potential of organizing, and captured by the American dream. Women subject to the slave marts "present a study in contradictions," Baker and Cooke wrote. "Largely unaware of their organized power, yet ready to band together for some immediate personal gain either consciously or unconsciously, they still cling to that American illusion that anyone who is determined and persistent can get ahead." Echoing Burroughs, who called for domestic workers to unionize, and reflecting an attitude similar to that of Burroughs and other nineteenth-century club women who worked across social classes, Baker and Cooke called for organizing, cooperation across class lines, and racial egalitarianism in labor unions. They concluded:

> The roots then of the Bronx slave market spring from: (1) the general ignorance of and apathy toward organized labor action; (2) the artificial barriers that separate the interest of relief administrators and investigators from that of their "caseloads," the white collar and professional worker from the laborer and domestic; and (3) organized labor's limited concept of exploitation, which permits it to fight vigorously to secure itself against evil, yet passively or actively aids and abets the ruthless destruction of Negroes. To abolish the market once and for all, these roots must be torn away from their sustaining soil.[34]

Baker's perspective as illuminated in this article correlates with what became a three-prong credo of her life's work: affirming human dignity, organizing for change, and seeking egalitarianism in human community.

Baker's Community Work, Her Religious Values, and the Civil Rights Movement

In 1941 Baker began her more than thirty-year formal participation in what became the civil rights establishment when she took a position as Assistant Field Secretary for the NAACP. From her earliest days with the NAACP Baker emphasized democratization and egalitarianism.

Attempting to empower local people through organizing, she "proposed that local branches have a say in the programs and policies of the organization" and initiated leadership training for local officers. At the same time Baker "lobbied for regularization of personnel policies, linking this with her pursuit of more democratic procedures."[35] For Baker, democratization and egalitarianism meant both changing practices of the NAACP hierarchy and emphasizing the potential and responsibility of local communities. In contrast to the NAACP's method of seeking change through national legal victories, Baker wanted persons in local areas to take charge of issues confronting them instead of waiting for deliverance from outside. Because "Black people who were living in the South were constantly living with violence," Baker concluded such changes were necessary:

> Part of the job was to help them to understand what that violence was and how they in an organized fashion could help to stem it. The major job was getting people to understand that they had something within their power that they could use, and it could only be used if they understood what was happening and how group action could counter violence even when it was perpetrated by the police or, in some instances, the state. My basic sense of it has always been to get people to understand that in the long run they themselves are the only protection they have against violence or injustice. . . . People have to be made to understand that they cannot look for salvation anywhere but to themselves.[36]

In travels across the South as Assistant Field Secretary, Baker encouraged what she said was the "prevailing attitude." It " 'is no longer one of hoping and waiting for the effects of national victories to trickle down to the South,' " she wrote in a 1942 field report, " 'but it is increasingly one of working and fighting for victories against local injustices and discrimination.' "[37] For Baker this sometimes meant attending to egalitarianism as a priority of local organizing. Baker often sought to overcome social class tensions and other impediments to local NAACP chapters' giving attention to issues facing all African Americans. "There's always this problem in the minority group that's escalating up the ladder in this culture," she once observed. "Those who have gotten some training and those who have gotten some material gains, it's always the problem of their not understanding the possibility of being divorced from those who are not in their social classification." There were, for example,

> those who felt they had made it, would be embarrassed by the fact that some people would get drunk and get in jail, and so they wouldn't be concerned too much about whether they were brutalized in jail. 'Cause he was a *drunk!* He was a so-and-so. Or she was a streetwalker. We get caught in that bag. And so you have to help break that down without alienating them at the same time. The gal who has been able to buy her minks and whose husband is a professional, they live well. You can't insult her, you never go and tell her she's a so-and-so for taking, for *not* identifying. You try to point out where her interest lies in identifying with that other one across the tracks who doesn't have minks. . . . So what you do is to cite examples that have taken place somewhere else. . . . You cite it, you see. This can happen to *you*. . . . As long as the violations of the rights of Tom Jones could take place with impunity, you are not secure. So you help to re-establish a sense of identity of each with the struggle.[38]

Reflecting a similar concern to what she felt as a child for Mandy Bunk, Baker persistently encouraged egalitarianism. She tried to help realize in these communities the mutuality and concern for others she saw her mother and grandfather practice. Connecting new ideas about radical democracy to religious perspectives and practices of her childhood, Baker said, the "deep sense of community that may have developed in that little place" where she lived "didn't always carry over." Some persons, she said, "lost their roots." In such instances Baker hoped people would "begin to think in terms of the *wider* brotherhood"[39] and attend to human need across social classes. This value as embodied in Baker's work prefigured what Gilkes observed among some Black women community workers, who, Gilkes said, identified with persons they served as peers. According to Gilkes, these community workers moved up professional opportunity structures to help their Black communities.[40]

In 1943 Baker was named National Director of Branches.[41] Yet in spite of her efforts Ella Baker did not feel the NAACP sufficiently addressed issues of egalitarianism. By 1946 she became dissatisfied with what she viewed as its antidemocratic and disempowering practices and resigned her post. She felt the NAACP was too hierarchical, failed to attend to the masses, and "was overly concerned with recognition from whites."[42] Later that year Baker began work for the New York Urban League and by 1947 was a leader in the local New York Branch of the NAACP. In 1940 Baker married an old college friend, T. J. Robertson (Roberts). During the next year she focused considerable energy on school desegregation as chair of the branch's education committee, and she participated with her husband on their tenants committee and other local community work. Baker never changed her name, and the couple later parted amicably. Six years after her marriage, Baker took custody of her nine-year-old niece, Jacqueline Brockington.[43]

When the Montgomery Bus Boycott began in the mid-1950s, around the time her niece entered college, Baker was a founding member of In Friendship, a Northern group that raised funds and arranged other support for Southern civil rights activities. After the boycott ended, Baker and her two primary associates of In Friendship, Bayard Rustin and Stanley Levison, encouraged Martin King Jr. and others to form an organization to capitalize on the boycott's momentum. In Friendship helped sponsor the first meeting of what became the Southern Christian Leadership Conference (SCLC). Baker was drafted as the logical choice to get the new organization off the ground, and in 1957 she moved south to Atlanta. She worked out of a hotel room to set up the SCLC's office and get under way its first major voting-rights program, the Crusade for Citizenship. Overseeing the Crusade was frustrating for Baker, since she wanted to enlist mass participation by organizing voter registration drives (to include instruction, transportation, and other support), while SCLC leaders seemed content to sponsor a program that consisted principally of mass rallies and grand exhortations by ministers without any follow-up.[44] Baker also advocated education programs for the Black masses to expedite voter registration. In this she conflicted with the clergy-led body over its heavy dependence on charismatic leaders and mobilizing instead of organizing. In spite of the conflict, Baker was successful in initiating contact that connected Septima Clark's Citizenship Education Program with the SCLC's Crusade for Citizenship, a relationship that developed into the most significant factor in increasing Black voter registration across the South.[45]

The Crusade for Citizenship was only one issue over which Baker conflicted with the SCLC Board. The SCLC never fully recognized

Baker's expertise, in spite of her long tenure and broad experience as a community organizer. She spent two years working as chief administrative officer of the SCLC. Although she had proven organizing skills and foresight, she officially served only as "acting" executive director because she was not a part of the "preacher's club" and was a woman. The Reverend Wyatt Tee Walker was named to replace her in 1958. As Baker said later, "I knew from the beginning that as a woman, an older woman, in a group of ministers who are accustomed to having women largely as supporters, there was no place for me to have come into a leadership role." Baker did not contest her status in the SCLC. "The competition wasn't worth it," she said.[46] Baker also conflicted with Board members who she felt exhibited traditional tendencies that disempowered lay persons. Baker thought charismatic leaders often stood in the way of talents brought by the masses.

When Black college students began almost spontaneously to sit in at lunch counters across the South in 1960, Baker saw an opportunity and convinced King and the SCLC to sponsor the Raleigh Conference, a gathering of the leaders of the sit-ins. Attended by over two hundred students of different races from the North and the South, as well as leaders of major civil rights groups, the meeting culminated in founding the Student Nonviolent Coordinating Committee (SNCC). Thanks to Baker's intervention, the students were not annexed as a youth wing of the Congress on Racial Equality (CORE), NAACP, or SCLC. Back at SCLC headquarters in Atlanta, Baker found a place for SNCC's first working space and made the SCLC's mimeograph and mailing facilities available as well.[47] Baker, by now in her fifties and beginning to sever ties with the SCLC, served as an adviser to the students. She influenced SNCC to adopt a group-centered style of operation and to focus on empowering and training leaders indigenous to local communities.

Some of SNCC's most significant work arose through contacts Baker made when she worked for the NAACP in New York. It was Baker who connected SNCC leader Bob Moses with Amzie Moore, a longtime advocate for Black advancement in Mississippi. The campaigns of college students in Mississippi during Freedom Summer, the Mississippi Freedom Democratic Party challenge at the 1964 Democratic Party Convention, the legacy of Fannie Lou Hamer, and much more originated from conversations in which Moore convinced

Moses to consider sending students to work in Mississippi.[48] Through SNCC, Baker influenced a generation of young people who initiated significant strides of the Civil Rights Movement in the Deep South, who became authors of various developments that unfolded in Black communities, and who became leaders in a number of New Left movements, including the Students for a Democratic Society (SDS), which adopted an organizational style and supported a form of political participation aimed at the broadest inclusion possible, a version of Baker's participatory democracy. Baker's influence was evident from close to the beginning of the Civil Rights Movement to its end. She was able to accomplish what she did by persisting in organizing around her religious, philosophical, and political commitments to human dignity and egalitarianism.[49] Ella Baker died in 1986 at age 83.

Baker's Moral Vision

In Ella Baker's life and work, human dignity and egalitarianism in human community reflect a combining of norms of racial uplift and social responsibility. For Baker, attending to human dignity meant both overcoming devastations deriving from practices of racism *and* opposing obstructions to human flourishing as full members of society. Likewise, in Baker's view, egalitarianism related both to intra-race class tensions, thereby affecting racial uplift work, *and* to justice in human community, which Baker articulated as working for "the cause of humanity." In her racial uplift and social responsibility practices, Baker sought to address "the cause of humanity" by empowering local people, or assuring as fully as possible a strong form of participatory democracy. Civil rights social historian Charles Payne has written that Ella Baker's efforts reflected her lifetime perspective of "looking for ways to reestablish among Blacks and other dispossessed groups the self-sufficiency and community of her youth."[50] While her perspectives on human dignity and egalitarianism originated in religious values of her youth, they also reflect nonsectarian and leftist ideas she encountered during her early years in New York and incorporated into her religiosity. Socialist ideas fortified and enhanced Baker's religious perspective. In New York, Baker added critical social analysis to her religiously intuitive evaluation of social injustice. Moreover, as a result of engaging socialism, Baker came to understand organizing as the primary means by which people could effect social change. In this regard, Baker's religiosity developed into a positive humanism,[51] asserting strongly the responsibility of individuals to make changes on the basis of what they could themselves accomplish.

The influence of religion in Ella Baker's activism is most apparent in the influence of her early religious context on her concept of human dignity (which included her concern that everyone have opportunities for realization of human potential) and egalitarianism in community (which developed into her concern for radical democracy). Among two religious influences that continued throughout Baker's life were her belief in God's expectation that people do good works and her use of Christian scripture to support her views of human community. Both maintained a role in informing and explaining Baker's ideas throughout her life.[52] Beliefs and practices in her childhood community instilled in Baker deep appreciation for every person's sense of self-worth and potential. Reflecting on her beliefs, Baker said, "I think these are the things that helped to strengthen my concept about the need for people to have a sense of their own value, and *their* strengths." Owing especially to the influence of her mother and grandfather, Ella Baker came to equate religion, particularly Christianity, with practicing egalitarianism and respecting human dignity. "Where we lived there was no sense of hierarchy, in terms of those who have, having a right to look down upon, or to evaluate as a lesser breed, those who didn't have," she reflected.

> Part of that could have resulted . . . from two factors. One was the proximity of my maternal grandparents to slavery. They had known what it was to not have. Plus, my grandfather had gone into the Baptist ministry, and that was part of the quote, unquote, Christian concept of sharing with others. I went to a school that went in for Christian training. Then, there were people who "stood for something," as I call it. Your relationship to human beings was more important than your relationship to the amount of money that you made.[53]

In Baker's correlation of being Christian with conviction, "[standing] for something" is the assertion that having conviction precipitates certain practices. The extent to which practices derived from this

"Christian concept of sharing with others" permeated and remained a part of Baker's self-understanding is evident in the almost apologetic way she included her father in this practice through her recollections about it at age seventy-seven: "My father took care of people *too, but see, my father had to work, poor little devil!*"[54]

Baker's encounter of social analysis and socialist ideas deepened thinking already evolving when she arrived in New York. As early as her college years, Baker began critical thinking about public life, developing her own views on human dignity and human community and about the importance of living one's convictions. During college she led protests opposing policies she interpreted as repressive and demeaning and decided against teaching as a career. Baker's protests and career decision reflected her maturing sense of human dignity as including opportunity for self-expression and self-realization. Early in her life she decided on the importance of these for herself (and for others) and determined the means to practice her own self-realization throughout her life. Having been reared in a context where persons practiced what they professed, Baker said her early critical thinking derived from "'what I saw as contradictions in what was said and what was done.'"[55] Her concern for congruence between professed belief and ordinary practice probably was deeply influenced by what she understood as her mother's and grandfather's witnessing to their faith.

For Baker, the absence of material security and exercise of human liberty reflected contradictions of religious and political proclamations that assert human value and liberty as priorities. "I think this has been a major factor in 'disturbances' of recent years," she said in a 1970 interview.

> Many people feel that they will never be recognized as human beings.
>
> A poor child, who is also black, senses in our society an inherent attitude of disrespect for poor black people, an attitude that regards them as being so different that they are incapable of being considered equals. The contradiction of having children salute the flag and learn the prevailing slogans of equality—that all men are created equal and endowed with inalienable rights, that all Americans have equal opportunity—and then have these children confront the realities of their lives is bound to produce

> an indigenous bitterness that grows and grows as their awareness of the society becomes more acute.
>
> Is it any wonder that we come across what they call the disruptive child?[56]

Baker's lifework affirmed human dignity and egalitarianism and sought practical congruity between these values and social life in the United States. This meant that Baker spent time addressing both material security and exercise of human liberty. After she moved to New York, her earliest community activism involved both. Baker's concern for congruity between belief and practice reflected her recognition of dual considerations in her conception of human dignity and egalitarianism. She was concerned about the material well-being of people, most surely arising from the religious duty she came to understand in her childhood community, and she was concerned to express and realize her worldview that full human life and liberty involve actualizing human potentialities in relationships with others.

The influences of religion (reflecting a theological origin of this view) and of socialist ideas are evident in a 1964 speech: "I always like to think that the very god who gave us life, gave us liberty. And if we don't have liberty, it is because somebody else stood between us and that which god has granted us."[57] For Baker, the desire for human dignity (including *freedom to* self-expression and self-realization, and *freedom from* degradation, material desperation, and need) springs from the divine origin of human life. "No human being relishes being spit upon like an animal. . . . Natural resistance is already there," she said.[58] Asserting the responsibility of individuals to participate in actualizing the divine gift of liberty, she continued, "so we have come here tonight to renew our struggle: the right to be men and women, to grow and to develop to the fullest capacity with which [God] has endowed us."[59]

Unlike the characterization by womanist theologians of Black religious women's expectation of God's making a way, Baker did not emphasize divine intervention for relief. Rather, her outlook stressed a theological positive humanism emphasizing what people can achieve cooperatively by their own organized initiatives on the basis of capacities given to them by God. She believed deeply in and frequently emphasized the responsibility and potential of organized groups, especially local communities, to change their own lives. In late 1964, she said to a group of civil rights advocates, "the only group that can make you free is yourself, because we must free ourselves from all of the things that keep us back."[60] As a consequence of this perspective, Baker says she put "'a greater degree of real concentration on organizing people. I keep bringing this up. I'm sorry, but it's part of me. I just don't see anything to be substituted for having people understand their position and understand their potential power and how to use it. This can only be done, as I see it, through the long route, almost, of actually organizing people in small groups and parlaying those into larger groups.'"[61]

Drawing on her religious roots, Baker used Christian scripture to admonish listeners to fight "for the freedom of the human spirit for freedom." "Let me quote one of my favorite thoughts in scripture," Baker told her audience. "And it has to do with the whole struggle I think: 'For now we are nearer than when we first believed but let us cast aside the works of darkness, and put on the armor of light.'" In what immediately followed, Baker equated "works of darkness" with long-term "tacit" agreement with practices that contributed to Black oppression; she called for not only freedom of African Americans but also "a larger freedom that encompasses all mankind."[62]

Baker's use of *human* freedom seems to signify her understanding of human dignity. For Baker, the meaning of human dignity relates both to her belief in the right of individuals to express themselves freely and the basic right of people to realize as fully as possible the capacities with which they have been endowed by their Creator. This includes people having the opportunity to work out for themselves the meaning of realizing their capacities. Ella Baker also felt that freedom of expression and freedom to actualize potentiality were constituted through full recognition and participation in the benefits and burdens of human community. While much of her work focused on African Americans, Baker's understanding of human dignity and egalitarianism always derived from her theological understanding about all humans. She said her work for freedom was for "a larger freedom that encompasses all mankind."[63] Explaining this, Baker said, "as far as I'm concerned, I was never working for an organization[;] I have always tried to work for a cause. And the cause to me is bigger than any organization, bigger than any group of people, and it is the cause of humanity. This is the cause that brings us together.

The drive of the human spirit."[64] Baker insisted on this principle through her lifetime of work to empower individuals, ranging from addressing issues of hunger and education to helping organize local communities and other groups for political participation. While these ideas were rooted in Baker's childhood community experiences of egalitarianism and care, they were expanded and became more fully developed through socialist ideas and through experiences she encountered as a young adult in New York.

Ella Baker worked for more than fifty years as a human rights activist. From her earliest days of organizing cooperatives to combat hunger and educating people about food quality, she expressed consistently a twofold perspective about human dignity and egalitarianism: first, that every human being deserves respect, and, second, that every person and community has within it whatever it needs to address its own social problems. Originating in racial uplift practices of her childhood, Baker carried forward these values in her own practices of racial uplift and social responsibility, and passed on these norms to others, who passed them on through their work. She focused on organizing local people to empower them to take charge of their own lives.

Septima Poinsette Clark: Education for Citizenship

Septima Clark, like Baker, was also concerned with empowering local people; Clark's focus was education for enfranchisement and citizenship. Through exercise of the franchise Clark saw opportunities for persons to participate in political processes that could improve their lives.

The religious self-understanding of Septima Poinsette Clark was deeply tied to her identity as a Christian and a church woman. Clark grew up in Old Bethel Methodist (later United Methodist) Church in Charleston, South Carolina, where her mother held membership, where she was baptized as a baby, where she was confirmed around age thirteen, where she chaired the youth group, and where, during all the years she resided in Charleston, she also held continuous membership. When Clark lived away from Charleston, she took up active membership in the local churches nearby. Clark once said of herself, "I've been working in the church all my life."[65] In addition to her local church participation, which she took very seriously, Clark was an active member with the United Council of Church Women and participated with other church women in various civic groups in what may be described as the legacy of the social gospel movement among religious women.[66] In this regard, she was like many nineteenth-century Black religious women social activists who related religious piety to racial uplift and social responsibility practices. Clark's participation in the Civil Rights Movement was, for her, an extension of the Christian civic activism in which she was already involved. She became predisposed to this through religious influences in her early life. Clark began her practice of religious activism before 1920 at her first teaching assignment by fulfilling what she likely understood as Christian duty to serve community members who came to her for assistance in becoming literate. By the 1950s her adult literacy work evolved into the Citizenship Education Program, a method of teaching literacy for voter registration that was replicated across the South and became significant to massive Black voter registration.

Clark's Moral Formation: Social and Religious Influences in Her Early Life

Septima Poinsette was born May 3, 1898, in Charleston, South Carolina, to Peter Porcher Poinsette and Victoria Warren Anderson Poinsette. Septima, named for her maternal aunt, was the second of eight children.[67] Like Ella Baker's grandfather, Septima's father had been a slave. Peter Poinsette's mother, who also was a slave, came to Charleston "from the Bahamas and he thought he may have been born there rather than on the Poinsette plantation."[68] Reared on the farm of Joel Poinsette, Peter took that name after becoming emancipated. While he lived on the Poinsette plantation, Peter's main responsibility was to take his slave master's children to and from school. Septima said her father was comfortable with the job, and, moreover, did not oppose the system of slavery. "Well, my father never found any fault with him [his white slave master] whatsoever," Clark said. She continued, "In fact, he didn't find any fault with any white people at that time; he was just that way." During the Civil War, Clark said, Peter "took water to the soldiers who were fighting to keep him a slave, to fight against the people in the harbor who were coming to free him. He really felt that it was perfectly all right." In addition to this, her father carried "wood to stoke the cannons to shoot the balls at those ships."[69]

Septima's knowledge of her father's disposition during the antebellum era likely derived from what he told her and her siblings when they were children. In a 1976 interview, Clark said Denmark Vesey, organizer and leader of the failed slave revolt in Charleston,

> would not have been a friend of his [her father's], because he didn't have that kind of a feeling. . . . [Vesey] could see what was happening. But [Vesey] had had some experience away from plantations, you know, and I guess that helped him. My father had such a . . . Well, I guess they had *Christianized* him. . . . He was one of the house servants—they used to say "house [niggers]"—and they felt themselves so much better than those who worked in the field. He didn't work in the field. So when slavery was over he found a job working in a ship.[70]

Although Clark characterized her own citizenship work as Christian, she also distinguished "Christianizing" (the slaveholder practice of inculcating passivity and docility) from living what might be called a conscious Christianity. While she expressed reserved criticism of her father's perspective as a slave, Clark said that she valued "his genuine love of people," demonstrated as a father and community member,[71] and that she learned from his instruction. "There were three things I learned from my father," she explained:

> One was that he wanted you to always be truthful. Next, he wanted you not to exalt yourself, but to . . . investigate how you could improve yourself towards [others]. Then, too, he talked about having Christ in your life. . . . I feel that sitting around that pot-bellied stove he really gave us three very good things to look forward to—being truthful, strengthening people's weaknesses, and seeing that there is something fine and noble in everybody.[72]

She came to understand her father both as a class-conscious house servant who felt himself better than fellow slaves and as a gentle, nonviolent person whose disposition influenced her ability to advocate the nonviolent philosophy of the Civil Rights Era.

When Peter Poinsette came out of slavery, he became a cook on ships sailing from New York to Florida, where he met and married

Victoria Anderson.[73] Although Septima valued the patience and temperament she learned from her father, in many ways she was more deeply influenced by her mother.

Victoria Warren Anderson was born in 1872 in Charleston of what "she proudly termed free issue. She had some education from books; my father had none," Clark said.[74] After marrying Peter Poinsette, she lived with him in Charleston, where he became a caterer while she took in laundry at home.[75] Unlike the humble conciliatory personality of her father, Clark said Victoria Poinsette was careful to present herself as a dignified person who opposed slavery. "My mother was something else. She was fiercely proud," Clark said. "She boasted that she was never a slave."[76] In addition, Mrs. Poinsette triumphed in having received some measure of education. "She was haughty, very much so," Clark continued. "She'd grown up in Haiti, and seemingly, in learning to read and write, she'd also learned something about the government." Taken together, Victoria Poinsette's education and being born of "free issue" influenced her perspective and behavior in relationship to slavery, domestic work, and race relations. She abhorred slavery, "terribly so, and she just actually hated the name of it, [and] always claimed that she never was a servant, and she wasn't going to be one." Although Victoria Poinsette took laundry and ironing work into her home, Clark said, "she used to boast about 'I never gave a white woman a cup of coffee.'"[77] The distinction may appear to be splitting hairs, since Mrs. Poinsette took in washing from whites; however, in spite of the meager pay and necessity of the work, taking washing into her home as opposed to going into white people's homes as a housekeeper afforded Mrs. Poinsette some level of autonomy, and clearly contributed to a sense of self-worth and dignity that she sought to maintain.[78] She opposed things that she considered undignified or that "she felt would make her a servant." For example, Clark recalled,

> vegetable carts used to come through the street, and she would never go out of her door to go to the wagon to purchase vegetables. Not her. That was not the culture of a lady. You'd sit in your door—they had these little well-holes, like, on the steps—and the man brought the vegetables in to her, and she'd choose what she wanted, and then they went back out. And she always wanted somebody—like you say "Jacquelyn," no—[to] put a

> handle on her name. She was always wanting people to say "Miss" or "Mrs." In speaking to us about my father, she just said "your father" or "Mr. Poinsette."

In addition to these practices of gentility, Clark recalled her mother demonstrating her sense of self-worth and dignity through practices that opposed or directly challenged racial oppression in her neighborhood or specifically addressed to her family. On the street where they lived, Mrs. Poinsette rebuffed attempts to confine Black children's activity and to disrespect her home. "Henrietta Street was really mixed, and it was just a one-block street. There was a Jewish family, a German one, and Irish and Italians. But the children didn't mix. The white children played in front of their door, and the black children played in front of their door. If we would skate by that Irishman's door, he would come out there and threaten to whip us." Clark recalled her mother's disputing this man as opposition to racial discrimination and as an act of courage: "I really appreciate her courage, because, in the days when segregation was very great, she had courage enough to speak against it to us." When the Irishman would threaten the Black children, Mrs. Poinsette "would always have something to say about it . . . just tell him that the street didn't belong to him. He said, 'Well, I paid for in front of my door.' You had to pay for paving the front of the door. But she said, 'That doesn't allow you the right to tell these children they can't skate past that door.' But we were afraid of him. . . ."[79]

As a woman, Mrs. Poinsette could not always overtly challenge the threats or indignities leveled at her and her family. In some instances she determined covert forms of resistance. Clark remembered her mother's actions to secure her home from trespassing or what she considered disrespect. This occurred repeatedly, Clark said, with persons illegally selling alcohol in her neighborhood:

> There was a group of, I guess they were eight Germans or Irish right across from me, and they had a car out in the street and they sold this bootleg, and they would come and sit on our step, you know, and when people'd come up you'd see them going in to this car, you know selling the bootleg liquor from that car. I really didn't know what they were doing at that time. My mother didn't want them to sit on her step. I guess she understood what they were doing. And she would lock the door and

> then take some water and throw under the door, and they couldn't understand where this water was coming from. That's the way she did. . . . Throw it very quietly. Yes. They'd be getting up and looking, wondering where this water was coming from.[80]

On another occasion, Mrs. Poinsette withstood a police officer who was looking for the Poinsette dog, which had scratched the face of a white neighbor's son. Clark said, "she told him that she didn't know where the dog was, and she'd put the dog up in the attic. . . . And he wanted to come in to look, and she refused to let him. She said, 'Don't put your feet across the sill of my door; . . . if you come through here, something's going to happen to you.' . . . She meant that, too. She would fight if she had to. . . . And she had that tone she would talk with all the time, and people understood it."[81]

Among those "people" who understood Mrs. Poinsette's tone were her children. "My mother was the disciplinarian in that family," Clark said. Her mother

> had a schedule for every child and for every day of the week. She had to wash and iron to help with the income. . . . Every day we had special chores. In the morning when I cooked the breakfast my sister had to take care of the little ones—get them dressed for school. When she cooked, then I had to do the dressing of the smaller children. My brother, who was younger than I, had to sweep down the steps and cut paper for the outdoor toilet. That was his work, and then rake the yard sometimes.
>
> Each of the older children always had a younger child as our ward to see that that child was fed, had clean clothes, didn't have holes in his clothes or anything of that type. If he had, then the older one got the whipping. That's the way my mother did it. I know if Lorene had a hole in her underpants, I'd get the whipping. I was expected to mend the hole.[82]

The Poinsette children could only play on Friday afternoons. Although neighborhood children could play ball and other games on Sunday afternoons, Mrs. Poinsette would not allow her children to do so.

> We went to Sunday Schools, one in the morning and one in the afternoon. When we came back in the afternoon we sat on the porch and they served us some peanuts and candy, and we could sing around an organ that we had. My sister could play the organ, but we never could go out in the yard and play ball, because that

> was against the religion to do anything like that on Sunday. Of course, we didn't have radio or television then, so the only thing you could do was sing, or go walking, and then go to bed.

Mrs. Poinsette even felt it irreligious to whip her children on Sundays. "If you did anything wrong on Sundays . . . she wouldn't whip you on Sunday"; however, the Sabbath did not bring absolute reprieve because "she'd whip you early Monday morning."[83]

Mrs. Poinsette's stringent perspective expressed in disciplining her children pervaded much of her moral practice and belief. She was active in her church, Old Bethel Methodist, and demonstrated her strict perspective regarding religious practice, among other ways, through her loyalty to that church. "The money she got from her washing and ironing she used to keep up her church dues," Clark recalled. "She wasn't going to let the church go lacking. If she needed a piece of ice . . . and she had money for insurance or money for church, she would rather drink the water hot. That's going to be for the church, that for the insurance. She kept it just like that."[84]

In social life, as was true of many nineteenth- and early twentieth-century religious women, Mrs. Poinsette related her religious perspective to morality and her sense of self-worth and dignity. This view influenced Mrs. Poinsette's behavior in regard to the practice of Black female concubinage and surrogacy left over from the antebellum and Reconstruction eras. "On our street," Clark said, "were four women with families who were mistresses of white men." Mrs. Poinsette warned her daughters against "sinful relationships" and disallowed their earning money by nursing white children because "she felt that in a white home a situation might develop in which there would be temptation with the man of the house or delivery boys or even men on the street." Mr. Poinsette agreed with his wife's assessment of the need to guard their children, especially the daughters. Her father, Clark said, "would never allow me, for instance, to work in a hotel or in domestic service; he feared the temptations and possible dangers sometimes associated with that sort of work."[85] Mother Poinsette also forbade playing with children born out of wedlock. Living across the street from the Poinsettes were a man and woman with a family of eight. "But still we didn't play with them because the mother and father weren't married. 'Being a kept woman,' that is the way my mother used to say it. We went all the way uptown and played with our cousins instead of playing with the children on that street." In addition, Clark and her siblings were prohibited from talking to unmarried adults who cohabited. She said, "my mother used to always say: 'You can't go to the Kallenbecks'.' Because the mother was not a married woman, the black people felt that you couldn't talk with them."

Despite her severity, however, Mrs. Poinsette was not entirely insensitive to her neighbors. When Ms. Kallenbeck became very ill while Septima was still in grade school, Mrs. Poinsette responded to Ms. Kallenbeck's request for companionship. "She wanted me to come and read the Bible to her, and my mother did let me go to do that."[86] Mrs. Poinsette admonished Septima to give assistance where she could. "If people sent you to the store or to get water, she didn't want you to take money for it. She always said you must learn to share your service."

Septima Clark's own religious self-understanding, sense of dignity, and sense of duty to help others derived from her parents' morality and beliefs. In her autobiography, written near the end of her work for the Southern Christian Leadership Conference, Clark wrote: "Many a day I have thanked a kind Providence for my parents, for the fact that they were persons of strong character, of great personal integrity, for the pride they had in their family and themselves. What they have bequeathed to me of those qualities has stood me in good stead in all the struggles that have marked so many of my years."[87] While she grew and developed her own sense of self, Clark was deeply influenced by her parents, beginning with a lifelong understanding of herself as a church person. In spite of opposing and later differing with her mother, Clark says her religious perspectives originated in her mother's teaching and in her mother's church. "I was christened in my mother's church," she says, and even though during revival at another congregation she "felt a difference" when she "was thirteen years of age, and so . . . became born again," Septima went "for several months [to] be trained up into the workings of my church. After that I was confirmed on an Easter Sunday in my church [Old Bethel Methodist]."[88]

She grew into an active membership in this congregation. "In the Sunday School when I got big enough I became chairman of the youth group," Clark recalled. "A little bit later on our church bought an organ. The lady who was chairman took sick, and raising money for that organ fell on me. I went from house to house raising over

$4000. That was when I was eighteen years of age."[89] By then a young adult with a teaching certificate, but uncertain about how to move forward in the profession, Septima experienced in this congregation what she called "a real pastor" who helped determine her life's possibilities. "Fortunately for me," she said, "we had as pastor of the Methodist church of which we were members a man who was a real pastor warmly concerned with the welfare of each member of his flock. His name was Burroughs, the Reverend E. B. Burroughs. . . . Mr. Burroughs, it happened, knew some of the trustees of the schools on nearby Johns Island. He communicated with one of these men and interceded for me. Then he asked me to write this trustee and apply for a job, which I did. I got the job."[90] Three years later, in 1919, Septima had what may have been her first date at Old Bethel when she invited the young man who would later become her husband to go to church with her there.[91]

In addition to passing on the religious perspective and orientation to help others, Mr. and Mrs. Poinsette motivated Septima's striving to become educated, as well as her decision to become a teacher. This influence on Septima's educational achievements reflected the Poinsettes' participation in the practices of racial uplift that emphasized education. Clark said both her parents insisted that their children do well in school. Although Mr. Poinsette usually deferred to his wife in matters of discipline in the home, when it came to the children getting an education, he was equally fervent. "One thing he wanted was for us to have an education," Clark said. "This was the only thing that I know he would whip you for, if you didn't want to go to school."[92] Like her husband, Mrs. Poinsette was resolute about their children's schooling. Although Septima was qualified with a teaching certificate after finishing seventh grade, she said her "mother positively refused to allow me to end my schooling in order to seek a teaching position. 'You must get some more education,' she declared. 'You'll go to Avery next year.' . . . Mother didn't know just how she was going to contrive to send me, because it was going to mean some money, but nevertheless she said I was going. 'And you start getting ready,' she instructed." As things worked out, Septima's tuition at Avery came from her first job working for a Black couple who moved into the neighborhood. The husband traveled frequently as a railway clerk, and his wife, who was afraid to stay alone, asked Septima "to stay with her and help her as house maid."[93]

While the Poinsettes insisted that their children be educated, realities of the family's financial condition also motivated Septima's striving for education and her decision to become a teacher. In her autobiography, Clark wrote: "My father made very little money and it was always difficult for him to earn enough to keep his wife and four daughters and four sons going. But with Mother's help he not only fed and clothed us and kept that roof on Henrietta Street over our heads, but also sent us all to school. And it was in those early years of my schooling that I determined I would be a teacher. So I feel that it was my parents' interest in our getting the best education we could obtain that steered me into my life work."[94] Aware of her parents' financial difficulty, she felt becoming educated and becoming a teacher would help:

> My mother was renting all the time. My parents didn't own their home. . . . [The owner] lived right in back of us on another street, and he'd come through an alley way and knock on our door to collect his rent. It was $5 a week that she had to pay for that house. One day she didn't have the money to pay him, and boy, he serenaded her. I heard him, and I felt, 'If I could be a teacher, I could have this money, and my mother wouldn't have this kind of humiliation.' Right from that time I wanted to be a teacher, and I must have been either nine or ten years old then.[95]

When Septima started school in 1904, free public education for Black children in Charleston was limited and poor. Her parents sent her "to a private school from first to third grade, then to public school from fourth to sixth, then to Avery Normal School, a private school for educating black teachers operated by the American Missionary Association." The extent to which the Poinsettes sacrificed to provide their children opportunities they thought education would bring reflects the value of education to them and coincides with the perspective of many other African Americans of the period. Her parents' role in instilling education as valuable for improving life was evident throughout Clark's life. Their understanding of education as racial uplift deeply influenced Clark's own practices of racial uplift and social responsibility.

At Avery, Septima became engrossed with the regular curriculum and library, and, because the school was a program of the American Missionary Association, Avery both complemented and expanded the religious instruction she received at home and at church. "To me Avery was a paradise. We studied astronomy, and my child's mind began to expand and question and consider as with mounting astonishment and awe I learned a little of the illimitable stretch and embrace of God's creation." Not only did she relate the study of astronomy to her own religious development, she also thought the astronomy course "fit well with the emphasis Avery put on religion. Each morning we had worship service, and twice a year the school had what they called a religious emphasis week," she said. "During these periods meetings were held by men who came down from the national office to conduct them. And in the ninth grade we had a regular course in the study of the Bible."

Upon completing Avery, Poinsette wanted to attend college at Fisk University, but her family could not afford it. Even though teachers encouraged her, Clark said, "I knew what a struggle we were having to get along even at that time and how hard it was to get the $1.50 a month for the Avery tuition, and I couldn't see how my parents could possibly send me to Fisk."[96] Since she could not attend Fisk, Septima completed her third teaching certificate and at age eighteen began looking for her first job, which she found on Johns Island, just off the coast of Charleston, with help from her pastor at Old Bethel Methodist Church. Poinsette recalled that both she and her parents "were happy that I had got the teaching job. Teaching was an honorable work that ranked well above most other work available to Negro girls. And it would be a life of service; I think this appealed particularly to my father, who as I have said, had an almost passionate love of people."[97] In addition to appeal of the job as honorable work and providing service, it also brought financial support for the Poinsette family. Septima made thirty dollars per month as a teaching principal. While it was fifty-five dollars less than white teachers holding comparable certificates, she was able to pay for her room and board and send home twenty dollars; she "allowed" herself two dollars for spending, most of which she used to send food home to her family.[98]

Clark's Early Practice of Community Work as a Moral Value

Although a young teacher at age eighteen, Septima knew the value of being known and accepted in the community. Furthermore, not only did she consider it her responsibility to provide "service" through teaching; she also assisted the community in other ways. On Johns Island she joined in community life by attending church, the main non-work activity on the island. "They'd have church this Sunday at a church here, then you'd go to another church; sometime you'll row across the creek to another church. That's the way I did. I went all around when I was over there. So all the people knew me."[99] When Poinsette arrived on Johns Island, it had "dismal economic, social and health conditions." She "lived in an attic room with no inside toilet. Workers signed contracts and were employed in tasks on large plantations. Women carried their children to the fields and placed them in boxes at the end of the row where they were working. A 'sugar tit'—lard and sugar—was placed in the babies' mouths to squelch crying. A health problem began as a result of the flies and mosquitoes that bit the babies, often causing malaria." Almost immediately Poinsette began seeking improvements. Because so many babies died before age two, she assisted in "bringing health reforms to the Sea Islands," which included conducting workshops on health issues.[100]

In addition, she spent extra time after school tutoring adults when some began to ask for her assistance.

> There were very few people over there who could read. They wanted to speak in church or at a large meeting, and they did not know how to read at all. So for my own pleasure at nights I would teach the adults how to read and to write. It was really a kind of recreation for me to work with them at nights after they got out of the field.[101]

In addition to wanting to speak in church, other Johns Islanders began to develop concern about civic activities. Soon after Poinsette

> went down to Johns Island, I discovered that some of the men were beginning to get interested in a movement that was to mean much for the island folk. . . . The Odd Fellows was a big thing. . . . The men had to know the rituals, had to make speeches to their fellow members, even had to keep books. And to do these things it was almost necessary to be able to read and write. . . . Some of the men began coming to the other Negro teacher and me for help.[102]

Poinsette taught adults to read by the same methods she used with children during the day. There was no blackboard and very little chalk or other school supplies. She and her colleague used dry cleaner's bags to write things for students to copy. "When I taught reading," she said,

> I put down "de" for "the," because that's the way they said "the." Then I told them, "Now when you look in a book, you're going to see 'the.' You say 'de,' but in the book it's printed 'the.'"
>
> Anyway, to teach reading I wrote their stories on the dry cleaner's bags, stories of their country right around them, where they walked to come to school, the things that grew around them, what they could see in the skies. They told them to me, and I wrote them on dry cleaner's bags and tacked them on the wall. From the fourth grade through the sixth grade they all did that same reading. But they needed that because it wasn't any use to do graded reading when they had not had any basic words at all.[103]

Although she had not had formal training in curriculum development, Septima Poinsette designed a method of relating the world of her students to the words they learned. In doing so she both taught them to read and affirmed the life with which they were familiar. The development of the citizenship schools for which she became so well known during the Civil Rights Era began with the necessity of creating tools for and making sense of her work as a teacher in this first job on Johns Island.

After two years at Johns Island, Poinsette took a one-year appointment at her alma mater, Avery Normal School, in 1918. Although the salary was the same as on Johns Island, thirty dollars per month, it was advantageous because she saved on board by staying at home and had better living conditions. She said later that Avery was a turning point in her life and that she "was providentially sent to Avery that year." It was at Avery during the 1918–19 school year that Poinsette first became actively involved with the NAACP. Poinsette joined the NAACP's drive to collect ten thousand signatures to present to the South Carolina legislature, demonstrating a desire of Black Charlestonians to have Black teachers in Charleston's public schools.[104] In the city of Charleston, African Americans could only teach in private schools. Clark described her concern:

> White teachers taught both black and white students, but they taught them in separate buildings. . . . We had white teachers

> who . . . didn't like for black children to speak to them in the streets; I guess they didn't want other people to know they were teaching blacks. They were embarrassed to be teaching black children and they would have you whipped.
>
> That was one of the things we had to work against. When I finished high school and had a teaching certificate and went to teach, the first thing I worked on was getting black teachers in public schools in Charleston, because I felt that it was such a disgrace to have children whipped just because they said, "How do you do, Miss Gibbs?" or whoever the teacher was.[105]

Thomas E. Miller, a Black leader and former Reconstruction Congressman, led efforts of the NAACP to have Black women teach in Charleston public schools. During that school year, Miller requested that Principal Cox at Avery ask his teachers to canvas door-to-door obtaining signatures for the petition. Septima Poinsette was among those who volunteered, and taking some of her students with her, in no small measure she helped fill the "tow sack" presented to the legislature with more than the ten thousand required signatures.[106] The law was changed the next year so that African Americans began teaching in Charleston's public schools in 1920.

During that school year, another of Poinsette's volunteer activities brought a dramatic change in her life. As a port city, Charleston was one of the places from which servicemen departed or to which they returned during World War I. Civic groups in Charleston asked teachers to serve on social committees to entertain returning servicemen. Poinsette worked with the Black USO group, and in January 1919 met Nerie David Clark, a sailor from the *USS Umpqua,* whom she invited to attend church with her family at Old Bethel Methodist.[107] Although her mother objected to Clark's being "somebody she didn't know" and being "of a darker-brown complexion than were members of [her] family," Septima Poinsette married Nerie Clark in 1920.

The couple had two children, a daughter who lived only twenty-three days and a son.[108] After the death of her daughter, Septima Clark said she had "a real hard time," because she thought that God might be punishing her for disobeying her parents and marrying a man of whom she knew little. "I really had that feeling," she said. "I thought it was against the will of God, according to the religious laws that I learned of it, and I felt very strongly about that. . . . Night after night, I had to pray about it."[109] Her husband was still serving as a sailor, and Septima was "too proud" to go to her parents, so she went to live near her in-laws in Hendersonville, North Carolina, and eventually went to live with them in Hickory, North Carolina.[110] When her husband left the Navy, Clark moved with him to Dayton, Ohio, where he returned to work as a country club waiter. Shortly after their move to Dayton, however, Nerie Clark became ill with a kidney disorder. He died in December 1925. Clark never remarried.[111]

Although she experienced difficulty moving away from Charleston, Clark also began to have an enlarged view of religiosity as a result. For her in-laws, being Christian did not mean "there were so many different rules you adhered to" as in Charleston. "My in-laws were all members of the African Methodist Episcopal Church. And I felt that I'd better join, too, and be with them or else I would not be considered too high with them."

> This proved to be a very fortunate move for me. I found them to be good people, with a healthy attitude toward life and people about them, white and Negro. They had what I felt was a more advanced idea of what being a Christian really means than the more strict code under which I had been reared had taught me to believe it was.[112]

In addition to living and worshiping with her in-laws, Clark continued her education, taking courses at North Carolina A&T College in 1922. That fall she took a teaching job in the North Carolina hills.[113] Along with the time she spent with her husband's family, Clark grew from other travel and encounters.

> As I started getting experiences in various places, my religious ideas changed. When I went to Dayton, Ohio, common-law living is great up there. . . . And there was a woman across the street who became very friendly with me and helped me with my baby, because . . . I had a fever, and couldn't nurse this boy. And she would come over and get the clothes and things and do them. And she was living in a common-law life. . . . And just experiences of people like that . . . I started looking for the differences. I never wanted to do those things myself, though. . . . And all of those things made me feel, you know, there isn't any one [way].[114]

Clark returned to Charleston in 1926, taking a job teaching at her former school on Johns Island. On Johns Island, Clark also returned to the work of adult literacy with which she had been involved previously. After one year, she sent her son to live with her in-laws because life on Johns Island was so difficult. In 1929, she took a teaching job in South Carolina's capital city, Columbia, where she lived until her mother became ill in 1946.[115]

In Columbia, Poinsette's perspectives and experiences became ever more broad. Like Baker, she took advantage of being exposed to new ideas and opportunities. She continued her education as she had done throughout her life. During the summer of 1930 Clark studied curriculum development at Columbia University in New York. In 1937 she took a course with W. E. B. Du Bois at Atlanta University. Clark persisted in her study, finally receiving a bachelor's degree from Benedict College of Columbia in 1942, and continuing with summer study until she completed a master's degree from Hampton Institute.[116] She participated in teacher-training programs through her school district, engaged in an array of civic activities, and took advantage of invitations teachers received to hear "well-known speakers" at local colleges, often white institutions, for lectures or other programs. While living in Columbia, Clark joined a local chapter of the Federated Women's Club of South Carolina, which sponsored various projects to relieve poverty. She also participated in the Black Columbia Young Women's Christian Association, the state teachers' association, and the Columbia chapter of the NAACP. For much of her time in the evenings Clark worked with Wil Lou Gray in the state's Board of Education program teaching adults to read and write. She also joined J. Andrew Simmons, her principal at Booker T. Washington School, in acquiring affidavits to support the NAACP's court case seeking to equalize Black and white teachers' salaries. Clark called this her "first 'radical' job" since it was her "first effort in a social action challenging the status quo, the first time [working] *against* people directing a system for which I was working." Clark valued opportunities to provide service to others, and again said her time in Columbia "was providentially sent," since it was so important to preparing her for later work with the citizenship schools. "My participation in the programs of the various civic groups not only strengthened my determination to make my own life count for something in the fight to aid the underprivileged toward the enjoyment of fuller lives, but also gave me excellent training in procedures that could be used effectively in that struggle."[117]

In Columbia, her son, Nerie Jr., lived with her again, but when she had difficulty providing for him, she sent him back to his grandparents in North Carolina, where he stayed until he reached adulthood.

In 1947 Clark took a job teaching seventh grade with the Charleston County Schools, returning in order to care for her ailing mother. Back in Charleston Clark continued activism and expanded her work to promote community advancement. Her Charleston civic work included supporting efforts of the Tuberculosis Association; the Young Women's Christian Association, where she chaired the administrative board; the Community Chest; the Charleston Federation of Women's Clubs; the Metropolitan Council of Negro Women; and the NAACP. She also served as president of her sorority's local chapter, Alpha Kappa Alpha's Gamma Xi Omega chapter, initiating what became a broad children's health program.[118]

Clark's work with the YWCA soon led to her notoriety. As chair of the Black YWCA Administration Committee, she coordinated preparations for the group's annual meeting. Clark suggested inviting as a guest speaker Mrs. J. Waites Waring, wife of former U.S. District Court Judge J. Waites Waring, a native Charleston aristocrat who opposed segregation and whose 1947 ruling struck down the state's all-white primary. Many white Charlestonians disliked Mrs. Waring, apparently because she was the judge's second wife and a Northerner and because she agreed with Judge Waring on race issues. Leaders at the Charleston Central YWCA resisted Mrs. Waring's appearance at the Black YWCA celebration. Clark said

> when the women in the central YWCA learned what we had done—we had a dual system with white and Negro groups separate—they were greatly perturbed, and they called a special meeting . . . to find out just how the invitation might be quietly recalled. . . . I still remember how strange I thought that meeting was. The woman who had conducted the devotional program had talked about walking in the light and walking with faith and walking with courage. And then after listening to her pleading for courageous walking, they had professed their desperate fear of having a woman speak to them. . . . I said to them, I personally

> knew nothing of the things they had been telling me and certainly I would not be willing to sign a letter to her asking not to speak to us. . . . But they weren't willing to let me alone. The executive director of the YWCA asked me to come into her office. I went in and found that she had a statement prepared which she wished me to sign; it was a statement to the newspapers saying in effect that we did not intend for Mrs. Waring to speak. I declined to sign that, too. I told them that I was sorry but that I just couldn't stand up on that sort of platform.[119]

As Clark persevered in refusing to recall the invitation to Mrs. Waring, "newspapers carried stories, the telephones buzzed, the gossipers had a field day."[120] Preparing for the meeting, Clark and others took precautions to avoid troublemakers causing problems. When the hour arrived, the meeting overflowed because of the publicity. Mrs. Waring, perhaps responding to assaults upon her and Judge Waring, "laid the whip to the backs of the people of Charleston and the South" for their treatment of African Americans. Clark continued to receive calls from as far away as New York, and local papers printed the speech extensively, resulting in a deluge of letters to the editors. One result was that Clark's friendship with the Warings grew.

As controversy over the Warings continued, both whites and Blacks began to oppose Clark's affiliation with them. In one instance, Clark's principal emphasized to her "his feeling that 'the time just isn't right' for [her] doing what [she] was."[121] Soon all Clark's civic activism was challenged as she was accused of subversive affiliations. Her relationships with the United Council of Church Women, which supported liberal causes, and with Myles and Zilphia Horton, who ran an interracial center at Monteagle, Tennessee, came under question. "I know they felt that I was really a Communist then. I was too much of a head woman, a controversial leader," Clark said.[122] In 1954, Clark attended a summer workshop at the Hortons' Highlander Folk School, founded as an interracial laboratory for teaching local people, especially the poor, how to cooperate and attend to social and political problems confronting them.

Highlander sought to help persons in local communities combat issues affecting them. This work excited Clark:

> Persons who came to Highlander to participate were concerned with specific problems. . . . They came up to the mountains to

> discover and consider ways of attacking these problems in their own communities. . . . Highlander workshops weren't set up merely to theorize and ponder problems; they expected and demanded that theory and discussion and decision be galvanized into action and achievement.[123]

Impressed with Highlander's work, Clark took a group of others from Charleston to a workshop later the same year. She invited the Hortons to lead workshops she developed for parent-teacher groups in Charleston and on Johns Island. Clark also invited Myles and Zilphia Horton to help organize a teachers' credit union. According to Clark, banks feared implications of the *Brown* decision, and "teachers who had done three or four years on a master's degree would have to start all over if they didn't get money to go that summer." The credit union helped finance their continuing education.[124] By the summer of 1955 Clark both attended and directed workshops at Highlander and continued taking groups from Charleston and Johns Island to experience the Highlander program.[125]

Clark's Civil Rights Participation as Living Out Religious Belief

In 1954 the NAACP won its protracted battle to desegregate the country's schools. In *Brown v. Board of Education* the Supreme Court struck down as unconstitutional a former Court's ruling that legalized separate schools for Black and white students. Around the country and particularly in the South, state and local legislatures acted quickly and vehemently to circumvent the ruling. In South Carolina this included developing a state committee on segregation and a 1956 statute that made "unlawful the employment by the state, school district or any county or municipality . . . of any member of the National Association for the Advancement of Colored People, and to provide penalties for violations."[126] In time the Waring controversy subsided but was not forgotten, as Clark continued civic activism and especially as she continued work with the NAACP. "I knew from the conversations going around that I was being discussed freely, and . . . I was expecting at any moment to be dismissed as a teacher." In spite of this expectation, Clark remained composed, asserting that "trying to do what I think is right" bolstered her. "I was trying to do what I felt was my duty. I was trying then as I had tried through the years before and have been trying in the years since to contribute something to the advancement of our southern community by helping elevate the lives of a large segment of it."

Pursuant to the *Brown* decision, like many other teachers across the state and the South, Clark completed a questionnaire that required listing organizational affiliations. Clark said, "I refused to overlook my membership in the NAACP, as some of the teachers had done, and listed it." That spring Clark was dismissed quietly, and her pension was lost when, after more than thirty years of employment with the state's public schools, she received no contract for the fall term. "Before the June 3 deadline in 1956 I received the letter announcing that I was not being considered for the term beginning that fall. No reason was given for my dismissal. It was simply a curt announcement that I was through." Clark said she sent "a registered return letter to ask them why. And the only thing they said to me was . . . no principal, no superintendent, no president of a college had to tell you why; your services are just not needed. That's what they said."

Shortly after her termination, Myles Horton invited Clark to direct workshops at Highlander, continuing work she had done during two previous summers at the center. Clark again said she believed "providential direction" intervened in carrying her to work at Highlander.[127] For the next five years, Clark moved about the South, as Ella Baker had done in the 1940s, initiating what became the civil rights Citizenship Education Program. Again, like Baker, she emphasized empowering local people and taught local leaders to teach their relatives, friends, and neighbors "to write their names, balance check books, vote in elections, and write letters." Through this work Clark served as a catalyst for transforming Southern political life.[128] In her emphasis on basic reading and writing as preparation for citizenship, Clark contrasted herself with Baker, saying her (Clark's) focus "had to do with teaching people to read and write first. And I think she [Baker] was trying to get over to them to become first-class citizens without reading and writing. . . . Because she was concerned about not being recognized."[129] Clark realized the need to help African Americans overcome the literacy requirements used throughout the South as barriers to Black enfranchisement. The purpose of adult literacy, Clark said, was to teach "them to read and write so they could register and vote."

All of these states had these stringent registration laws. They had to write their names in cursive writing here in Charleston and read a section of the election laws. In Georgia they had thirty questions they had to read and give answers to. In Alabama they had twenty-four questions they had to read and give answers to. In Mississippi they had twenty-four questions. And in Louisiana there were thirty questions that they had to read and answer. Now eastern Texas did not have that; in eastern Texas they had to pay a poll tax, and we had to work with them to get them not to pay the poll tax. And they had to do that each year. So we had these differences all around. And in each state we had to do different things.[130]

The "citizenship schools" began on Johns Island, growing out of Clark's community work there. While driving a bus between Johns Island and Charleston, Esau Jenkins, one of the adults with whom Clark had worked and whom Clark had taken to a Highlander workshop in 1954, successfully helped one of his passengers become qualified to vote. After this success others approached Jenkins for assistance. As a result Jenkins sought to develop a school "to interest the islanders in equipping themselves for citizenship, and . . . to combat adult illiteracy." He discussed the idea with Clark, who, as director of workshops at Highlander, assisted him in purchasing a building. After the building was secured, Clark sought a teacher.

I was directing the work at Highlander, and that work took me into so many different places that I would not have the time to do the day-by-day teaching. Besides going into the deep south states, holding meetings, getting people to realize that we should have Citizenship Schools, I was also going to the north, the midwest, and the west fund-raising for the Highlander Folk School.[131]

A local beautician and dressmaker, Bernice Robinson, took the job as teacher, and the school opened on January 7, 1957. In a 1980 article reflecting on the work of the citizenship schools, Clark described the criteria for teachers:

Our major requirements are that the persons be able to read well aloud, and that they write legibly on a blackboard. It has been our experience that these persons, without a great deal of formal training, can be taught to teach a few basic things, and that often they make better teachers than persons with a great deal of aca-

> demic background. Their approach is a "folk" approach to learning rather than a classical one. Their vocabularies are similar, and there is usually an existing relationship upon which we build.[132]

Success of the first school was immediate: "every single one of our pupils who had attended school those five months was able to get his registration certificate!" Clark recalled. Soon, Black residents of other coastal Charleston islands followed Johns Island's model. In the summer of 1958, after hearing of Johns Island's success, Wadmalaw Islanders also requested assistance. In October, Edisto Island asked to start a citizenship school, and eventually, a program opened on Daufuskie Island as well.[133]

To develop curriculum for citizenship schools, Clark used methods she learned from experience while teaching at Johns Island and from work with Wil Lou Gray in Columbia, combating adult illiteracy for the state's Board of Education. "We were teaching words," Clark said, "but the words were words of an adult world and they were words an informed citizen, a participating citizen, would often be using."[134] Moreover, because the barriers to enfranchisement varied widely from state to state, curriculum content was tailored to needs in each state. "We used the election laws of that particular state to teach reading. We used the amount of fertilizer and the amount of seeds to teach the arithmetic, how much they would pay for it and the like," Clark said. "We did some political work by having them to find out about the kind of government that they had in their particular community. . . . Each state had to have its own particular reading, because each state had different requirements for the election laws." Clark also developed a general workbook discussing election, registration, and voting laws, social security laws, tax laws, and other important topics.[135]

As Highlander continued interracial meetings, and Clark continued directing Highlander's workshops, Tennessee authorities sought to interrupt the school's operation. In July 1959, while Horton was away teaching in Europe, Tennessee State Police raided Highlander and charged Clark with possession of whiskey. The charge was a ruse, since "most of the people I worked with knew that I was a teetotaler."

> When I was director of the educational program at Highlander, they didn't have any beer. That's one thing I spoke about with

> Myles. The men did like to drink beer, but I felt as if we didn't need to have the beer, because I saw quite a few of the union men that the beer made almost crazy. They didn't act like themselves. Some of them couldn't get out of bed to come to the workshop the next day, and I didn't want to be wrestling with people with beer. When Myles had to go to Europe on a trip, I certainly put my foot down that I was not going to have any beer-selling.

Nevertheless, after the arrest, Clark was convicted. In spite of the raid, training at Highlander continued. By 1961 "eighty-two teachers who had received training at Highlander were holding classes in Alabama, Georgia, South Carolina, and Tennessee."

Assaults on the Highlander Folk School continued, however, and by December 1961, Tennessee revoked the school's charter and auctioned its property.[136] Anticipating the shutdown, Horton had conversations with Martin Luther King Jr. about transferring the Citizenship Program to the SCLC, an idea Ella Baker initiated that came to fruition during the summer of 1961. As Clark explained,

> After the raid on Highlander in July of 1959, Dr. King and Myles Horton got together to see if they could use the program that we had already planned, and they decided they could. Andy Young came to the SCLC at that time, sent by the United Church of Christ in New York. . . . So I went to Atlanta. I stayed in Atlanta on weekends; on Monday morning I would get into a car and be driven somewhere in the South. I would stay for a week or two.

Funds the Marshall Field Foundation granted Highlander for citizenship schools transferred to the SCLC along with Clark as director.[137]

At the SCLC Clark continued developing the citizenship school movement. Andrew Young secured housing for the program in a United Church of Christ facility, the Dorchester Cooperative Community Center in Liberty County, Georgia, about 295 miles south of Atlanta. Young and Dorothy Cotton worked with Clark as citizenship program staff. "Three of us . . . drove all over the South recruiting people to go to the Dorchester Center," Clark recalled. "Andy Young was the administrator, Dorothy Cotton was the director or the educational consultant, and I was the supervisor of teacher training. The three of us worked together as a team, and we drove all over the South bringing busloads of folk—sometimes seventy people—who would live together for five days at the Dorchester Center."

Although most persons participating in training to lead citizenship classes came to Highlander School or the Dorchester Center, on occasion it was necessary to take the program into Southern communities where people lived. Sometimes before a workshop could be held, Clark spent weeks "just talking and talking to people." In most cases, she eventually set up schools using local people as leaders. Teachers received a modest wage to attend training sessions and a monthly stipend to lead classes. Ever mindful of the desperate circumstances of Black people during that time, Clark said, "They were always in debt. We felt that if they didn't make anything on the farm, we had to pay them."[138] They used funds from the Field Foundation to encourage attendance and to help alleviate distresses of their poverty.

By 1961 work preparing African Americans to vote increased exponentially as the Kennedy Administration sought to diffuse violent retaliation and tension against direct action campaigns like the sit-ins and Freedom Rides. Engineered by U.S. Attorney General Robert Kennedy to direct civil rights energy away from direct action projects the Administration perceived as confrontational, the Voter Education Project focused on Clark's citizenship program as a means of vastly increasing Black voter registration. Funded by the Taconic, Field, and Stern Foundations and administered through the Southern Regional Council, the Voter Education Project officially began in 1962 with separate programs of the SCLC, SNCC, CORE, and the Urban League to prepare and register Black voters. Over the next four years the programs trained about ten thousand teachers for the citizenship schools. During this period almost seven hundred thousand new Black voters registered across the South. Moreover, after the 1965 passage of the Voting Rights Act, Black voter registration increased very rapidly. At least a million more Black people registered by 1970, the year Clark retired from her work with the SCLC.[139]

Clark's Religious and Moral Perspectives

Throughout her life, Septima Poinsette Clark held quite traditional evangelical Christian perspectives deeply connected to her self-understanding as a church woman. Clark took very seriously her identity as a church person and what she perhaps understood as a responsibility to have a relationship with congregations wherever she lived. It is likely that this reflected both her identity as a church woman and her concern that others perceive her as such.

After Septima married and moved from Charleston to Hickory, North Carolina, she joined her in-laws' congregation. Yet she held continuity of her church membership as important. When she joined the Clarks' congregation, she took the formal step of having the two churches correspond with each other. "Well, I had a letter to go to the African Methodist when I was up there living with them, and then when I came back I had another letter to come back here, is what I did."[140] In Monteagle, Tennessee, where she established the work in citizenship education at the Highlander Folk School, Clark was a regular congregant at the "only place I could go to church . . . up at a town called Sewanee. Up there I went to the church they had designed for seminarians to preach to the Black people who worked on the grounds. The other churches in the town of Monteagle I could never go to. I simply couldn't go."[141] After she retired from Highlander and moved back to Charleston, Clark became fully active again in Old Bethel Methodist Church, where she served on several local church boards and did not hesitate to speak her views on church matters.[142] In going back to Old Bethel, Clark returned to the place where beliefs that undergirded her activism originated in the ritual of regular church participation and instruction of her parents.

As a participant in Black religious communities throughout her life, Clark expressed perspectives coincident with Black religious traditions. In keeping with beliefs Delores Williams identifies among Black women, Clark held that God "makes a way for life and flourishing." This is reflected in her frequent references to "providence" as providing opportunities, direction, and care throughout her life. She wrote in her autobiography that, after losing both teaching job and pension, "I was not nervous and not afraid. I was somewhat surprised, of course, and considerably hurt. But I was not frightened. I felt then—and I feel now—that a kind *Providence* directs us when we strive to do what we think is right, and I have sought all the years since as an eighteen-year-old girl I went over to Johns Island, to do what is right, not only for my own people but for all people." Clark described providential participation in her appointment to teach at Avery and in her teaching career in Columbia. Likewise, she identified providential direction in her work at Highlander, even though the invitation came from the school's director and evolved as a natural next step in her activism. "I was out of a job," Clark said later; however, "this I do believe—*Providence* directed me."[143] Clark held that God wills human observation of divine intention, "destining" persons to cooperation and community, but humans succumb to powerful systems that subvert this intention.[144]

In a speech delivered after her retirement from the SCLC, titled "Why I Believe There Is a God," she said, "I was sure that the seed for my belief in God's existence had actually been sown in my childhood by Christian parents who told me about God and made me know that He was a living reality for them."[145] As she grew older, as conditions changed, and as she experienced life beyond the world of her parents, her perspectives about the nature of God and about God's expectations evolved and became less severe. As a young person, Clark feared God's punishment of disobedience.[146] In contrast to the focus on personal morality as the demand of Christianity that her parents passed on to her, as an adult Clark reinterpreted the meaning of religious duty as having quite explicit implications for participation in social and political life. She cites both living with her in-laws, who were less strict about the meaning of practicing Christianity, and exposure to other persons and perspectives as contributing to the broadening of her own views. Unlike Ella Baker, who fashioned beliefs that fit more fully with her growth through exposure to new ideas and experiences, Clark maintained a fairly close adherence to traditional Christian doctrine throughout her life. Baker developed a reasoned, strongly pragmatic, deeply political understanding of the nature and meaning of religion and civil rights practices; in some sense, Septima Clark maintained a precritical perspective about faith and connected her practice directly to the example and teaching of Jesus.

Still, for Clark, who regularly observed rituals like worship attendance, prayer, and scripture reading, living her belief meant observing daily practices in keeping with what she understood as religious duty, expressing Christian principles in an interracial context. She felt her behavior as a Christian should reflect the life of Jesus. This is particularly how she characterized her work at Highlander and with the Citizenship Education Program.

> I do not like to be described as a Negro leader fighting for the integration of the schools, the churches, the transportation facilities, the political parties, or whatnot. I don't consider myself a fighter. I'd prefer to be looked on as a worker, a woman who

> loves her fellow man, white and Negro alike, and yellow, red, and brown, and is striving with every energy, working—not fighting—in the true spirit of fellowship to lift him to a higher level of attainment and appreciation and enjoyment of life. I hope that I have—surely I wish to possess and I do strive to attain—something of the spirit of the lowly and glorious young Man of Galilee, who, as I read him and understand him and worship him, saw no color or racial lines but loved with a consuming devotion all of the children of God and knew them all as his brothers.
>
> I like to think of Highlander as a place where the simple but profound ideals of Christianity were not only preached but practiced.[147]

While Baker seems to have examined, interrogated, and reinterpreted the faith of her family and community, Clark remained close to the faith of her mother and father, although she did reinterpret the meaning of living that faith. Describing her own religious feeling, Clark said her faith and activism represented the flowering of what was planted in her by her parents and community and also by God. "This feeling that God exists is a feeling that I share with all mankind," she wrote. "Nothing seems more universally woven into the consciousness of all men in every age than an apparent compulsion to acknowledge divinity. It was this disposition, this incurable religious feeling in me that caused the seed of belief sown by my parents and society to flourish."[148] The extent to which Clark maintained a traditional interpretation of Christian faith, in contrast with Baker, is also seen in her language and descriptions of experiencing God. Clark described the survival and recovery of an aunt struck by a car as a miracle from God and a contribution to the flowering of her faith.

> My own religious experiences have given me insights into the reality of God that would have been unattainable otherwise. On a rainy soaked street I saw my mother's sister knocked down by a speeding automobile and her great-grandchild who was holding her hand just escaped going into the tidal drain. We were all leaving church getting into our cars[, and] I asked God to send her back to her children and although she was in her late seventies with a broken hip, a concussion of the head, and a broken collar bone[,] after many months in the hospital and at home she

> came back safe and sound. . . . My belief in the power of God was greatly strengthened whenever I visited her and thought of the miracle God had wrought.[149]

While not fundamentalist in her perspectives about Christian scripture, Clark's approach to Scripture often was a kind of literal translation of ideas and even words from Scripture for use coincident with ideas and circumstances of her work. In this regard, Clark's interpretation of Scripture coincides with the legacy in Black Christian traditions to evaluate the Bible based on its relevance for daily life.[150] When assessing the relevance of the relatively small number of persons who participated in citizenship workshops on Edisto Island, Clark used a verse from 1 Corinthians to identify the anticipated impact of the small group's work on the whole community. A "total of thirty-eight men and women enrolled. That was a large group, but small in comparison with the size of the group of illiterates not interested in advancing themselves through study of the ABC's of learning. Nevertheless, as the Scriptures point out, often a small bit of yeast will be the leaven that raises the large loaf."[151] She also used ideas and words of New Testament letters to describe the interracial and inter-class sense of community that developed among workshop participants at Highlander. Clark wrote that "because they are sharing ideas, they are enjoying a true unity of purpose, and I might go on to add, with the Apostle Paul, a unity of faith, hope, and love. And sometimes even there is a unity in sacrifice, too."[152] Finally, Clark generalized the movement of history as in accord with pronouncements of Christian scripture, saying she was encouraged by what she saw in the correlation.

> When I would be discouraged by the seeming triumph of injustice and wrong in our world or my life at any given time, the Bible and the broad sweep of history which validates what the Bible says about the nature and destiny of men and institutions not only come to my rescue but also strengthen my belief. When I survey the broad sweep of history and watch the winged flight of Christian faith from an obscure province in Asia Minor through severe persecutions at Rome to the decay of the Dark Ages, the challenge of the Enlightenment to its present sway over the life and thought of men I cannot help but believe there is a God.[153]

In spite of her allegiance to traditional evangelical Christian perspectives, Clark never was limited to the viewpoint that being Christian simply meant personal piety and praying. In keeping with another emphasis of her parents, on service and religious duty, and correlating with traditions of Black religion to execute racial uplift and social change practices, Clark strove to live out in daily life what she saw as the meaning of her religious convictions. In doing so, she was propelled into public life and public activism, a realm far beyond the interpersonal and immediate local community service her parents conceived as Christian duty. For Clark, racial uplift and Christian duty included offering traditional works of charity, challenging persons to move out of oppression, and struggling against conventions and systems that oppose human dignity. Describing the civic work she did with the NAACP and other groups in Charleston, Clark expressed her concept of duty as a life calling: "I was trying to do what I felt was my duty; I was trying then as I have tried through the years before and have been trying in the years since to contribute something to the advancement of our southern community by helping elevate the lives of a large segment of it."[154]

While Clark was specific in addressing her work primarily to African Americans excluded from exercise of the franchise, from full citizenship, and from full human flourishing, she conceived the work she did as universal, calling it work toward "a new and fairer day for all God's children."[155] In the dedication of her autobiography, using language comparable to Baker's, Clark describes her activism as working in "the struggle for human dignity."[156] This struggle for Clark meant attending first to those persons who experience least the meaning of being fully human as defined in the society of which they are a part. "The ability of the United States to cope with racial difference within her borders," Clark wrote, "is the key to her role as a leader of a world that is made up largely of colored peoples. Our day of judgement may well be decided by the way we treat the least of these, our brothers, within our midst." During the Civil Rights Era, this logically indicated attending to African Americans and segregation: "For, after making every allowance, every fair-minded and informed citizen must know that segregation is in itself evil that has done our nation—not simply the Negroes or other peoples segregated—untold harm and has held back by many years the rightful development of the South." Clark believed that she should expect nothing less than that the socially proximate meaning of justice be available for all society's citizens.[157]

Clark's Emphasis on the Least

The size of the segment of the Southern community Clark sought to elevate reflects the focus of Clark's racial uplift and social responsibility practices on the masses of persons whom she felt were most oppressed by Southern race and class conventions. In keeping with what womanist theologians Jacquelyn Grant identifies as attending to the least and Cheryl Townsend Gilkes calls responding to the most oppressed and deprived, Clark felt the masses often were in no position to help themselves. They were, she wrote, "lonely and lost, those frantic to find a future endurable, those who have stood by helpless and watched loved ones being destroyed by merciless power structures and unprincipled individuals who were destined instead in the providence of God to be their brothers."[158] Clark saw work of uplifting the oppressed as work that Christians ought to do in the world.

Clark equated the citizenship program with Jesus' ministry to the least. For her, it was in attending to the needs of the masses that the entire society improved.

> Despite the fact that during virtually my whole adult life I have been fighting the dominant citizenship of my Low Country—though I feel that actually I am fighting for them as well as for the less privileged and the silent—I love them, all of them. I want to see their lots, as well as the lots of the less fortunate, improve steadily. And I am convinced that the advancement of our lowly ones to the opportunities of first class citizenship also will lift to a better life those who now enjoy a higher status. . . . I work among the Negro people, who, we must agree, have the fewest of the democratic freedoms and many of whom have inadequate education or none at all, who live constantly under the fear of intimidation, insult and violence, I am reminded that here is the continuing test of our democratic form of government. In the recent rise of the image of hope for the segregated black man and his deliverance from this state of pseudo-slavery I see clearly the form of challenge. If permanent social patterns are to be created that are truly democratic, I maintain, then the most lowly being must enjoy equally with every other American the fruits of

> democracy. Only then will the Negro, and particularly the Negro parent, see the glimmer of light ahead, only then will he see a way out of his dilemma.[159]

For Clark, attending to needs of the least meant more than providing traditional gifts of charity. Like Baker, who advocated human responsibility in changing society, Clark thought attending to the least also included empowering and challenging "the least" to overcome and move beyond their present circumstances.

> Christians can never be content with token progress by a fortunate few. They must continually remain sensitive to the will of God for the redemption of "the saints of rank and file," the people of the land around whom Jesus centered his earthly ministry. The Citizenship Education Program is attempting to provide an opportunity for these people to help themselves and their neighbors. By training one or two persons from each community we are able to help them to teach their neighbors about the American way of life and the way in which the ballot is used to create and continue the rule of liberty and justice for all (even dark-skinned persons in Mississippi).[160]

Still, for Clark, it was not enough to prepare persons to seek the advantages of full citizenship. It was also necessary, she said, to address social structures that operated against their flourishing.

> The first words of Jesus' public ministry were quoted from the prophet Isaiah. "The Spirit of the Lord is upon me, because he hath anointed me to preach the gospel to the poor; he has sent me to heal the brokenhearted, to preach deliverance to the captives, and recovering of sight to the blind, to set at liberty them that are oppressed." Throughout the New Testament, the concern for the poor and underprivileged is expressed as one of the fruits of grace. Where there is obedience to the gospel, there will be concern for the less fortunate. "The *least* of these my brethren *are* no less *brothers* in Christ than one's social counterparts."
>
> Long experience in Christian missions has taught us that this love and concern for others must be made concrete. Our missionaries could not be content preaching the gospel to hungry folk. They had also to teach them new agricultural methods and help them to provide food for themselves and their families. They provide clinics and hospitals to improve the health of the people, and established schools for the education of these new converts.

Clark held that Christian ministry involved attending to things that prepare persons for self-sufficiency as well as confronting structures that cause persons to be "deprived."

> In recent years we have realized that still another step is necessary. To feed or educate or heal an individual with no thought for the type of community life, or system of government which has contributed to the deprived state of the individual, is too shortsighted indeed. If we really are to contribute to the "deliverance of the captives" it is necessary to do something to redeem the system which keeps them in captivity.[161]

At the same time, Clark was quite provincial in her understanding of the origin and ultimate meaning of human liberty. Whereas Baker began deeply rooted in and committed to traditional Christian missions as a remedy for social ills and transcended this perspective as she grew in experience and engaged socialist ideas, Clark was quite critical of the context and practices that caused oppression, but throughout her life she remained wedded to traditional Christian perspectives about human life and liberty and to a nationalistic understanding of Christianity. At age eighty-two she wrote:

> In every corner of the globe, there is now heard the cry for freedom. Our Christian Mission stations at home and abroad have done a great deal to plant concepts of freedom, justice, and equality in the hearts of men. Now the march is on to actualize these concepts. At times it scares us, as in the Congo where untrained masses are turned loose with little preparation for running a government, but we realized that this is a part of a dream which is both Christian and American in its inspiration—our fear should be transformed into concern.[162]

Clark and Black Religious Institutions

Although Clark's racial uplift and social responsibility activism originated and developed through civic participation and employment at Highlander Folk School, a marginally para-religious institution, Clark engaged Black religious institutions directly in her civil rights organizing. She often worked through and sometimes depended on churches to house and provide other support for citizenship schools as she worked with persons who were often church members. However, the most intense period of her involvement with Black religious institutions occurred when her work moved from Highlander Folk School to the SCLC. The character of Clark's experiences with these institutions included local support *and* fear of the work she did; patriarchal oppression, particularly shown through opposition to women's leadership; and a hierarchy correlating with patriarchy that opposed or devalued local people and local leadership.

Pursuant to Clark's earliest civic activism, she encountered fear among church members who thought she was too radical in her approaches to racial issues. When Clark was fired for her civic activism and support of Mrs. Waring, her sorority held a testimonial benefit for Clark. The sorority sisters, however, many of whom were teachers, feared taking pictures with her at the event, and members of Clark's home church, Old Bethel Methodist, did not attend. "They were too afraid," she said.

> When I was dismissed from school and my sorority gave that testimonial for me, all of my church women were afraid to do anything about it. And I was on their trustee board and working with the missionary group, but not one of them would come and say a word. They sent a little girl [laughter] out of the youth group, and she read a little paper and she could hardly read it.[163]

However, the pastor of Old Bethel Church did attend the event.

As Clark set about developing citizenship programs in local communities, she often depended on churches for assistance. Many provided initial meeting places. In Huntsville, Alabama, for example, Baptist and Methodist ministers were Clark's initial contacts; they helped her gather persons to begin conversation about citizenship schools. On Edisto Island, a local Presbyterian church provided space for the citizenship program to meet. In addition to local religious institutions, Clark's Citizenship Education Program also was supported by Christian denominational bodies, such as the United Church of Christ, which initially sponsored the Reverend Andrew Young as field support for Clark while she worked at Highlander. The United Church of Christ later provided a facility to house the program when Clark left Highlander and moved the program to the SCLC.[164]

In other instances, however, local Black ministers and some congregants feared supporting Clark and her work. "It's simply a contradiction," she said later. "So many preachers supported the Movement that we can say it was based in churches, yet many preachers couldn't take sides with it because they thought they had too much to lose." Although she had some support from clergy in Huntsville, she said another clergyman and church members were afraid to support her. In Selma, Alabama,

> black preachers would say, "Who's going to pay for this? Who's going to do so-and-so?" Back of it was the fact that they didn't want the white people to know that we were teaching blacks to write their names, for then the merchants would stop giving the preachers their anniversary gifts. They wanted those gifts. Material things were more to them than the human value of things. . . . Of course, I understand those preachers. I know they were dependent on white people's approval. Even with their congregations' support, they could be run out of town if the white power structure decided they ought to go. Often they weren't against the Movement; they were just afraid to join it openly.[165]

In those instances where church persons, particularly ministers, clearly supported the Civil Rights Movement, Clark encountered other difficulties consistent with Baker's experience at the SCLC. This included male clergy's and other men's antagonism toward women's leadership, trivializing women's contributions, and opposition to developing and enabling local leaders. During the Civil Rights Era, men were almost always in charge in Black churches. "It was just the way things were," she recalled. However, the reality of this convention, like others she opposed, disturbed Clark. "I see this as one of the weaknesses of the civil rights movement, the way the men looked at women. I used to feel that women couldn't speak up. . . . Of course, my father always said that a woman needs to be quiet and just be in the home. . . . I changed my mind about women being quiet when they had something to say."[166] Moreover, Clark asserted, women's participation often was responsible for initiating and sustaining civil rights activities and practices in local areas: "In stories about the civil rights movement you hear mostly about the black ministers. But if you talk to the women who were there, you'll hear another story. I think the civil rights movement would never have taken off if some women hadn't started to speak up."[167]

In her own work with Black ministers, Clark directly confronted traditional perspectives about women's leadership. Her role as an executive within the SCLC frequently was questioned, and, as was the case with Ella Baker, her suggestions and contributions often received no serious consideration. "I was on the executive staff of the SCLC, but the men on it didn't listen to me too well," Clark recalled. Her position on the SCLC staff derived from the important role she played in connecting the organization with local people across the South, translating ideas about social change into practices that energized and involved many people. While it had been a goal of the SCLC to build a South-wide base and program, Clark's work with the citizenship schools was essential to many SCLC local programs. "They liked to send me into many places, because I could always make a path in to get people to listen to what I have to say. But those men didn't have any faith in women, none whatsoever. . . . Rev. Abernathy would say continuously, 'Why is Mrs. Clark on this staff?' Dr. King would say, 'Well, she has expanded our program. She has taken it into eleven deep south states.' Rev. Abernathy'd come right back the next time and ask again."[168]

Although King was supportive of Clark's work with citizenship education and its significance to the SCLC's effectiveness, Clark said, "like other black ministers, Dr. King didn't think too much of the way women could contribute."[169] Describing the reaction of Dr. King and other SCLC leaders to the presence of women during SCLC executive staff meetings and to ideas she presented, Clark commented that during "executive meetings, if [women] had anything to say, maybe we could get to say it at the end of the session, but we never were able to put ourselves on the agenda to speak to the group."[170] When seeking to present ideas to the entire executive board during meetings failed, Clark tried sharing her thoughts directly with King through letters and reports. Similar to Baker, Clark sought to convince the SCLC and local SCLC supporters of the relevance of empowering local persons.

> When I heard the men asking Dr. King to lead marches in various places, I'd say to them, "You're there. You going to ask the leader to come to everywhere? Can't you do the leading in these places?"
>
> I sent a letter to Dr. King asking him not to lead all the marches himself, but instead to develop leaders who could lead their own marches. Dr. King read that letter before the staff. It

> just tickled them; they just laughed. . . . If you think that another man should lead, then you are looking down on Dr. King. This was the way it was. . . . Here was somebody from Albany, from Waycross, Georgia, from Memphis, Tennessee, from Chicago, from Detroit—all wanting him to come to lead a march. I felt that it wasn't necessary. I thought that you develop leaders as you go along, and as you develop these people let them show forth their development by leading. That was my feeling, but that was too much for them. They didn't feel as if that should be.[171]

The reaction to Clark's idea not only reflected the view at that time of many Black clergy toward women, but also revealed the disempowering nature of religious hierarchy to laypersons and the tendency of civil rights celebrity to detract from and weaken the role of local people.

By the early 1960s Clark expressed concern about dissolution of citizenship schools because there was no follow-up from SCLC staff. In one report to King, Clark wrote:

> Many states are losing their citizenship schools because there is no one to do follow-up work. I have done as much as I could. In fact, I'm the only paid staff working doing field visitation. I think that the staff of the Southern Christian Leadership Conference working with me in the Citizenship Education Program feels that the work is not dramatic enough to warrant their time. Direct action is so glamorous and packed with emotion that most young people prefer demonstrations over genuine education.

In some ways, coincident with Baker's feeling that organizing (as opposed to mobilizing) people was essential, Clark felt teaching was indispensable. The deeper similarity between the two women is the emphasis both placed on determining ways to enable people at the grassroots to be self-determining.[172]

> I don't think that in a community I need to go down to the city hall and talk; I think I train the people in that community to do their own talking. This is what I do. But he [King] couldn't see it. I would not have ever been able to work in Mississippi and Alabama and all those places if I had done all the talking. And when I worked with those young people who came down, the college students, I would say to them, "Don't go and cash the check for this woman. Let her do it; you can go with her, give her

> that much courage. But make her cash her check and do her own talking so that she can have the feeling that she can confront."[173]

In her interaction with college students who were civil rights volunteers, Clark, like Baker, emphasized empowering local people, probably reinforcing the idea that Baker had been teaching the students as well. The SCLC's patriarchy did not relent during Clark's tenure. She retired from its staff in 1970.

Empowering Local People as a Moral Value

Religious belief and religious practice were fundamental components of identify formation for both Baker and Clark. Baker came to identify with her mother and grandfather's model of religiosity, which emphasized an essential connection of personal belief and piety to moral practices that express care and concern for others. Unlike the traditional notion of Christian charity, wherein concern for others often means neglecting their agency and responsibility, Baker's models (especially that of her grandfather) anticipated that other persons would also express a religiosity less dominated by emotional arousal and more clearly expressed as a practical responsibility to oneself and others. As a child Baker participated with her mother and grandfather in living out what might be called this witness to their faith. As an adult she continued to do so, even as she expanded her understanding of how to live out her witness by drawing on conceptual resources beyond Christian scripture.

Influenced by her parents' model of traditional practices of charity and true concern for others, and particularly by her mother's devotion to her church, Clark came to understand herself as a church woman with a single-minded duty to live out the principles she learned from her parents and the church. As an adult Clark's steadfastness in living these principles and her competence as an educator meant the circle in which she practiced her faith became increasingly wider. Her work with the citizenship schools across the South was—on a much larger scale—a continuation of her first volunteer work helping adults learn to read and write on Johns Island.

Both Baker and Clark willingly used personal ingenuity in practicing their religiosity as they translated, improvised, and innovated traditions in order to fulfill what each saw as religious duty. This willingness to be creative probably helped each of them to become quite at ease with the necessity of unconventionality as they became more and more involved in changing the larger society beyond their local communities. As they became more important to the evolution of the Civil Rights Movement, Baker and Clark translated their parents' religious teaching on giving assistance into a focus on helping those most in need of assistance. While Baker emphasized organizing and Clark stressed educating, the signature of both women's work was seeking to empower local persons to take charge of and improve the quality of life in their communities.

While mobilizing suited one important aspect of the Civil Rights Movement—gathering and deploying large numbers of persons toward a common end—mobilizing did not ensure lasting, broad, or continual change. Ella Baker and Septima Clark focused on organizing and educating persons to leave local communities empowered and, therefore, open to ongoing evolution after outside civil rights workers left. Baker and Clark emphasized the reality that real change for African Americans (for racial justice in the United States) would not result instantly from successful (read *large*) marches, rallies, or demonstrations. Through their work they asserted that change would result from ongoing racial uplift and social responsibility practices, deriving from new visions, new abilities, and new structures originating in and nurtured by local people who are organized and educated for change and who themselves become organizers and educators for change. Both women saw this as helping local people become self-determining and enabling people to take responsibility for their own lives, as small groups and then communities became equipped to evaluate, participate in, and then transform society. As they emphasized preparing persons to take charge of their own circumstances, Baker and Clark reflected the perspective that substantial comprehensive change in the United States would occur in an evolutionary manner. This meant that they both practiced and sought to instill in others a form and exercise of fidelity—identified by Katie Cannon as "quiet grace"[174]—that outlasted the ability to see or foresee what would result from one's practices.

3

Giving the Movement Life

Black Women's Grassroots Activism

Because they were educated, Ella Baker and Septima Clark had relative access to the middle and upper classes among both African Americans and other groups in the United States. Notwithstanding financial and racial limits on their choices, the factor of education and the era in which they lived presented Baker and Clark professional and civic opportunities and access to travel that were unheard of for slave and free antebellum Black women, as well as for women of the Reconstruction era. Moreover, their education and access to the Black middle classes positioned them for their travel and work, while also making possible the nature of their civil rights contributions. In spite of these influences of social class, however, religious and ideological commitments stimulated Baker and Clark's activism as practices of racial uplift and social responsibility. Throughout their lives both Ella Baker and Septima Clark sought to improve circumstances of African Americans and organized and educated persons in efforts to change society. Emphasizing the importance of empowering the masses—local people—they conceived, carried out, and passed on values and practices that came to define and in some measure systematize programs of the Civil Rights Movement.

Because of their important role as architects of the Movement, Baker and Clark did not also manage and execute each strategy. As Clark once observed, "I was directing the work at Highlander, and that work took me into so many different places that I would not have the time to do the day-by-day teaching."[1] The work of executing Movement strategies, like "day-by-day teaching" in citizenship schools, proceeded as other Movement participants engaged the paradigms they established. Unfortunately, as many local participants engaged these paradigms, they encountered physical and economic reprisals for civil rights involvement. In addition to making possible their specific contributions to the Civil Rights Movement, Baker and Clark's education, exposure, and access also insulated them from the brutalities often experienced by those who took up the practices they set in place. Fannie Lou Hamer and Victoria Way DeLee were two persons who experienced retaliatory violence firsthand as they encountered values and replicated practices Baker and Clark set in place. Having endured the Southern sharecropping system, both Hamer and DeLee grew up in poverty, lived in rural communities, and had limited formal education. Both women's intuitive sense of justice brought them into the Civil Rights Movement. Their introduction to civil rights practices, and, perhaps most importantly, their coming to interpret the religion embedded in Southern Black culture as consistent with and even requiring civil rights activism, sustained each woman's vision of a different, better life. As each grew to realize more and more the potential of her agency, her role as local community worker evolved into civil rights leadership. Although their roles differed from Baker's and Clark's, grassroots activists like Hamer and DeLee were leaders in their own right and helped sustain the movement by activity they initiated in local areas.

Fannie Lou Hamer: Realizing Promises of Religious Faith and Hope

Some might say examining the role of religion in the civil rights activism of Fannie Lou Hamer is nothing less than exploring the miraculous. Perhaps one of the most unlikely persons to reach and participate in the summit of U.S. political life, Hamer, a poor, barely educated woman lived the life of Black tenancy in the Mississippi Delta for forty-four years. She rose within two years from the level of a local sharecropper standout among other tenant cotton pickers to challenge the meaning of democracy and freedom in the United States. From her life of plantation tenancy she was deeply significant in changing her society's political and moral landscape. Hamer's story also is an example of the power of human community and the potential (though unrealized) of democracy.

Fannie Lou Hamer's understanding of religion and its connection to social and moral conditions pervaded her worldview. As a child, she prayed about her family's circumstances. She related religious belief to social life through the use of gospel music and prayer from her earliest civil rights activism. And she said she saw immediately the connection among getting the vote, freedom, and what "the Lord required." Hamer's faith perspective continued throughout her activism, and in looking back after the heyday of the Movement, she reflected on the role of religious faith in her work, saying, "'The Lord has helped me to help my people.'"[2]

Hamer's Moral Formation: Social and Religious Influences in Her Early Life

The youngest of twenty-two children of sharecropping parents Lou Ella Bramlett Townsend and James Lee Townsend, Fannie Lou Townsend was born October 6, 1917, in Montgomery County, Mississippi.[3] Hamer said both her parents were examples as religious persons. "My mama and daddy were some great folks," she recalled. "Daddy was a minister—a deeply religious man."[4] James Lee Townsend was a Baptist preacher *and* bootlegger, and, exhibiting pragmatism about the reality of survival issues, Fannie Lou apparently saw no contradiction between her father's dual roles. In fact, for a time, to ensure her own family's survival during winter months when it was especially hard to secure enough food, Hamer said she and her husband sometimes "made liquor."[5]

Although her father was a minister, it was Lou Ella Townsend who most profoundly influenced the youngest child's moral and religious perspectives. Perhaps Hamer identified with her mother's struggles as a Black woman seeking to survive the horrific Mississippi sharecropping system. Describing her mother's prayers for children in a manner reminiscent of Sojourner Truth's narrative, Hamer said, "My mother was a fantastic woman; I used to hear her get on her knees and pray that God would let all of her children live. Praying she'd see all of them grown. And I understand now, what she meant. She didn't want to leave her kids with somebody else. That wish was granted because when she died in 1961, she had seen every one of her children get grown."[6] Hamer said her mother inspired her, and spoke frequently and fondly of her mother's teachings and toils for her family.

"My mother was a great woman," she said. "To look at her from all the suffering she had gone through to bring us up—20 children: 6 girls and 14 boys, but still she taught us to be decent and to respect ourselves, and this is one of the things that has kept me going, even after she passed. She tried so hard to make life easy for us. Those are the things that forced me to try to do something different . . . when this Movement came to Mississippi."[7]

Although they wanted to make life easier for their children, farming in the inequitable sharecropping system generally failed to support the Townsend family sufficiently. Racial violence cut short the one opportunity when potential for improving the family's lot appeared. "My father, year after year, didn't get too much money and I remember he just kept going. Later on he did get enough money to buy mules. We didn't have tractors, but he bought mules, wagons, cultivators and some farming equipment. As soon as he bought that and decided to rent some land, because it was always better if you rent the land, but as soon as he got the mules and wagons and everything, somebody went to our trough—a white man who didn't live very far from us—and he fed the mules Paris Green, put it in their food and it killed the mules and our cows. That knocked us right back down. And things got so tough then I began to wish I was white."[8]

The Townsends never recovered from this loss and spent the rest of their lives barely eking out an existence. "We worked very hard and a lot of times, we didn't have a whole lot of food. In fact, sometimes we didn't have too much of nothing. But somehow mama would try." To provide sustenance for the family, Mrs. Townsend used foods creatively:

> I seen my mother go out in the garden and she would get tops off of greens; she would get the tops off of white potatoes. She would get the tops off of beets and all this kind of stuff. And she would cook it. She would make different kinds of gravies without any kind of meat in it. She always had some kind of little thing that would be very good for us. When I think about my teeth, I'm 53 years old, never had a tooth pulled in my life. I think, then, that some of the things that she was doing for us was natural food.[9]

In addition, Lou Ella Townsend worked as a domestic and did various other odd jobs to help with the family's income.[10] She took her children along to glean fields after harvests asking "landowners to let us scrape the cotton fields." Going from one field to another, Mrs. Townsend and the children sometimes gathered as much as a bale of cotton. Mr. Townsend would "haul the cotton to the gin and they would sell that bale and then she would buy food."[11] One of Mrs. Townsend's other supplementary jobs eventually caused her loss of sight. "We worked all the time," Hamer said, "just worked and then we would be hungry and my mother was clearing up a new ground trying to help feed us for $1.25 a day. She was using an axe, just like a man, and something flew up and hit her in her eye. It eventually caused her to lose both her eyes and I began to get sicker and sicker of the system there."

Memories of her mother's life impressed Hamer indelibly. As an adult she recalled "'the way I'd see her at night, patching our clothes so we'd have something to wear. And her own clothes—they'd been patched and patched over so much till they looked too heavy for her body to carry. All I could think was why did it have to be so hard for her.'"

As was true for young Septima Poinsette, so too for Fannie Lou Townsend: seeing effects of poverty on her parents, and especially her mother's vision loss, developed in Fannie Lou a resolve to improve her mother's life. "I vowed that when I got bigger, I'd do better by her, and this vow I carried out, for I took care of her for ten years before she died, after I was grown."

Her family's difficulty also motivated Hamer's determination to change life in Mississippi. As a child she began to analyze the injustice of her family's life as sharecroppers and pledged that someday she would change things. Young Fannie Lou determined that "if I lived to get grown and had a chance, I was going to try to get something for my mother and I was going to do something for the Black man of the south if it would cost my life; I was determined to see that things were changed."[12]

In addition to motivating her youngest child's resolve to make changes, Lou Ella Townsend also modeled a courageous and independent sense of herself that Fannie Lou embraced. Again, similar to Septima Clark's mother, Victoria Poinsette, in spite of her life of oppression and racial subordination, Lou Ella Townsend was fiercely defensive of her children. This was true to the point, Hamer says, of Lou Ella's carrying a weapon to protect them:

> People would say she was crazy because she didn't allow no white man to beat her kids. You know, every day she would go to the field with a pan on her head and two buckets in her hand. One of these buckets would always be covered up. One day, I kind of peeked in that bucket and mama had a 9mm Luger in there. She would carry her gun to the field every day. She was very strong. She was a deeply religious person, but she didn't allow anybody to mess with her children.
>
> One day this man had come out to the field, he was on a horse because they didn't have cars like they have now. So he was on this big horse, a big Black, slick horse, this horse was named Charley and he told my mother he was coming out there to get one of her nieces. And he told my mother, "You know, I come out here to get Pauline today and I'm going to make her go back home but I'm goin' to give her a good whipping first." My mother just stood there, popped her cork and said, "You don't have no Black children and you not goin' to beat no Black children. If you step down off of that horse, I'll go to Hell and back with you before Hell can scorch a feather." And he didn't get down. But she would have done just what she said. This was the kind of way she felt.

In another instance, Mrs. Townsend and a plantation owner "wrestled to the ground" after she objected to the man's hitting her youngest son. Seeing this in her mother, Hamer says, influenced her own sense of self-worth: "I really feel that that had a lot to do with me being what I am today, whatever that is."[13] Lou Ella also encouraged her daughter to be proud of her Black identity. As a child, continuously observing the ease of white life as compared with that of Blacks, Fannie Lou once said "'to make it you had to be white.'" Mrs. Townsend responded, "'don't ever let me [hear you] say that again. . . . Be grateful that you are Black, because [if] God had wanted you to be white, you would have been white, so accept yourself for what you are.'"[14]

Notwithstanding pervasive difficulties, young Fannie Lou did have moments of pleasure during her childhood. As a girl, she enjoyed singing and school. One biographer records that when "she was really, really small, people would stand her on a table to hear her sing out: 'This little light of mine, I'm gonna let it shine. . . .'"[15] It was this song that Fannie Lou sang as a child that became one of the ways by which she was most well known among the civil rights community.

Although she enjoyed school, Hamer received only six years of formal education. Conventions limiting school terms of Black children to coincide with planting and harvesting seasons circumscribed the time and attention allowed for Hamer's education. "We never had too much chance to go to school," Hamer said. "We would have December, January, February and March and most of that time, we never had shoes." When Hamer was old enough to attend school, she wanted "'to get a real good education, and to go some place else to get it'"; however, she said, "'by that time, my parents was down—they were kind of old when I was born. Papa'd had a stroke and Mama was blind, so I had to stay and help them out.'"[16] Nevertheless, Fannie Lou went to school when she could and excelled at it. She was a standout in spelling and reading.[17] She said her parents tried to support their children's efforts in school, but poverty and the sharecropping school term of four months for Black children overpowered the Townsends' efforts.[18] Fannie Lou did learn to read and write, and she tried to pass on to her mother some of the benefit by teaching Mrs. Townsend to write her own name.[19]

Hamer's experience was consistent with other "cotton belt" children of the era. She lacked clothing and other basic provisions, so she seldom went to school and had to begin fieldwork early in her life to help support the family. For Hamer this meant her early entry into the perpetual indebtedness of sharecropping life. During her most active civil rights work, Hamer frequently retold a story of the seduction that shackled her with this burden. "I started working when I was 6 years old," she said.

> I was playing beside a gravel road and the land owner drove up and asked me could I pick cotton. I told him I didn't know, and he told me he wanted me to try anyway. He said, "If you go out in the field and pick 30 lbs. of cotton this week, I'll carry you to my commissary store." He then called off the different kinds of things like Crackerjacks and cake he would give me. I'd never had that in my life, so I went out in the field and told my mother and daddy. They told me that I would have to pick the 30 lbs. of cotton myself, they wouldn't give it to me. So I went out that week—the first time with a little cloth flour sack, I filled that up real fast. So then they got me what was called a croaker sack, some call them grass sacks, and I picked that 30 lbs. of cotton.

Hamer received and enjoyed the promised treats after picking that first 30 pounds of cotton; however, what transpired with her taking sweets, as Hamer later realized, was her initiation into long-term obligation to a life of sharecropping. "I found out what actually happened," Hamer said, "was he was trapping me into beginning the work I was to keep doing and I never did get out of his debt again." Subsequent to this initiation, Hamer spent her childhood, youth, and young adulthood laboring as a sharecropper alongside her parents, siblings, and others in the African American community. "Life in Mississippi was really something else. We would have to cut stalks like men. . . . We would have to break the corn stalks, rake 'em up in heaps and then take a match and burn it. It was very hard. We worked. Wasn't no two ways about it."[20]

As a child of sharecroppers entering the lifestyle at an early age, Hamer encountered customs of the era, including the violence common in Mississippi and across the South. Lynching was one violent custom, perhaps more common in Mississippi than in some other Southern states; since Mississippi was second among the states in murders committed by white citizens to uphold "law and order."[21] As a speaker during her civil rights activism, Hamer frequently told the story of Joe Pulliam, another sharecropper who, Hamer said, was "robbed . . . of what he earned." When Pulliam tried to correct the wrong done to him, the white farmer with whom he had the dispute went to Pulliam's home and shot him in the shoulder. Pulliam retaliated with his own rifle, killing his assailant, Hamer said, and the other "white fellow" ran to town to rally a mob. Pulliam ran into a forest and hid "in a hollowed-out stump." The posse located and killed Pulliam after exchanging fire with him; in the exchange thirteen whites were killed. The forest where Pulliam hid was burned, causing him to crawl out of the stump. When the group found Pulliam, Hamer said, they "dragged him by his heels on the back of a car and they paraded about with that man and they cut his ears off and put them in a showcase and it stayed there a long, long time—in Drew, Mississippi." This memory, and others like it, made even stronger Hamer's desire to change Mississippi. "All of those things, when they would happen would make me sick in the pit of my stomach and year after year, every time something would happen it would make me more and more aware of what would have to be done in the State of Mississippi."[22]

Although what she encountered was common to local Black life, as a child, Fannie Lou Townsend questioned the injustice of what was happening.

> I really didn't know what everything was about but I just couldn't understand why Black people worked so hard and never had nothing. I just couldn't understand why the white people that weren't working were always riding in nice cars, two or three cars, and a truck. I just couldn't understand. They had everything, and it seemed that we worked all the time and didn't have nothing.[23]

Hamer looked forward to adulthood when she could address injustices she saw. "I began to make promises to myself," she said, "'cause I didn't really know who to make a promise to, and . . . I just really asked God because I believe in God; I asked God to give me a chance to just let me do something about what was going on in Mississippi."[24] While she had a strong sense of injustices as a child and yearned to change them when she became a woman, Hamer did not have significant opportunities to respond until she was well into her adult life. In the meantime, whenever she could, she extended kindness and tried to help persons in her community in other ways.

Hamer's Practice of Community Work as a Moral Value

When she was around twenty-four years old, Fannie Lou Townsend married Perry (Pap) Hamer. Perry and Fannie Lou developed a friendship in the cotton fields, where they met. He was a tractor driver for the W. D. Marlowe plantation, where, after their marriage, Mrs. Hamer also took a job doing fieldwork and serving as plantation timekeeper. Hamer's life into her middle years was, as she said, similar to that of Lou Ella Townsend: "My life has been almost like my mother's was, because I married a man who sharecropped. We didn't have it easy and the only way we could ever make it through the winter was because Pap had a little juke joint and we made liquor." In addition, as her mother did to supplement her family's income, Hamer cleaned Marlowe's house when she was not working in the fields.[25]

In spite of difficulties in her life as a child and an adult, Hamer grew to understand herself as a Christian whose responsibility included caring for others. She and Perry Hamer adopted two children whose families could not provide for them. An older daughter was left with the Hamers by a single mother who had no resources. They adopted a younger girl at five months old because she had been burned and her family who also had few resources could provide no medical care. The Hamers were themselves quite impoverished, but by comparison, Mrs. Hamer said they "had a little money so we took care of her and raised her." In addition to their two adopted daughters, the Hamers also took care of Mrs. Townsend after she became too ill to care for herself.[26]

Hamer expressed her concern for people in other ways. As plantation timekeeper she was responsible for recording the work hours, the weight picked, and the pay due each worker. This job was a position of authority from which Hamer watched out for the interests of her peers in the fields. She noted the plantation owner deliberately defrauding sharecroppers at the end of the season by miscalculating figures and by using an overloaded counterweight for weighing cotton the workers picked. Hamer resisted this whenever possible: "I would take my pea [counterweight] to the field and use mine until I would see him coming, because his was loaded and I know it was beating people like that."[27] As Mrs. Hamer's notoriety for such acts grew, their home became a gathering place, and she became a leader in the sharecropper community.

This caring continued when she became a civil rights activist. Moreover, questions about injustices nascent in Hamer's childhood persisted into her adult life. As Mrs. Hamer endured the toil with others at plantation work for little reward, she continued to question the obvious inequities. "'Sometimes I be working in the fields,'" she said, "'and I get so tired I'd say to the people picking cotton with me, hard as we have to work for nothing, there *must* be some way we can change this.'"[28] This perspective about injustice in their social life and the desire for change stayed with Hamer, perhaps predisposing her for entering and leading in the Civil Rights Movement. When the promise for change presented itself, Hamer responded spontaneously and fervently, immediately interpreting civil rights activism as corresponding with her understanding of Christianity.

Hamer's Civil Rights Participation as Living Out Religious Belief

Fannie Lou Hamer first engaged in practices that became defining of the Civil Rights Movement in 1962, one year after her mother died.

Hamer was forty-four years old. She heard from a neighbor and friend, Mrs. Mary Tucker, that student workers would hold a meeting about voter registration at Williams Chapel Missionary Baptist Church in Ruleville, Mississippi, on August 27. After hesitating because she had doubts about the effectiveness of the students' plans, Hamer decided to attend. Three members of SNCC, James Forman, Bob Moses, and Reginald Robinson, and James Bevel of SCLC told the group gathered about their rights as citizens of Mississippi and the United States. Preaching from the Bible passage Luke 12:54, Bevel admonished listeners to recognize the signs of the times. Near the end of the meeting, when students asked for volunteers to go to the courthouse in Indianola and attempt to register the following Friday, Hamer volunteered, along with seventeen others. "I didn't know anything about registering to vote," Hamer recalled. "They were talking about we could vote out the people that we didn't want in office, we thought that wasn't right, that we could vote them out. That sounded interesting enough to me that I wanted to try it. I had never heard, until 1962, that Black people could register and vote."[29]

Hearing about the possibility of affecting the system that had oppressed her all her life empowered and excited Hamer. "Just listenin' at 'em," she said, "I could just see myself votin' people outa office that I know was wrong and didn't do nothin' to help the poor. I said, you know, that's sumpin' I really wanna be involved in."[30] It was at this meeting that Hamer first heard civil rights freedom songs ("I had never heard freedom songs before," she recalled),[31] which she apparently straightway connected with her own love of singing.

Although they had volunteered to try registering, when Hamer went with the others to the county courthouse in Indianola, "most of the people were afraid to get off the bus." However, as one SNCC worker recalled, Hamer's leadership role in the community became relevant at once. Charles McLauren said Hamer was the one who "'just stepped off the bus and went right on up to the courthouse and into the circuit clerk's office.'"[32] The others slowly followed her. Hamer described what came after:

> We went on into the circuit clerk's office, and he asked us what did we want; and we told [him] what we wanted. We wanted to try to register. He told us that all of us would have to get out of there except two. So I was one of the two persons that remained inside, to try to register, [with] another young man named Mr.

> Ernest Davis. We stayed in to take the literacy test. So the registrar gave me the sixteenth section of the Constitution of Mississippi. He pointed it out in the book and told me to look at it and then to copy it down just like I saw it in the book: Put a period where a period was supposed to be, a comma and all of that. After I copied it down he told me right below that to give a real reasonable interpretation then, interpret what I had read. That was impossible. I had tried to give it, but I didn't even know what it meant, much less interpret it.[33]

Hamer's first attempt to register was unsuccessful, but when events unfolded as repercussions for seeking to register, that first attempt proved to be life-changing for her. Recalling that day, Hamer said, she had some sense that profound change was imminent: "I don't know why, but I just had a feeling because the morning I left home to go down to try to register I carried some extra shoes and a bag because I said, 'If I'm arrested or anything, I'll have some extra shoes to put on.' So I had a feeling something might happen; I just didn't know. I didn't know it was going to be as much involved as it finally was. But I had a feeling that we might be arrested."[34]

The first reaction came instantly. From their arrival at the courthouse until they headed back to Ruleville, police scrutinized the bus and its riders. When they had driven halfway back to Ruleville, police stopped them, told everyone to get off, then back on the bus again, and, arresting the entire group, ordered their return to Indianola. Hamer helped the group cope with the uncertainty by humming and then singing: "We just started singing 'Have a Little Talk with Jesus.'" Upon returning to Indianola, the driver was taken away while police determined a charge. As the group waited for a decision about the bus driver, Hamer continued to sing gospel songs. Others joined her as she led "This Little Light of Mine," "Freedom's Coming and It Won't Be Long," and "Down by the Riverside." Police finally charged the driver with operating a bus of the wrong color—it looked too much like school buses, they said. The group combined their cash to pay the thirty dollars officers agreed to accept as bond.[35]

Problems for Hamer were just beginning, however. Mississippi law required listing in local papers for two weeks names of persons who took registration tests. This, of course, subjected Blacks to diverse retaliatory activity. Publicity of Hamer's attempt to register preceded the next printing of local papers, reaching Ruleville before she returned on the bus that same day. "Everything happened before my name had been in the paper," she recalled with some astonishment. After she got off the bus, as Hamer walked to the Marlowe plantation where she had lived and worked for eighteen years, her "oldest girl met me and told me that Mr. Marlowe, the plantation owner, was mad and raisin' Cain. He had heard that I had tried to register."[36] Marlowe returned to the Hamers' home shortly, telling Mrs. Hamer to withdraw or leave. In a manner that emulated her mother's determination and forthrightness, Hamer said to Marlowe: "Mr. Dee, I didn't go down there to register for you. I went down there to register for myself." Of course, this enraged Marlowe, but Hamer said she "knowed I wasn't goin' back to withdraw, so wasn't nothin for me to do but leave the plantation." That evening her husband took her to the home of a friend, Mrs. Tucker, the woman who originally invited Hamer to the mass meeting. Perry Hamer was allowed to remain on the plantation. He thought doing so would secure the family's belongings. And Marlowe also needed Perry Hamer's help through the end of the season.

Over the next several days, Mr. Hamer "began to feel nervous when he went to the [maintenance shop on the plantation] and saw some buckshot shells," Mrs. Hamer said. "They don't have buckshot shells to *play* with in August and September, because you ain't huntin' or nothin' like that." Ten days later, on September 10, night riders repeatedly shot into the Tucker home. Such violence continued as homes of others attempting to register were also terrorized. To ensure his wife's safety, Perry Hamer took her to stay with her niece in neighboring Tallahatchie County.[37] "I stayed away, 'cause things then—you could see 'em at night. They would have fires in the middle of the road. . . . You wouldn't see no Klan signs, but just make a fire in the middle of the road. And it was *so dangerous,* I stayed in Tallahatchie County all of September and then October, and then November I come back to Ruleville."

During the two and one-half months she stayed with her niece in Cascilla, Mississippi, Hamer had a kind of conversion experience, deciding not to run any longer but to return home and fight the oppression. Hamer remembered her determination to make changes in Mississippi and reasoned that her actions were not unjustifiable.

She was supported in this regard by SNCC workers, who, following Ella Baker's influence, affirmed local people in changing their lives. While Hamer was in Cascilla, Baker understudy Bob Moses, who launched SNCC's Mississippi work, sent Charles McLaurin to find the courageous lady who sang the hymns in Indianola. When McLaurin found her, Hamer responded out of her faith, as if she expected divine intervention. "I'm looking for Fannie Lou Hamer," McLaurin said. Hamer, who was putting wood in a stove, "turned around and said, 'I'm Fannie Lou Hamer.'" McLaurin recalled telling Mrs. Hamer "that Bob Moses and the people at SNCC asked me to pick her up and take her on to the Nashville [SNCC] conference. And she got up and went to getting her stuff. . . . She couldn't have known whether I was kidnapping her or what. But she just got right up and came."[38]

With SNCC's support, Hamer returned to Ruleville: "I was comin', I didn't know why I was comin', but I was just sick of runnin' and hadn't done nothin'."[39] Hamer explained her decision and resolve to her children, saying, "this is what you got to look at. I'm not a criminal. I hadn't done one thing to nobody, I went down to register for myself and I got a right to live in Ruleville because its people there have done way more thing[s] than that, they still here, and I'm going back to Ruleville regardless."[40] When Hamer returned to Ruleville in late November she first secured shelter and furnishings for a family home. In spite of Perry Hamer's hopes when he stayed behind at the Marlowe plantation, the family lost all their belongings. On December 3, 1962, with help from community members, the Hamers moved into a three-room house that they rented from an African American woman for eighteen dollars per month.

The next day, Hamer went back to retake the registration tests. In an interview with Howell Raines, Hamer said when she presented herself for the literacy test that day, she had all the resolve and freedom she needed to pursue registration without fear. She told the registration agent, "'Now, you cain't have me fired 'cause I'm already fired, and I won't have to move now, because I not livin' in no white man's house. . . . I'll be here every thirty days until I become a registered voter.'"[41]

While in Cascilla Hamer worked with SNCC studying the state's constitution in preparation for the test. By 1961 Septima Clark had affiliated with the SCLC, and SNCC student workers, who often interacted with SCLC workers, adopted Clark's citizenship preparation method for use across the South. "Some of the people from the Student Nonviolent Coordinating Committee would help us to try to interpret it, so that time I gave a reasonable enough interpretation," Hamer later recalled. "When I went back to see about it in January, I had passed the literacy test. So I didn't take the test but twice."[42]

Completing the registration entailed more than Hamer's presenting herself in December and checking results in January, however. Her and others' attempts to register, Hamer said, "made us look like criminals. We would have to have our lights out before dark. It was cars passing that house all times of night, driving real slow with guns, and pickups with white mens in it, and they'd pass that house just as slow as they could. . . . This was the kind of stuff." In addition, the poverty with which Hamer lived was even more severe because of stresses caused by their loss of jobs when she began seeking enfranchisement. "That was a rough winter," Hamer recalled. "I hadn't had a chance to do any canning before I got kicked off, so I didn't have hardly anything. I always can more than my family can use 'cause there's always people who don't have enough. That winter was bad, though. Pap couldn't get a job nowhere 'cause everybody knew he was my husband. We made it through, though, and since then I just been trying to work and get our people organized."[43]

Leading voting registration efforts and other general civil rights practices became full-time work for Hamer before she received her own registration certificate. Subsequent to the SNCC conference held at Fisk University in Nashville, Tennessee, Hamer became a SNCC field secretary. She also began leading local citizenship education classes in the tradition that Septima Clark established: "I started teachin' citizenship class, and I became the supervisor of the citizenship class in this county. I moved around the county to do citizenship education, and later on I become a field secretary for SNCC—I guess being about one of the oldest people at that time that was a field secretary, 'cause they was real young."[44] She described herself as starting civil rights work "as soon as I was fired from the plantation. . . . It just kind of materialized together. I didn't have anything else to do."[45]

Hamer's civil rights work brought reprisals against her personally, against other Blacks who were seeking to change their conditions, and against the entire community. On many occasions potential voter registrants changed their minds because, Hamer said, "land owners . . . white people would get to them." African Americans were threatened with loss of jobs or homes or both for civil rights participation. "Well, it was rough because we would go places, go in to do voter registration in places, and we talked to people. We would walk the streets in different little areas, and we would tell them we were coming back the next day. And by the next day somebody would be done got to them, and they wouldn't want to talk with us, and this kind of stuff. Some days it would be disgusting, some very disappointing. So very disappointing."

Along with the work of preparing and motivating people to register, Hamer also helped secure and distribute food and clothing to combat losses Black citizens experienced as a result of their efforts. In the Mississippi Delta, as in other areas across the South, local churches often housed mass meetings, citizenship classes, and other civil rights activities. Hamer recalled that destroying churches was one means of exacting vengeance against communities for their civil rights activities. When "we'd go to churches, and occasionally along, they was burning up churches. These are the kinds of things we faced."[46]

Perhaps the most severe retaliation Hamer endured occurred during late spring 1963. In June, she was one of five Mississippians traveling with SCLC worker Annelle Ponder to complete one of Septima Clark's citizenship training workshops at the McIntosh Center in Georgia. On their return bus trip, the group was physically removed by local police for entering the "whites only" waiting room during a rest stop in Winona, a small town near Greenwood, Mississippi. When Ponder reminded officers of the 1961 Interstate Commerce Commission ruling that desegregated public accommodations and attempted to take down license numbers of the police cruisers, the entire group was arrested and taken to the local station house, where several were beaten violently. Hamer described her beating:

> They come to my room, and one of them men told me, "Get up from there, fatso," and he carried me outa that cell. . . . "You from Ruleville, all right." Said, "You, bitch, you, we gon' make

> you wish you was dead." And let me tell you, before they stop beatin' me, I wish they would have hit me one lick that could have ended the misery they had me in. They had me to lay down on this bunk bed with my face down, and they had two Black prisoners. You know, a lot of folks would say, "Well, I woulda died before I'd done that." But nobody know the condition that those prisoners was in, before they were s'posed to beat me. And I heard that highway patrolman tell that Black man, said, "If you don't beat her, you know what we'll do to you." . . . So they had me lay down on my face, and they beat [me] with a thick leather thing that was wide. And it had sumpin' in it *heavy*. I don't know what that was, rocks or lead. But everytime they hit me, I got just as hard, and I put my hands behind my back, and they beat me in my hands 'til my hands . . . my hands was as navy blue as anything you ever seen . . . that blood, I guess, and then beatin' it 'til it just turned black. And then after the first one beat, they ordered the second one to beat me, and when the second one started beatin', it was just—it was jus too much. I started wiggling . . . you know, kickin' my feet back there. The highway patrolman walked over there and had the first one had beat, told him to sit on my feet . . . while the second one beat. . . . But anyway, they finally told me to get up, and I just couldn't hardly get up, and they kept on tellin' me to get up. I finally could get up, but when I got back to my cell bed, I couldn't set down. I would *scream*. It hurted me to set down.[47]

In addition to her own brutalization, the trauma of the night included Hamer's listening to others being beaten. As word of their disappearance spread, civil rights leaders sought assistance locating them, including unsuccessful efforts to get FBI intervention. SNCC Field Secretary Lawrence Guyot, who went to investigate the arrests, was the first outsider to reach the Winona police station where they were held. When Guyot arrived, he also was arrested and beaten. Hamer continued, describing what she heard of others:

> They whipped Annelle Ponder and I heard her screamin'. After a while she passed by where I was in the cell and her mouth was bleedin' and her hair was standin' up on her head and you know it was horrifyin'. Over in the night I even heard screamin'. I said, "Oh, Lord, somebody else gettin' it, too." It was later that we heard that Lawrence Guyot was there. I got to see him. I could walk as far as the cell door and I asked them to please leave that

> door open so I could get a breath of fresh air every once in a while. That's how I got to see Guyot. He looked as if he was in pretty bad shape. And it was on my nerves, too, because that was the first time I had seen him and not smilin'.[48]

Although most of them had been beaten badly, the group kept themselves from becoming completely demoralized by singing. June Johnson, a teenager with the group, said Hamer led the song "When Paul and Silas Were Bound in Jail." Hamer also repeated Bible verses that she thought appropriate to help keep others and herself calm.[49] Hamer even attempted to influence jailers with her religious views. As Hamer was escorted to her trial by the jailer who helped beat her, she asked him, "[Did you] ever think or wonder how you'll feel when the time comes you'll have to meet God?" Fully embarrassed, the jailer tried to deny Hamer's inquiry. "Who you talking about?" he replied clumsily.[50] Tragically, during the four days the group was held, another Mississippi civil rights worker, Medgar Evers, state NAACP Field Secretary, was murdered. "After I got out of jail, half dead, I found out that Medgar Evers had been shot down in his own yard," Hamer said.[51]

On the day of their release, Andrew Young and James Bevel helped carry Hamer to a Greenwood doctor who washed off her body and stitched and bandaged her wounds. They then took Hamer to Atlanta, where she convalesced for several weeks. Both Hamer and other civil rights leaders kept her family away to prevent their seeing how terrible she looked. "After I got beat, I didn't hardly see my family in 'bout a month," Hamer said, "'cause I went to Atlanta, from Atlanta to Washington, and from Washington to New York, because [we] didn't want my family to see me in the shape I was in. I had been beat 'til I was real hard, just like a piece of wood or somethin'. A person don't know what can happen to the body if they beat with something like I was beat with."[52]

After Winona and her recovery, Hamer became even more deeply rooted as a civil rights leader. She spent less and less time attending to local day-to-day citizenship preparation and development work, and began to step onto the state and national political scene. By the summer of 1964, Hamer said, "I didn't go much to the [freedom] schools because I was out on the road most of the time, going to mass meetings in different areas and different places. Like they'd want me to come from place to place to speak, and that's what I was doing."[53] In fact, earlier that year, during the spring of 1964, Hamer began her run for U.S. Congress. Ironically, the election during which Hamer ran for Congress was her first opportunity to vote, even though she qualified for registration in January of 1963. Not having poll tax receipts from two previous election cycles prevented earlier exercise of her enfranchisement.[54] "The 20th of March in 1964, I went before the Secretary of State to qualify to run as an official candidate for Congress from the 2nd Congressional District," Hamer said, "and it was easier for me to qualify to run than it was for me to pass the literacy test to be a registered voter." Although Hamer successfully qualified and ran for Congress, she lost the primary in June. Her loss in a predominantly Black district underscored the continuing difficulty African Americans faced in registering to vote.

> We had four people to qualify and run in the June primary election but we didn't have enough Negroes registered in Mississippi. The 2nd Congressional District where I ran, against Jamie Whitten [the incumbent], is made up of 24 counties. Sixty-eight percent of the people are Negroes, only 6-8 percent are registered. And it is not because Negroes don't want to register. They try and they try and they try. That's why it was important for us to set up the "Freedom Registration" to help us in the Freedom Democratic Party.[55]

Freedom Registration gave to Blacks whom the state denied enfranchisement an opportunity for full political participation through a Freedom Ballot held in November of 1963. Moreover, through the Freedom Ballot, civil rights workers demonstrated that given an opportunity, African American citizens would register and vote. NAACP worker Aaron Henry and white Methodist minister Edwin King ran as alternatives to regular candidates for governor and lieutenant governor, respectively. Held in churches across the state, and especially in the Delta, the Freedom Ballot recorded over 80,000 votes of primarily African American citizens.[56] Combined success of the Freedom Registration and Freedom Ballot were the major impetus for the Freedom Summer effort.

Coordinated primarily by the Council of Federated Organizations, a collaboration of civil rights organizations working in Mississippi, Freedom Summer attempted both to accomplish a massive registration effort and to call national attention to civil rights work in Mississippi by bringing in hundreds of volunteers, most young and white, to help with registration. During June of 1964 Hamer taught one of the two-week sessions in Oxford, Ohio, for college students going to Mississippi for Freedom Summer. She told the young people, "Mississippi Blacks took their religion seriously, and any antireligious sentiments that they had should be kept to themselves." Hamer also warned students that retaliatory violence for their work should be expected, and pointed out the need to be especially careful at night. "'Out in daylight he don't do nothin'. But at night he'll toss a bomb or pay someone to kill,'" she said.[57]

By the time of Mississippi's regular Democratic Party precinct meetings, over "63,000 people registered on the Freedom Registration form," Hamer said. The numbers did not impress Mississippi's Democratic Party leaders. They continued to restrict African Americans from regular party participation and voter registration. "And we tried from every level to go into the regular Democratic Party medium," Hamer recalled. "We tried from the precinct level. The 16th of June when they were holding precinct meetings all across the state, I was there and there was eight of us there to attend the meeting, and they had the door locked at 10 o'clock in the morning. So we had our own meeting and elected our permanent chairman and secretary and regulars and alternates and we passed a resolution as the law requires and then mailed it to Oscar Townsend, our permanent chairman."[58] Alternative precinct meetings, like the one Hamer described, were held for African Americans and others across the Mississippi Delta. They were organized as part of the Mississippi Freedom Democratic Party challenge to the regular state party's practices.

During the spring, in anticipation of the regular Democratic Party's failure to admit African Americans, civil rights workers organized the Mississippi Freedom Democratic Party (MFDP) to provide opportunities for full political participation by Blacks and to challenge regular Mississippi Party delegates at the National Democratic Convention in Atlantic City, New Jersey, in August. Hamer, elected MFDP vice chairperson, was made a spokesperson for the group. Going into Atlantic City, the MFDP had sufficient support from state delegations around the nation to raise as a realizable possibility unseating and replacing the traditional all-white Mississippi delegation. Consisting of Black sharecroppers, students, ministers, and other Black and white progressive men and women, the MFDP delegation significantly reflected the racial, economic, and gender breadth of the state. Unfortunately, as preconvention proceedings unfolded, President Johnson and powerful supporters quashed MFDP hopes by issuing threats and collecting favors in an attempt to secure a Johnson/Humphrey ticket and smooth convention.[59] By opening of the convention, the possibility of recognizing the MFDP, which had seemed realizable a few months earlier, was not seriously considered. The National Party Credentials Committee offered as a compromise the honorary seating of two MFDP delegates not chosen by MFDP members. Hamer and the MFDP refused the compromise and returned to Mississippi dejected and wiser.

Although a formal failure, the MFDP effort precipitated major social changes. Hamer's nationally televised testimony before the 1964 Credentials Committee was pivotal in this regard. In a compelling narrative, she recounted the deprivation, difficulty, and violence of her life and that of others in Mississippi, as the country watched spellbound.[60] Pursuant to its Atlantic City Convention, the Democratic National Committee required delegations to be racially and gender inclusive, and the 1965 Voting Rights Act became law. After the Democratic Convention, Hamer traveled to Africa with ten other civil rights workers for a break from the intensity of the year's activities and some much needed rest.[61] When she returned to Mississippi, Hamer continued work for the MFDP, which broadened its base by collaborating with groups like the NAACP and the AFL-CIO. The broader coalition successfully challenged Mississippi Democrats at the 1968 National Convention, where Hamer was a delegate. Hamer also was a delegate at the 1972 convention.[62]

Around this time, Hamer's efforts turned decidedly toward local empowerment and quality-of-life concerns. She continued participation in political access work but also initiated several subsistence and economic development ventures to attend to urgent food, clothing, shelter, and other quality-of-life needs in Sunflower County. Remembering intermittent periods of hunger throughout her life and recognizing hunger and malnutrition issues that continued to face Mississippians, in 1968 Hamer founded a "pig bank" to begin immediately supplying food to hungry families while at the same time generating some level of independence. Using start-up funds from the National Council of Negro Women, Hamer purchased forty pigs, thirty-five of which were young females. The bank loaned pregnant pigs to families with the space for them. These families kept the offspring but returned the original pig to the bank and promised to give a pregnant pig to two other families during the next year. By 1969, over one hundred families received pigs, and in 1970 more than three hundred families benefited.[63]

After successful launch of the "pig bank," Hamer founded "Freedom Farms Cooperative" to address land access and ownership deficiencies. In 1969, only seventy-one of 31,000 Black Sunflower County residents owned land. With $1,300 raised by two Harvard researchers who visited and saw the county's poverty and malnutrition, Hamer began purchasing land, initially buying forty acres. She saw subsistence farming and land ownership not only as a cure for hunger problems, but also as a means of providing security against the hostile retaliation of the Mississippi sharecropping system when Blacks agitated for full citizenship. Hamer also envisioned developing alternative work and home ownership for Black citizens. As word about the cooperative spread, support came in from across the country. Within three years, Sunflower County Freedom Farms grew to three hundred acres, providing meat and fresh vegetables for thousands of poor people, Black and white, as well as cash crops to help support the program. In addition, by 1971, through Hamer's leadership the cooperative helped sixty-eight families acquire low-interest financing to build homes on co-op property.[64]

In succeeding years, Hamer continued the civil rights activism that had become her life's work. She opposed de facto school desegregation in Mississippi, continued political rights activity, and increased economic empowerment work. In spite of her considerable efforts working on behalf of others, Hamer and her family never escaped poverty. By 1974 her health began to decline severely. Hamer died in 1977 at age fifty-nine.

Hamer's Moral Vision

Fannie Lou Hamer's moral perspective was decidedly Christian. She was among the Black Mississippians whom she described as having "gone to church all their lives."[65] She was a regular member at

Williams Chapel Church, where she attended her first civil rights mass meeting.[66] Hamer's attendance and support of Black churches persisted throughout her life, even though she criticized churches (and clergy) for failure to respond sufficiently to the needs of communities, for missing opportunities of the Civil Rights Era, and for betraying African Americans to the Movement's opposition and collaborating with the opposition. "'Sometimes I get so disgusted I feel like getting my gun after some of these chicken eatin' preachers,'" she once said. "'I know these Baptist ministers. . . . I'm not anti-church and I'm not anti-religious, but if you go down Highway 49 all the way to Jackson, going through Drew, Ruleville, Blaine, Indianola, Moorhead, all over, you'll see just how many churches are selling out to the white power structure.'" In spite of her harsh criticisms, however, Hamer understood religion and religious institutions, specifically churches, as having contributed profoundly to sustaining African Americans. Moreover, her ability to criticize churches and church leaders while she identified the importance of churches to African American life reflects Hamer's strong sense of her self and her faith, and her mature religiosity. Hamer was able personally to conceive, articulate, and creatively encounter positive and negative aspects of Black religious life. In this she identified what womanist theologian Delores Williams later labeled dual traditions of sustenance and suppression in Black denominational churches, and she modeled what womanist ethicist Katie Cannon later called the practice of "unmasking" harmful and "disentangling" affirmative traditions found there.[67]

In a 1971 interview Hamer credited churches with giving African Americans the strength to survive. "I really think that people should return to some of the things that have made us strong for these many years," she said. "If we hadn't been a strong people, we would have crumbled long ago. I don't know which guy was singing 'only the strong survive,' but it's very true, you know. I think it's time to return to some of these things." Hamer believed that specific religious practices, like singing spirituals and attending church, were part of what made churches effective for African American life. She asserted the continuing value of churches in spite of their deficiencies. "Like people ashamed of singing spirituals and all of these things like the Church," Hamer said,

> it's been a part of our lives. So why not be a part of what's sustained you for all these years and kept you going? That's the reason I tell young people don't write off the Church and don't write off God. If something is wrong with the Church, stand up and change it and make it be relevant to the community. . . . We have to keep the Church in the community. The most beautiful people that I've ever met are people who come from a Church background. There's nothing wrong with the Church, it's a part of our history, it's a part of our heritage; it's a part of our strength.[68]

Throughout her public life, Hamer spoke of the Civil Rights Movement as reflecting Christian ideals and, similar to Septima Clark, frequently used Christian scripture both to construe the meaning of social problems, especially racial discrimination, and to encourage and explain activities of civil rights campaigns. Hamer's religious interpretation of the Civil Rights Movement appears to have developed through her activism. Unlike Clark and Baker, who consciously undertook racial uplift and social responsibility practices as a means of living out their moral perspectives, as Hamer became active she began to see congruence between civil rights practices and her belief that being Christian meant helping others. Although prior to the Civil Rights Movement she did not correlate social activism with her belief, she saw in the Movement the consummation of her faith. "My father used to read a scripture from the Bible," Hamer said,

> "Faith is the substance of things hoped for and the evidence of things not seen." We Negroes had hoped and we had faith to hope, though we didn't know what we had hoped for. When the people came to Mississippi in 1964, to us it was the result of all our faith—all we had always hoped for. Our prayers and all we had lived for day after day hadn't been in vain. In 1964 the faith that we had hoped for started to be translated into action. Now we have action, and we're doing something that will not only free the Black man in Mississippi but hopefully will free the white one as well.[69]

Perhaps Hamer's long-term participation in churches and religious practices with her community predisposed her to this interpretation.

Hamer assimilated the rhetoric and perspectives of SNCC and SCLC representatives, who described the Movement and its practices through the lens of Christian scripture and Christianity. This was, in fact, the context of Hamer's first encounter with the Civil Rights

Movement. Movement organizers' religious interpretations influenced Hamer significantly. When she told the story of first hearing of voter registration, she also recited the text and sermon James Bevel used to rouse people for voter registration. She told one interviewer:

> James Bevel preached that night . . . from the 12th chapter of St. Luke and the 54th verse, "Discerning the Signs of the Time," you know. He talked about how a man could look out and see a cloud and predict it's going to rain, and it would become so; but still he couldn't you know, in a sense; he couldn't tell what was happening right around him. He [was] looking at a cloud and he didn't know right then what was happening the next door to him. . . .[70]

In her own activism, Hamer frequently used a New Testament passage to describe (and offer prognosis for) the country's racial division. "But this white man who wants to stay *white,* and to think for the Negro," Hamer said, "he is not only destroying the Negro, he is destroying himself, because a house divided against itself cannot stand and that same thing applies to America. America that is divided against itself cannot stand, and we cannot say we have all of this unity they say we have when Black people are being discriminated against in every city in America I have visited."[71] On other occasions Hamer used scripture to oppose hatred and to predict the triumph of justice.[72] Her more frequent engagement of scripture was as interpretation of and sanction for civil rights activism. These uses of scripture ranged from motivating civil rights practices through metaphorical speech to analyzing activism as realizing a Christian telos or purpose. In one instance, when she was visiting a church and encouraging voter registration, after reading from a passage from Exodus the pastor invited Mrs. Hamer to speak. She said, "'Pharaoh was in Sunflower County! Israel's children were building bricks without straw—at three dollars a day! . . . They're tired! And they're tired of being tired! . . . And you, Reverend Tyler, must be Moses! Leadin' your flock out of the chains and fetters of Egypt—takin' them yourself to register—*tomorra*—in Indianola!'"[73] In this speech Hamer might have been consciously exploiting an opportunity to advance voter registration efforts, but she was also a Christian whose motivations deeply connected with perspectives derived from Scripture.

Reflecting on the significance of the Christian faith and canon for her own self-understanding, in 1966 Hamer wrote that Freedom Summer campaigns were manifestations of God's promises in Scripture and answers to prayers. "I believe in Christianity," Hamer said.

> To me, the 1964 Summer Project was the beginning of a New Kingdom right here on earth. The kinds of people who came down from the North—from all over—who didn't know anything about us—were like the Good Samaritan. In that Bible story, the people had passed by the wounded man—like the church has passed the Negroes in Mississippi—and never taken the time to see what was going on. But these people who came to Mississippi that summer—although they were strangers—walked up to our door. They started something that no one could ever stop. These people were willing to move in a nonviolent way to bring a change in the South. Although they were strangers, they were the best friends we ever met. This was the beginning of the New Kingdom in Mississippi. To me, if I had to choose today between the church and these young people—and I was brought up in the church and I'm not against the church—I'd choose these young people. They did something in Mississippi that gave us the hope that we had prayed for so many years. We had wondered if there was anybody human enough to see us as human beings instead of animals.[74]

In addition to using Christian scripture to interpret the environment of the Civil Rights Era, Hamer saw her activism as following the example of Jesus, reflecting what she understood as the meaning of Christianity—acting with concern for others. "Christianity," she once said, "is being concerned about your fellow man, not building a million-dollar church while people are starving right around the corner. Christ was a revolutionary person, out there where it was happening. That's what God is all about, and that's where I get my strength."[75] She said being Christian meant not only saying "I'm a Christian," but acting in particular ways, "putting that claim to the test, where the rubber meets the road."[76] In fact, Hamer felt God enabled Christian activity, and she asserted that God assisted in her efforts on behalf of African Americans.[77] In her emphasis on practical implications of professing Christianity, Hamer reiterated perspectives pervasive in the earliest religious traditions of Blacks in the United States. Similar to religious leaders of the antebellum era,

Hamer understood religious belief as practically and pragmatically related to everyday life, and especially to concerns facing African Americans. In this regard, her perspectives and practices, like those of many other religious Black civil rights participants, reflected a reinvigoration of this focus in Black religion and exhibited congruence with initial performance of racial uplift and social responsibility practices as Christian duty.

Hamer held an egalitarian moral perspective, valuing human personality above racial identity. She asserted the need to attend to racial discrimination in order to realize the larger goal of building a good society. This perspective, she said, derived from her religious belief. "Ain't no such thing as I can hate anybody and hope to see God's face," Hamer told one interviewer. "I'm goin' to do all I can for every oppressed person," she said, "because if I try to do something for one and oppress the other, that is not right."[78] She felt the MFDP—which included persons of all races, ages, economic standing, and education levels—embodied this ideal. An effort like the MFDP was "the only solution that's going to do anything for us in the South. And that's not only Blacks, that's Blacks and whites."[79]

Still, Hamer worked intensely in opposition to racism, and her criticism of the country for racial oppression was harsh.

> We can no longer ignore the fact that America is NOT the 'land of the free and the home of the brave.' I used to question this for years—what did our kids actually fight for? They would go in the service and go through all of that and come right out to be drowned in a river in Mississippi. I found this hypocrisy is all over America. . . . I see so many ways America uses to rob Negroes and it is sinful and America can't keep holding on, and doing these things.[80]

Hamer was disappointed when she traveled beyond Mississippi and experienced the racial and social class hierarchy that obstructed democratic participation. Subsequent to the 1964 Democratic Party Convention, Hamer began to characterize the problem of racism as a national problem. "This problem is not only in Mississippi," she said. "During the time I was in the Convention in Atlantic City, I didn't get any threats from Mississippi. The threatening letters were from Philadelphia, Chicago and other big cities."[81]

> In 1964 we registered 63,000 Black people from Mississippi into the Freedom Democratic Party. We formed our own party

> because the whites wouldn't even let us register. We decided to challenge the white Mississippi Democratic Party at the National Convention. We followed all the laws that white people themselves made. We tried to attend the precinct meetings and they locked the doors on us or moved the meetings and that's against the laws they made for their ownselves. So we were the ones that held the real precinct meetings. At all these meetings across the state we elected our representatives to go to the National Democratic Convention in Atlantic City. But we learned the hard way that even though we had all the law and all the righteousness on our side—that white man is not going to give up his power to us. We have to build our own power.[82]

While the experience was frustrating, one result for Hamer was to incorporate considerations of social class into her own worldview. Her perspectives on gender and class prefigured what have become tenets of womanist theology that examine how class oppression disproportionately affects women, and that oppose patriarchy in Black churches and Black communities, while also asserting the need to attend to ways oppression affects all African Americans. In a 1971 speech, Hamer noted class distinctions between herself and college-educated Black women, but concluded that racism was a common part of Black experience that necessitated collaboration across class lines. Moreover, Hamer said Black women's collaboration should be to the benefit, not exclusion, of Black men, who also share the experience of racial oppression.

> A few years ago throughout this country the middle-class Black woman didn't even respect the kind of work that I was doing. But you see now, baby, whether you have a Ph.D., D.D., or no D, we're in this bag together. And whether you're from Morehouse or Nohouse, we're still in this bag together. Not to fight to try to liberate ourselves from the men—this is another trick to get us fighting among ourselves—but to work together with the Black man, then we will have a better chance to just act as human beings, and to be treated as human beings in our sick society.[83]

Consideration of social class standing not only influenced Hamer's views about intra-race relations, but also informed her rhetorical and practical construction and her understanding of her own civil rights activism. While social and economic circumstances caused her to focus on African Americans, Hamer came to see her work as related to the good of the entire country. In another 1971 speech she said:

> My whole fight is for the liberation of all people because no man is an island to himself; when a white child is dying, is being shot, there's a little bit of America being destroyed. When it's a Black child shot in America, it's a little bit of America being destroyed. If they keep this up, a little of this going, and a little of that going, one day, this country will crumble. But we have to try to see to it that not only the lives of young and adult Blacks are saved in this country but also the whites.[84]

As Hamer's activism evolved, she attended particularly, though not exclusively to economic circumstances of persons in Sunflower County. Her Freedom Farms Cooperative provided food, shelter, and alternative sources of employment for many people. In her economic development work as with her civic participation activism, Hamer continued to understand herself as completing work that issued from her identity as a Christian, which was formed, as she said, by being "brought up in the church from an early age" and being "taught to love."[85]

Victoria Way DeLee: Community Activism as Religious Practice

Victoria Way DeLee is another example of a grassroots activist whose community leadership preceded and engendered her civil rights practices. Responding to what she felt was God calling her to "help those who can't help themselves,"[86] DeLee worked to improve people's lives by seeking justice in her local community as a means of serving God. DeLee initially led protests, boycotts, pickets, and later, as she became more aware of civil rights activities, organized voter registration campaigns and school desegregation efforts to improve life for African Americans, in particular, and poor people, generally, in Dorchester County, South Carolina. Coming of age in the rural South amidst the post-Reconstruction legacy of racial oppression and subjugation, DeLee, like Hamer, was a social activist fueled by Christian upbringing. DeLee's activism was motivated by a particular religious fervor deriving from her strong commitment to a spiritual belief in holiness. By her early twenties, she saw civil rights work as God's work.

DeLee's Moral Formation: Social and Religious Influences in Her Early Life

Victoria Way was born April 8, 1925, to Essie Way in the town of Ridgeville, Dorchester County, South Carolina. Essie Way did not marry Victoria's father. Victoria, two sisters, a male cousin, her mother, and her grandmother Lucretia Way were tenants of a local white farmer. Essie worked as a maid for her landlord and other local white households to support the family. Helping her daughter support their family, Lucretia Way reared the children and worked as a field hand. Lucretia further supplemented the family income by taking in laundry, as did Septima Clark's mother.[87] Victoria was greatly affected by seeing her mother and grandmother labor relentlessly for as little as twenty-five cents per day. Remembering those times, she once said, "Well, really, we were treated like slaves, because when the white people came in and said that you had to go to work, you had to work whether you wanted to or not." Again, similar to Hamer, DeLee determined as a child to try to change her family and community's circumstances: "It was in my mind from a little girl when my grandmomma and them were being treated like that, I used to say 'well, one day I'm gonna fix it.'"[88]

While Victoria's early determination to "fix" things for her mother and grandmother derived from outrage about their mistreatment, as she entered adulthood her activism issued from convictions about justice fueled by religious influences of her grandmother and church life. Lucretia's practice of regular family prayer throughout Victoria's childhood was a significant influence. Lucretia Way prayed with her grandchildren every evening. Affirming her own practice of praying as an adult, DeLee recalled participating with her grandmother in evening prayers as "when I learned to pray. My grandmomma always taught me how to pray." As a child, however, Victoria questioned the efficacy of entreating God for help. "I didn't believe in God all the time," she recalled.

> 'Cause, you see my grandmomma say God would fix it. He knowed how. 'N' she would be just prayin' and cryin' all in the night. 'N' then I went to wonderin' what kind of God is that? If

> he gon' fix it, why would He let the people do what they was doing to her? Why she had to work so hard? Why she work for 25 cents a day? Why we had to go out there and bring a bag of those white people old clothes and stuff home and things like that? And, then, she think God would, she jus' believe in God. I didn't believe in Him. And she would have me down on my knees, she'd be prayin' in the night, teachin' me the Our Father prayer, you know. I'd quote the Our Father prayer with her. And then after we done say the Our Father prayer, then she would pray. Oh, my Lord, and my grandmomma just cry and pray. And I'd be down there jus' cussin' away in my mind. I was sayin', 'Don't you worry, I'll fix it for my grandmomma. I'm gon' fix it.'[89]

While much of Victoria's childhood energy seemed focused on determining independently to attend to her grandmother, Lucretia persevered in imparting religious perspectives to her grandchildren. At Lucretia's insistence, regular church participation was also a part of Victoria's early life. Whenever Lucretia went to Bethel Methodist Church, she took her four grandchildren with her. "My grandmomma was a church-goer," DeLee recalled. Perhaps naming the origin of her own later attraction to pentecostal doctrine, DeLee said her grandmother practiced holiness: "When I was raised in the Methodist church, it was clean. Really and truly my, my grandmomma and those, they was sanctified people. They was so sanctified."[90] Throughout childhood Victoria attended Bethel Church with Lucretia, but by the time she was a preteen, Victoria became attracted to the active youth usher board at St. John Baptist Church, which traveled to nearby towns to sing. Moreover, some members at Bethel Methodist Church stigmatized the Way children because they were born out of wedlock. "Everytime we would go to this church," Victoria recalled, "they would always treat us bad. 'Cause back then when you have children and it was outta wedlock, everybody would slight you, you know, push you to one side."[91] So, with Lucretia's permission, Victoria and her siblings began attending St. John Baptist, where another of Lucretia's daughters served as youth usher board director.

While Victoria enjoyed the pleasures of a Black rural Southern adolescence singing and taking short trips with the church choir, much of her life remained tainted by the frustration she felt about the conditions of African Americans. In addition to the circumstances of her mother and grandmother, conventional violence against Blacks in Dorchester County profoundly influenced her: "They used to, back there in them days lynch people. They'd hang 'em. If a Black person did something, they would take them in the woods and hang 'em."[92] Recalling an occasion when she stood by as a child while the prospect of violence was used to intimidate her grandmother, DeLee told the story of a white landowner, Bub Cummings, riding an ox by her grandmother's house specifically to tell Lucretia of his opportunity to have the first shot at a Black man, Mr. Fogle, who would be killed in the nearby town of Dorchester for allegedly whistling at a white woman. "I can see it as if it was yesterday," DeLee said.

> My grandmomma had this beautiful flower yard in the front of her house, you know. And she had all these rose bushes and stuff. And we were out there in the rose bushes. . . . And he call out to my grandmomma. And he say, "Mom Cretia." 'Cause they would call her Mom Cretia or Aunt Cretia. It was Mom Cretia. And, uh, he tell her, "Come here." He say, "I'm in a hurry. I got to go 'cause they done promise me that if I git there they gonna give me the first shot at that niggah. And I'm going to git the first shot!" He was gon' be in the group of the first people to shoot.

After the lynching was over, DeLee said Cummings returned to further intimidate her grandmother by recounting details of the event:

> And all she could do was just sit there and listen. She wasn't allowed to say nothing back to him. And when he was gone, she just cried, and she just prayed and was crying how awful it was. And they said they [castrated him] and stuffed them in his mouth while they shoot him. And they shoot him piece by piece. . . . That thing stuck in my mind. Here this man being killed, and I overheard. He didn't care. He talked right in front of us. "If you do so and so, we'll have you killed, you niggers this and that. . . ." That's all they would call us back there was niggers, you know, they didn't try to butter it up at all.[93]

While such violence and intimidation made lasting impressions on Victoria, effects of what was meted out against her mother, grandmother, and other local African Americans were, perhaps, paralleled by Victoria's personal encounters with repression and violence.

Although she anticipated becoming an adult before taking meaningful actions to initiate change, Victoria began expressing dissatisfaction at a young age by rebelling whenever possible against oppressive racial customs. When children in the Way family were old enough to work, they went to the fields with Lucretia: "Whenever we would work in the field, my grandmomma them tell us what to do. Soon as her back would turn, I'd go contrary to it, and let the white man see that I could, I wasn't gonna be doing it the way he wanted it." Seeking to assert her dissatisfaction in this way caused another event that left an indelible impression on Victoria's mind.

> One particular time, this white man he told me that I was nabbing the cotton, leaving it back there, and I said, "I didn't." And he said, "Yes you is." And he told my grandmomma what I was doing, and he hauled off and slapped me out. That man knocked me in my head 'til I fell out. . . . And my grandmomma had to beat me, had to beat me until this man was satisfied. He said, "That's enough. That's enough." I'll never forget it.

Unlike Lou Ella Townsend, who physically fought to restrain whites striking her children, Lucretia Way whipped Victoria to prevent a beating from the angry man. Lucretia Way's action was an effort to protect Victoria from further violence. Reflecting on the event years later, DeLee said, "My grandmomma just, had to just beat me, 'cause she know if not he could, would have killed me." At that time, however, Victoria was not able to accept her grandmother's actions. "She told me afterwards, when we come home," DeLee said, "but I don't think right then I had ever forgiven her for beatin' me for that white man, 'cause I felt like she didn't had to do it. And I told her so. I said, 'I don't see where you had to beat me to satisfy him. I wouldn't beat one of my children to satisfy him.' She say, 'But you don't know. If I didn't, he would have killed you.'"[94]

Victoria's experience parallels that of other Southern Black children growing up at that time. Katie G. Cannon identifies what Lucretia Way did as practicing and passing on "functional prudence," the ability to preserve life in recognition of the dangers of racism.

Describing lessons that Southern African American elders sought to teach children during slavery and in the late nineteenth and early twentieth centuries, Cannon shows how the character Janie in a story by Zora Neale Hurston is taught functional prudence by her elders. Because certain attitudes could pose threats to physical survival, both Hurston and her character were reprimanded or punished by grandmothers (and fathers) for having "too much spirit," a "sassy tongue," or a "stiff neck."[95] Writer Maya Angelou tells of a similar experience in her autobiography. Recounting events following her interaction with two white women in a local Arkansas shop, Angelou records her grandmother's (called "Momma") response:

> "Mr. Coleman's granddaughter, Miss June, just called from the General Merchandise Store." [Momma's] voice quaked a little. "She said you was downtown showing out." . . . I decided to explain and let her share in the glory. I began, "It was the principle of the thing, Momma"—I didn't even see the hand rising, and suddenly it had swung down hard against my cheek. . . . "You think . . . these crazy people won't kill you? You think them lunatic cracker boys won't try to catch you in the road and violate you? You think because of your all-fired principle some of the men won't feel like putting their white sheets on and riding over here to stir up trouble?" . . . Momma's intent to protect me had caused her to hit me in the face, a thing she had never done, and to send me away to where she thought I'd be safe.[96]

In spite of Lucretia Way's intent, Victoria understood efforts to curb her will as more repression. In addition to racial repression, she said, "my grandmomma was so strict on me. She beat me all the time, and try to keep me straight." These circumstances and Victoria's "spirited" perspective led to her early marriage so she could begin to "get what I wanted done." By the time she was fourteen, Victoria developed a plan to run away from her grandmother's defensive severity to strike out violently against whites. Fortunately, Victoria's best friend thwarted the plan and convinced her that getting married would provide freedom from her grandmother. Victoria thought this was a good idea, and at age fifteen, on December 21, 1940, she married her suitor, S. B. DeLee.[97]

Through Lucretia's persistence and Victoria's socialization, church participation became a part of her self-understanding. As Septima

Clark indicated, being a churchgoer was integral to respectable Southern Black culture. Victoria was an active church member throughout her youth and, immediately after her marriage, began attending St. John Baptist Church, where the couple met.[98] Religious values inculcated in DeLee by her grandmother and nurtured by churches she attended pervaded DeLee's self-understanding. As these values evolved, they became important to DeLee's turning away from plans for violent revenge and toward community and political activism.

Although she did not immediately let go of her idea of revenge in favor of social and political action, changes in DeLee's life disposed her to refocus her energy. Important among these changes were the birth of her first child, Sonny B. DeLee, in 1942 and a compelling sermon she heard when Sonny was a baby. Recalling her excitement about her son and the sermon, DeLee said:

> Ooh when that baby born, I had love that baby! You know how, your first baby, ooh. And I went to church that Sunday with my first new baby. And the preacher preached a sermon. I'll never forget that. . . . I think it was all for me. And he was saying, "You could git by, but you wouldn't git away." . . . And I listen at that message. And every time I look at that baby. . . . And he said that whatever them white people do to you . . . God had they number, and He right way they live. And if they didn't git it, they children children children would git it. . . . and then he brought out that whatever we do, we might git by, but our children would reap what we sow. . . . And he just went on. And every time I looked at that baby, and looked up, and that preacher jus' went on. And ooh, my God, for the first time I see myself. And I say, "Oh, Lord, way should I turn?" 'Cause I already did some things [to whites]. And I still had . . . planned on killin' 'em. I meant to go about and kill some white people just like they had kill all them Black people. . . . And when that preacher preached that sermon that Sunday, I got converted to myself right in that church, right there. . . . And I say, "Ooh, there is another way. Uh huh, I can't do that, 'cause my baby gonna reap it. And I love my baby."[99]

DeLee was so powerfully affected by the sermon that she felt she needed guidance in responding to it. Later that day, DeLee walked three miles to Lucretia Way's home to seek her counsel. She said, "I walk and went to my grandmomma house that evenin' and tote that baby. And I told her, and I went and start tellin' her, and I went to cryin'."[100] Lucretia advised DeLee to seek forgiveness: "She said that before God would convert my soul I would have to love the white people. She said, 'You got to *mean* it.' And, sure enough, the Lord answered my prayer and I started to love white folks. But I stand up all right. I let 'em know that they wasn't goin' to run over me."[101] DeLee's going to see Lucretia Way reflects an appreciation of her grandmother as an elder. Even though she did not always agree with her grandmother's views, DeLee experienced her as a person who was persistent in her faith and whose life experience provided wisdom that would be useful to DeLee for confronting and surviving life's dilemmas. DeLee called the Sunday of this sermon a day of conversion. She began, she said, to remember lessons and Bible verses she learned as a child in Sunday school and to spend time praying for forgiveness.

> Then it come back to me for the first time, I remembered one thing I had learn in my Sunday school lesson. In the Methodist Church they had thing to say in the beginnin' was the word, and the word was God and—And that come back to me then, but I had never 'membered it befo'e. . . . So then I went to prayin'. I went to prayin'. From that day on I went to prayin'. I went and prayed for forgiveness. . . . I got converted that same Sunday, but you see converted is a turnaround. See. And I made a turnaround that same Sunday. . . . And I got up and testified that I was converted, 'cause I did. I didn't meant to do them things [to whites] no more. 'N I want[ed] a change in my life. And I went to doing things different.[102]

DeLee's religious desire for change and her decision to do things differently may have predisposed her to develop her perspective and practices in response to civil rights activities.

The DeLees continued participating as regular members of St. John Baptist Church for thirteen years. Leaving St. John after a conflict in the congregation, the family spent a year at Surprise Baptist Church in a town nearby before converting to pentecostalism. During their tenure with Surprise Church, Bishop James Ravenel of the House of God,[103] a pentecostal denomination, began a radio ministry and tent revival near Ridgeville. Ravenel's messages particularly appealed to the DeLees because he emphasized "holiness." DeLee recalled that, like others attracted to Ravenel's message, "we just . . . went out there to go hear him. It was going on a good while." Persuaded by Ravenel's "teaching in the scriptures," DeLee said "our eyes come open, then about holiness. And that you had to be holy. . . . And that, as I say, when we find out it was right, we received the baptism of the Holy Ghost."[104] The family became a part of Ravenel's ministry, and, consequently, Victoria and S. B. DeLee helped found the House of God congregation at Ridgeville. Perhaps of great significance to the intensity with which DeLee later carried out her activism was the combination of her natural assertiveness with a spiritual independence she began to embrace after she entered the House of God holiness denomination.[105]

DeLee's Practice of Community Work as a Moral Value

DeLee entered the public arena as a community activist, seeking to change conditions for people of her immediate community. Despite her previous rejection of the idea that God would make a real difference in her grandmother's life, DeLee encountered a powerful and creative outlet for channeling her energy in a religious context through preaching about voting rights in a rural Black church. The same minister who preached the sermon that challenged DeLee to refocus her life also introduced her to the Civil Rights Movement. Reverend R. B. Adams, pastor of St. John Baptist Church, preached about civil rights and urged his congregation to attempt voter registration.

When Adams's promptings caught DeLee's attention, she and her husband traveled fifteen miles by train to St. George, the Dorchester County seat, where registration was held. DeLee recalled that when they arrived, there was a room full of Blacks who "were given permission to register." An attendant was moving the process along by calling out "Next!" whenever another person was allowed to go to the inner office for registration. The DeLees moved into the room and sat with the crowd. When the attendant said "next," Victoria rose to her feet. Upon seeing her rise, the person who should have been next sat down because he thought he was out of turn. DeLee said, "But I got on up. I went like I was next. When I went in there to register, [the registrar] said, 'Who brought you?' I said, 'I brought myself.' I had on a black overcoat because I was pregnant with Vicky. I'll never forget. I had both of my hands in my pockets."

Because she had come without "permission," the registration agent told DeLee he could not register her. She insisted that he would, and the two argued back and forth. Finally, standing in front of the door and keeping one hand in her pocket as if she had a weapon, DeLee told the registrar that he would not leave the room if she were not given her "civil rights." The agent finally complied, telling DeLee not to let others know of her success. DeLee said she would not consent to such a thing, and upon leaving the room she "went right on out there and went to talking right loud to everybody" about the registration.[106]

Empowered and encouraged by her own success, DeLee came to regard voter registration as one vehicle by which she could make a difference. "I'll never forget that day!" she said. "That was a good feeling day. I felt so good that I got, made that man registered me!" She became tenacious in efforts to register other persons. "Then I went out, and I start talking to people," she recalled. "I start tellin' 'em 'bout my registration certificate. I come back to the church, and I get up in the church and tell the preacher how I get my registration certificate. And the preacher went to telling everybody how they must do like I done."[107] Thus DeLee immediately began her life of civil rights activism. She started encouraging others to register to vote and leading additional activities for change in her community.

The next year, 1948, DeLee led a protest against the county school board to prevent the firing of a teacher whom she valued as someone who cared for "all the children." JohnEtta Grant, who began her teaching career at Clay Hill Elementary School in Ridgeville, commuted twenty-six miles by car from Charleston to teach in Ridgeville. When other teachers who boarded in town began to commute with Grant, local authorities told Grant that she must move into the county or lose her job. Upon learning of this, DeLee organized parents who together traveled by train to the county school board meeting in St. George.[108] As she later recalled,

> So they went to fire this teacher. And I got all the parents to come together, and we had a meeting one night. And we baffled that school board. And that's the first time Blacks ever stand up in this area to white people. And we got on that school board, and then they couldn't fire the woman. So that was the first thing that really, to me we accomplished.[109]

Perhaps equally as important as the protest for DeLee was her experience of the event as the first time African Americans of the area successfully challenged restrictive racial practices. This experience surely helped sustain in DeLee the possibility of cooperative community activity in later years. Community affirmation and support became a significant factor in DeLee's entry into civil rights activism. For example, her pastor's sanctioning her voter registration by telling others to follow her example, since it occurred so early in her life, affirmed DeLee's developing sense of herself. Moreover, Reverend Adams obviously felt it significant to encourage DeLee's activism. Adams later introduced DeLee to South Carolina NAACP Field Secretary, the Reverend I. DeQuincey Newman. Newman oversaw the NAACP's state registration drive and particularly promoted DeLee's activities. "So when I started working," DeLee says, "then they start to working with me. Oh, I had a lot of help from the outside, you know, to help me work with this."[110] Once she entered civil rights activity, DeLee experienced a refocusing of her energy away from violent retaliation back toward her original goal "to fix it" for Black people some day.

DeLee's Civil Rights Participation as Living Out Religious Belief

With support of the state NAACP, DeLee began to move beyond her local congregation to encourage African American voter registration across Dorchester County. When NAACP activities began to be severely scrutinized and restricted in South Carolina and across the South,[111] DeLee continued her efforts by founding a local organization, the Dorchester County Voters' League. She began the Voters' League by traveling around the county on Sundays, seeking permission from Black pastors to make appeals for participation by their congregants.[112]

In spite of her efforts, throughout the decade state and local statutes and conventions severely limited voter registration attempts. At one point DeLee became so frustrated with obstacles to Black voter registration that "she took two carloads of twenty people" to the Justice Department in Washington, D.C., to seek federal assistance.

The trip occurred as an improvisation, since DeLee felt she had exhausted all other possibilities. She told one reporter:

> We had just enough money to buy gas and have one hamburger and a drink on the way there and back. I came to Washington, and brother, did I raise said [*sic*]. I wanted them to send some federal men down to help register voters.
>
> They said, "go home Mrs. DeLee and we'll do something" and I said "the only way I'll understand is if you send someone." They didn't come for a week so I went back myself and went from door to door in the Justice Department and told them if they didn't send someone I'd bring everybody up there.[113]

The Justice Department responded by sending personnel to oversee voter registration activity of three South Carolina counties, including Dorchester, in which people complained about opposition to Black registration. Justice Department activity in the state caused reaction at the highest levels. Responding to the probes in South Carolina, Governor Ernest F. Hollings sought to protect "the state's sovereignty and [said] that the 'harassment' that the people of Clarendon, Dorchester and Williamsburg counties have been put through by the FBI is going to stop."[114] After years of persistence, meaningful differences in Dorchester County Black voter registration emerged. Between 1956 and 1968 the percentage of registered African Americans increased from 7.2 to 33.5 percent of the total county registered voters.[115]

Following voter registration successes, DeLee led work to influence Dorchester County elections. As with voter registration, local officials encumbered election efforts. In one instance, when illiterate and semiliterate African Americans sought assistance in voting, the "poll manager, claiming to be acting in accordance with instructions from the U.S. Attorney in Columbia [the state capital], refused to permit Negroes who had registered in 1965 to receive assistance in voting from anyone except the poll officials, all of whom were white." This practice contradicted state law that permitted assistance by a poll manager or any precinct elector of one's choice who was standing nearby.[116] Responding to such opposition, DeLee and other African Americans decided to begin entering Democratic Party precinct activity. Assisted by the state NAACP and implemented through the Dorchester County Voters' League, Black residents began running for offices in every voting precinct in the county. In early efforts, African Americans were quite successful because of conventionally poor attendance of precinct meetings. According to

DeLee, it was easy to organize enough Blacks to outnumber whites at precinct meetings. During one year, African Americans won the majority of major county Democratic precinct offices.[117] This strategy of surprise did not work well after its initial use, when local white Democratic Party members organized to restrict or exclude Black participation. During a 1966 Democratic Party precinct meeting in Ridgeville, ten local residents postponed calling the meeting to order so that "a large number of white persons, including families with their children," could gather to outnumber the African Americans present. Also, the precinct chairperson ruled African Americans out of order when they attempted to nominate persons for office. DeLee complained to the state Democratic Executive Committee, which told her she must first contest precinct meetings at the county convention. DeLee brought the complaint unsuccessfully to the county convention. She then appealed to the state Convention Credentials Committee. After a full hearing, the committee rejected the complaint and took no disciplinary action against the delegation.[118]

Activities in Dorchester County involving the exclusion of Black people from participation in the Democratic Party were replicated throughout South Carolina and across the South.[119] Citing abuses and repression by the state Democratic Party and the anti-African American "full-slate" law,[120] and calling for action to ensure "meaningful enfranchisement for Black people," in 1969 Black leaders and progressive whites across South Carolina decided to form a third party.[121] DeLee attended the organizational meeting for the United Citizens' Party (UCP) of South Carolina and was elected vice-president. Like the MFDP, which preceded it by four years, the UCP sought to "'speak for the "silent majority" of Blacks and poor whites who are vitally concerned with issues of survival.'"[122] This philosophy of attending to the needs of all excluded persons coincided precisely with DeLee's goals. The Party immediately entered races for local office and, by November of 1970, fielded candidates for governor and lieutenant governor.[123] After the death of South Carolina's First Congressional District representative, the UCP entered its second statewide race, unanimously nominating DeLee as its candidate.[124] In keeping with the UCP position and broadening her work to include participation and social access issues, DeLee said her candidacy "would be aimed at 'the red, white and Black man'" in the district, using her "real experience in Washington to help get something done for the poor."[125] Again, paralleling Hamer who lamented that there was no real representation for the poor of Mississippi, DeLee said, "I know the things people need and I feel the truly underprivileged have never had a representative in Congress."[126] Although DeLee lost the race for Congress, she won a number of precincts and upset the balance of power between Democrats and Republicans in three (including the largest) counties of the district.[127] Consequently, while unsuccessful in the Congressional race, the result of DeLee's candidacy was similar in impact to Hamer and the MFDP's 1964 attempt to unseat the traditional Mississippi Democratic Party. DeLee and the UCP's efforts precipitated substantial changes in state Democratic Party practices, leading in particular to more inclusion of African Americans.

As DeLee continued to lead state voting rights efforts, through the NAACP and other civil rights organizations, she encountered varieties of civil rights practice, including school desegregation activities. The major school desegregation activity in South Carolina began with the Clarendon County suit, one of the several decided in the 1954 *Brown v. Board of Education* ruling. Even though the Clarendon case was among those decided with *Brown,* South Carolina successfully resisted integration for at least another fifteen years after the U.S. Supreme Court decision.[128] In 1965 the U.S. Office of Education required South Carolina's school districts to submit for approval desegregation plans complying with federal statutes. Dorchester County Districts One and Three were among four state districts that did not file compliance plans by 1965. Moreover, Dorchester County Districts One and Three turned away thirteen Black parents who took their children to the first day of school that year.[129]

The DeLees initiated desegregation activities in Dorchester District Three in 1964, when they attempted to enroll two of their children at Ridgeville Elementary School. Other parents later joined the DeLees. School district officials repeatedly resisted these efforts by disqualifying some Black students from eligibility to attend the white schools or by allowing only a few students to enroll at any given time. By March of 1966 Dorchester County District Three submitted an acceptable voluntary desegregation plan.[130] That plan, like that of most other districts in the state, was called "freedom of choice."

Placing the responsibility of desegregation on African Americans, the plan allowed parents to choose which schools their children would attend. Under the burden of full responsibility for initiating and carrying through desegregation efforts, Black parents and children were squeezed between the nation's requirement and local segregationist sentiment, the latter causing economic and physical retaliation for desegregation activity. "Freedom of choice" began for Dorchester County District Three in the spring of 1966. Fearing severe reprisals, most Black parents and children in Dorchester County (and in other counties across the state) took the physically, financially, and emotionally safer route of leaving things as they were.

In March of 1966, DeLee, on behalf of her sons Van and Elijah, led a list of plaintiffs in a suit seeking to completely desegregate the district's schools.[131] The effort to desegregate county schools took more than five additional years of court battles, strategizing, and protesting. While none of DeLee's activity was met with enthusiasm from county residents, desegregation work proved to be extremely provocative.[132] It was during this period that the DeLee home most frequently was shot into and subsequently completely destroyed by fire. As she later recalled,

> [When] we went to integrate the schools, that's when the whites really started trying to kill us, [even though] they were trying to kill me for the longest. Before that house burned down, it would look like a polka dot dress where the bullet holes from where they would shoot in the house. . . . One night I was sitting in the chair, and I was rocking the baby. When I rocked back like that, the bullet went right through by my face and went in the wall . . . and just missed me. . . . And the sheriff couldn't find nobody, couldn't catch nobody.[133]

In addition to initiating court action, DeLee led demonstrations, encouraged other parents to oppose school segregation, and frequently sought to meet with school district officials to expedite change.[134] As DeLee continued to resist school segregation, the scope of her activity expanded to include Native Americans, whom she encouraged to join desegregation activity. Until that time, Native American children attended a third county school system geographically located within District Three. While the district's 1966 approved desegregation plan asserted freedom of choice, when

Native American parents sought to exercise choice, "those choices were uniformly denied even though the choices of Black children were uniformly granted." When officials refused Native American enrollment by freedom of choice, DeLee organized "demonstrations against [their] having to attend [the] inadequate school." Following several days of protests, the district superintendent agreed to admit fifteen Native American children "on the basis that that number would not overcrowd the white school."[135] District Court presiding Judge Robert Hemphill, who prevented full exercise of choice by Native Americans, also enjoined demonstrations by issue of an order upholding the superintendent's decision to admit only fifteen Native American children.[136] In addition, Hemphill acted to suppress DeLee's participation in further desegregation efforts. When she went with Native American parents to enroll the fifteen children admitted to Ridgeville Elementary School, marshals arrested her for disobeying the demonstration injunction. Judge Hemphill placed DeLee under a $10,000 bond and ordered her to show why she should not be held in contempt of court. In spite of consistent attempts by DeLee and others, schools in Dorchester County District Three were not completely desegregated until 1971.

DeLee's Moral Vision

Two norms guiding and supporting Victoria DeLee's civil rights activism were communal cooperation and religious holiness. Throughout her activism DeLee both expected and relied on divine sanction of her work and community support. Expecting the community's moral perspectives and social aspirations to be similar to her own, DeLee presumed that community support derived from a similar religious vision of a just society. In this regard, DeLee carried out and looked back on her activism as a divinely directed embodiment of communal expectations. She felt her successes would not have been possible apart from the support, cooperation, and complementary vision of many members of the local community. She understood her work as successful because the community worked together following God. "I didn't make the change by myself," DeLee once said, "'cause if it wasn't for they help, and God in front leadin' all of us, we wouldn't have made this change in Dorchester County."[137] Reflecting the interdependence necessary to national civil rights successes, the interplay of DeLee's individual goals with those of her community and the perspective of both leader and community that God ordained their work kept local Movement activity going.

While DeLee's community was not homogeneous in holding this viewpoint, people who held perspectives compatible with the community's vision supported civil rights work. "Just like you got 'em now, you got quite a few different groups of people, types of people," she said, "and one of 'em was at that time men folks that, who wanted some freedom and justice. . . . They backed me up 100 percent."[138] DeLee's analysis of the way gender affected community activities reflects her understanding of how community cooperation and a shared religious vision enabled civil rights victories. During her most intense period of activism, DeLee believed that Black men deferred to her leadership as a way of accomplishing communal goals through the means available to them.

> The reason they was willing to follow me, men folks would not get as far as I've gotten doing what I was doing. Because they was killing them men folks, see. They would kill Black men. They'd throw Black mens in jail. They'd beat 'em up, and all this sort of thing. Well, with me, they wouldn't come out, you know, that bold and just do me like that. So then the Black men supported me. . . . They couldn't do it, but they didn't fight me. They, they fought with me. . . . [And] if we went to jail, and they get the message, they was coming and get me outa jail. And if they couldn't get me out that jail, they wasn't go left that jail house. They would stay on that outside, 'round out there where, where I was in that jailhouse. 'Cause they figure if they'd a left there that them people woulda kill me, you know.[139]

DeLee concluded that Black women's cooperation in support of her leadership derived both from women's participation in the community's civil rights vision and being influenced by a common religious perspective guiding their work. For DeLee, norms of community cooperation and shared religious perspectives superseded potentially destructive concerns about gender mixing (a particularly sensitive area in some religious, especially holiness, contexts). Reflecting both her concern about personal holiness and the significance of community solidarity, DeLee said local Black women followers of the Civil

Rights Movement trusted her and were solidly behind her: "The Black women, they supported me so much, because of all my getting around. . . . I wouldn't be with women, the most time I would be with men folks. But the women had so much faith and confidence in me. . . . I've never been accused of nobody's husband, man or nothing. Never has!"[140]

DeLee was resolute, consistently professing her commitment to holiness throughout her activism. In one instance, similar to Septima Clark's statement that she was a teetotaler when she was charged with selling alcohol, DeLee referred to her practice of holiness as proof that local authorities were harassing her after she ran for Congress. Two days after the election DeLee was arrested "and charged with 'following too close, resisting arrest, striking a police officer, and cursing and abusing a police officer' following a four-car accident." DeLee denied all charges: "I don't use curse words since I was saved. I may have raised my voice when arguing with the officers but I didn't use any curse words."[141] Contending that it was raining, DeLee also disputed the officer's report that the weather was fair.[142] She recounted the events to a reporter:

> It would be different, she said, if they had charged that Victoria DeLee "wouldn't stop talking." People know that about her, she said. "Those other things are just not true," she said. . . . "I have never cursed since I was saved," she said. Her most emphatic denial was against assaulting a police officer. She said she would never strike out against someone with a gun and a stick. . . . At one point, Mrs. DeLee recounted that one officer said he had "a good mind to beat my brains out."[143]

Perhaps the most significant way DeLee experienced the interaction of community cooperation and shared religious perspective was through her work with local congregations. Several Black churches and Black church networks were among the most meaningful supporters sustaining protest activity in the county. As was the case across the Movement, the affinity of civil rights practice with religious belief and ideological perspectives of many civil rights participants yielded leadership, support, and camaraderie that reciprocally enhanced individual, community, regional, and national vitality of the Movement. For DeLee, this affinity was evident through long-term interaction with three ministers and their congregations, as well as through various relationships with other local congregations and leaders. R. B. Adams, the Baptist minister and NAACP member who first noted DeLee's community work, encouraged her efforts, planted the seed for her own enfranchisement, and inaugurated her interaction with state NAACP leadership. I. D. Newman, United Methodist minister and former South Carolina NAACP Field Secretary, encouraged DeLee and connected much of her local, regional, and statewide activity with his own efforts to realize state NAACP goals. Bishop J. Ravenel, DeLee's first pastor in the House of God Church, continued his support of her activity, as did Adams.

While DeLee understood personal faith as undergirding her work, it was the interaction of her faith and practice with the faith and practice of others that sustained her long-term activity. She observed that it was "the faith that I had in God" that motivated and energized her. For DeLee, practice of her faith in a local community was essential. "I always stuck to the church . . . because I was brought up in the church, and then after I got married, I still stuck with the church," she said.[144] Noting the support she received in local congregations, DeLee explained: "When I left from the Baptist Church, I went to the House of God Holiness Church. And God fix it so the leadership that I had there . . . Bishop Ravenel was the type of minister . . . believed in standing up and fighting for what you want. He believed in the NAACP . . . and he never discouraged me." Furthermore, DeLee articulated the significance of religious communal support to her work.

> And then, another thing, because if you know yourself, and . . . if you're going to a church, and you are doing something and the people approve of what you are doing and every once in a while they praise you, it makes you feel good at, you know, and you go on doing it. And Bishop Ravenel was good at that. He would always say, "Sister DeLee is, we got to respect her for her leadership because [of] what she is doing to help her people . . ." and this and that and the other. And it always was something to encourage me. He never talked anything negligent about me.[145]

Perhaps the most important religious communal support DeLee received was from her spouse. S. B. and Victoria DeLee engaged local congregations together. And Mr. DeLee supported his wife's efforts emotionally, financially, and physically, providing security and camaraderie that undergirded her work. Financially, Mr. DeLee's support literally made it possible for Mrs. DeLee to participate as a visible leader for change in Dorchester County. Mr. DeLee's employment outside the county at a federal agency, the Charleston Naval Weapons Station, sufficiently insulated the DeLees from local and even state economic reprisals, one means by which opponents suffocated Black leadership and activity across the South. Furthermore, Victoria DeLee never worked for wages during the majority of her years of civil rights practice. She was able, however, to transport registrants and voters, to attend Movement workshops and meetings across the county and state, to host myriad volunteers in her home (providing them with meals and often shelter), to travel across the county organizing and executing numerous types of work, and to perform a variety of other activities. These practices not only required time away from their ten children but also consumed the family's financial resources. Mr. DeLee's work provided the financial means for Mrs. DeLee's practice. Mr. DeLee's willingness to stay at home released Mrs. DeLee from some mundane family and household responsibilities. Moreover, he secured the place to which Mrs. DeLee returned daily after her battles against oppression.

Throughout her civil rights endeavors, DeLee's activism was motivated by four interrelated points of view. These viewpoints—about equality, membership, justice, and social participation—are discernible in activities DeLee undertook and in statements reflecting her ideas about a good society.

DeLee believed that all persons have equal value as members of the human community and, as such, deserve respect. Her ideas about the equal value of persons as members of the human community were evident from her youth. The observation that her mother and grandmother worked so hard for meager compensation or "old clothes," her objection to violence against African Americans, and her efforts to assert her dignity as a child reflect her appraisal of Black persons' value as human beings. As DeLee's perspective evolved, she began to relate her beliefs about the dignity and value of African Americans as human beings to the possibilities existing for other persons in her immediate context. This means that DeLee began to connect her ideas about human dignity to a notion of rights of community members. An important element of exercising one's rights as a community member and receiving respect relates to being able to make choices comparable to those made by others in society. Exclusion from opportunity to exercise the franchise and from access to equitable educational resources denies persons ordinary choices of community life and, therefore, denies the equal human dignity of those persons.

Coinciding with this view about human value is DeLee's standpoint about membership in society. DeLee presumed membership for those living in society. Further, her presumptions about choosing imply rights that appear to be specifically related to her ideas about human value: On the basis of their equal value as human beings and their status as members of society, people have license to social privileges, or civil rights. Two of the most important rights in her work include the right to fair treatment and the right to full social participation. Fair treatment for DeLee is relative to the ordinary possibilities experienced by others in the community or society. Her concern about the wages and work conditions of her mother and grandmother grew out of the incomparably better economic chances and life conditions of other people in the same community. DeLee's school integration work for African American and Native American children related directly to substandard conditions of nonwhite facilities in the same geographic district.

Closely related to her fair treatment ideas is the assertion that full social participation options should be available to all members of society. DeLee's work to ensure the right to full participation is evidenced both by her efforts to help secure voting rights for Black people and by campaigns to register voters once technical enfranchisement was possible. DeLee further asserted ideas about full participation through attempts to stop intimidation of Black voters. Engaging the Democratic Party and the United Citizens' Party also reflect this perspective. When the Democratic Party failed to provide opportunities to participate, DeLee helped found the UCP to provide an alternate vehicle for participation.

Beginning early in her life and continuing throughout her civil rights work, DeLee seems to have been motivated by a personal sense of what she felt was just. Her sense of justice led her to believe that unfair treatment and barriers to full participation should be challenged. Possibly arising from the conditions into which she was born, DeLee's sense of justice seems substantially bound to judgments about the conditions of the most marginalized in society. Reflecting her perspective about human value, DeLee consistently worked to ensure that the most marginalized should be heard, represented, and attended to. Her initiating efforts to bring Native Americans into school desegregation activity demonstrates this position. In Dorchester County Native Americans were relegated to a third, even poorer school system, and geographically and economically were more ostracized from the community than were many African Americans. DeLee asserted her belief in justice for the oppressed during her Congressional race, saying her candidacy was significant to "the truly underprivileged [who] have never had a representative."[146]

The above three viewpoints are best understood when correlated with DeLee's regard for the most marginalized. She says that even as a child her concern was for those whom she felt could not help themselves. In her adult life, DeLee maintained this concern. "There was so many people who couldn't git what they wanted," she says of the pre-Movement period, "and they couldn't stand up for themselves. That's the people I wanted to do something about. So . . . that was in my mind to make some changes there." Moreover, DeLee asserted that intervening in such circumstances is a central message of Christian scripture. "The Bible tells us help them who can't help themselves," she said.[147] She felt those farthest away from obtaining goods and services of society are least likely to have significant opportunities to realize ordinary possibilities in society. This concern for those "who can't help themselves" motivated DeLee's initial desire to make a difference for her own family, and became central to her activism as faith practices throughout her life.

Self-Realization as Moral Practice from a Grassroots Perspective

Both Fannie Lou Hamer and Victoria Way DeLee were involved in community activism seeking to improve local life before they encountered civil rights practices. Their roles and identities as community leaders already existed and in fact became the soil in which seeds of the Movement were planted and their activism thrived. Others who knew or noted these women's local leadership connected them with civil rights work as a way of both extending the Movement and expanding community work they already performed. Both Hamer and DeLee acted with intense religious fervor in organizing and leading civil rights activities. Their community activism reflected their religious devotion and expressed the certainty they felt about divine intention for the flourishing of Black life. While this sense of themselves preceded their more formal involvement in the Civil Rights Movement, it is the case that the Movement provided support and opportunities for each woman to realize possibilities of exercising her innate abilities and expressing intuitive values that may not otherwise have occurred. For Hamer and DeLee, there evolved a fruitful compatibility of their interpretation of Christianity and sense of urgency about the predominant conditions of their communities with the values, norms, and practices of the Civil Rights Movement.

Hamer and DeLee's religious self-understanding and nascent activism conformed so closely to Civil Rights Movement values and practices that each woman's work and influence extended far beyond her local context. Though Hamer's national recognition and political participation exceeded DeLee's, both women wielded considerable relative power and became influential leaders in ways that were unheard of for persons from their socioeconomic situations. Such an accomplishment is perhaps even more unlikely today, since contemporary practices of political participation require high levels of literacy and education. This convention constricts the possibility that grassroots leaders like Hamer and DeLee will be recognized and supported beyond local settings today.

The Civil Rights Movement provided the context in which Hamer and DeLee became more fully and freely themselves, each fulfilling her own yearning to contribute to a positive quality of life for Black people, in particular, and poor people, in general, through her work. Several elements of the Civil Rights Movement converged to make possible Hamer and DeLee's realization of possibilities that would not have occurred otherwise. These elements included, but certainly are not limited to, Movement practices brought to and replicated in their local communities, persons who introduced these practices and affirmed Hamer and DeLee's community work, members of their local communities and others who followed Hamer and DeLee's leadership, and initiative arising from the two women themselves. As an element contributing to their self-realization, the two women's personal initiative is particularly important. Originally, Hamer and DeLee became community activists as a means of affirming and realizing their nascent ideas about the value and dignity of their families and communities. At the same time, as members of these families and communities, Hamer and DeLee were affirming and asserting something about themselves. While the meaning of what she asserted was not fully developed for either woman, both Hamer and DeLee sought to improve their lives and the lives of others. Although the Movement context yielded various opportunities, without their initiative it is unlikely that either Hamer or DeLee would have moved forward as they did. At the same time, other Movement participants welcomed and encouraged the two women by engaging their work with Movement practices and ideas. Both Hamer and DeLee immediately saw civil rights activity as congruent with their understanding of living faithfully, and they engaged civil rights practices as a means to fulfill more completely their religious responsibilities and to realize more fully their identity as Christians. Each woman's attribution of divine intervention as important to her work reflects an understanding of herself as partner to divine work with responsibility to participate in changing social life. Taking up this responsibility—taking initiative in their communities—Hamer and DeLee began community activism and engaged Movement practices.

Because of the reciprocally beneficial interaction of work in the Movement and opportunities they experienced as a result of the Movement, Fannie Lou Hamer and Victoria Way DeLee realized new possibilities for themselves and bore witness to their beliefs in ways that they had probably never imagined. Like Baker and Clark, they passed on values about human community that continue to influence life today.

4

Clara Muhammad:

Supporting Movement Ideas outside Its Mainstream

Clara Muhammad and the Nation of Islam

Elijah Muhammad is typically credited as founder of the Nation of Islam through his taking up, passing on, and organizing around the teachings of W. D. Fard in Detroit in the early 1930s. It is not accurate, however, to name Elijah founder without also recognizing that Clara Muhammad, his wife since 1919, was de facto cofounder. Together they built an organization that during their lifetime numbered over 100,000 persons,[1] with assets in excess of $50 million. Through the teachings of the Nation of Islam (NOI), Clara and Elijah Muhammad influenced a generation of African Americans in taking up the posture of race pride that became integral to some developments in the Civil Rights Movement and beyond. In addition to her work alongside her husband, for several significant periods in the organization's early life, during Elijah's absence, Clara was in reality leader of the NOI, ensuring its continuing existence and development.

Initially, because of dissensions within the movement and later as a result of FBI harassment, during the Nation of Islam's emergence Elijah Muhammad often was secluded or frequently moving from city to city. This precariousness in Elijah's life meant Clara became a stabilizing factor for him, their family, and the NOI. Because of the duration and frequency of Elijah's absences and because detailed records of the ways Clara Muhammad guided the NOI do not exist, we may never know the full relevance of her steady perseverance. By all available accounts, she was a major contributor to the origin and development of what became a national movement that helped awaken and deepen the role of pride in Black identity during the Civil

Rights Era. Moreover, the Nation of Islam movement helped break open the perceived hegemony of Christianity as the only legitimate expression of religiosity not only for African Americans but also for other people across the United States.

While the ideology of the NOI under the Muhammads included the disparaging and controversial perspective that *all* white persons were devils, two other components of the ideology, stressing race pride and Black self-determination, were foundational to Civil Rights Era emphases on African American agency and autonomy as constitutive of full citizenship. Clara Evans Muhammad played a central role in cultivating and institutionalizing this perspective. As a leader in developing the NOI, she not only refashioned her own religious perspective, leaving Christianity to become a Muslim,[2] but also helped her husband build an organization that became the foundation for and mechanism through which thousands of African Americans first experienced affirmation of Blackness and through which thousands of persons descended from Africa and Europe encountered Islam and became devout Muslims.

Clara Muhammad was a woman of the same generation as Ella Baker and Septima Clark. Muhammad's life experience was quite different from theirs, however. Although all three women grew up poor, Muhammad contended with survival issues of a level and duration that Baker and Clark never encountered. In view of her early life circumstances, Muhammad's accomplishments are quite remarkable. She was a Black woman who completed only seven years of primary education in Perry, Georgia, who bore and reared eight children, and whose early life as a wife and mother often was beleaguered by abject poverty. Although she was not a part of what might be called the "mainstream" Civil Rights Movement, Clara Muhammad's role as one who helped construct the vehicle that transmitted notions of race pride to the Black masses made her a significant participant in the evolution of the Civil Rights Movement.

Religious and Moral Influences in Muhammad's Early Life

Although Clara Muhammad's role in the Nation of Islam (now the Muslim American Society)[3] was influential, significant details of her early life—as with accounts of her full contributions to the organization—are scarce. Born November 2, 1899, to Quartus and Mary Lou Thomas Evans, Clara Bell Evans was the third child and second daughter in her immediate family. She had an older brother, Carlton, and a sister, Rosalie. A halfsister, Mamie (born to Quartus Evans in a previous marriage), did not live with the family. Both Quartus Evans and Mary Lou Thomas entered the world during the Reconstruction era, born in 1871 and 1872, respectively. They married in their hometown of Perry, Georgia, as the century and any hopes for substantial and sustained Reconstruction were coming to an end. Family history and other oral accounts say the Evanses were sharecroppers in Howton County, Georgia.[4]

The Evans family, including young Clara, are described as "devout" Christians. They worshiped in a local African Methodist Episcopal congregation, where Quartus served as a steward and Clara sang with others in the church choir. These songs later became a source of strength for Clara as she helped guide the NOI. Accomplishing what was a full education for black children in many rural Southern communities, Clara completed grade seven. Quartus Evans, who also was literate, is described as having a "strong moral and work ethic."

After Elijah Poole met Clara Evans in 1917, he began regular visits to her family on Sunday afternoons. Although Elijah was also an active Christian (his father, William Poole, was a Baptist minister) who attended Zion Hope Baptist Church, Quartus Evans objected to him because Poole had completed only grade four and because his family was even more destitute than the Evanses and, thereby, held a lesser social status among the community of African Americans.[5] Clara Evans seemed to be close to her father throughout her life.[6] In spite of this close relationship, however, and against her father's protestations, Clara evidently fell in love with Elijah, and on March 17, 1919, the couple eloped and married in the nearby town of Cordele. After about a month of living secretly with Clara's brother in Weona, a few miles from her family home, Clara and Elijah renewed contact with Quartus and Mary Evans.[7]

The young Poole family lived for four years in Weona, where Elijah initially found work for the railroad and in local factories. This employment was not secure, however, since Elijah's repugnance for racial subordination, in at least one instance, caused him to lose work for offending his white employer. Clara Poole's later actions supporting Elijah's philosophy suggest that she held a similar disposition. Although their views restricted possibilities for employment and were dangerous in 1920s rural Georgia, Elijah's philosophy would later be consciously and widely embraced by many African Americans as it evolved into racial pride and assertions of Black nationalism.

Because of difficulty making a living in the South, in 1923 the Pooles moved North—part of the great migration of Southern blacks—to Detroit.[8] Initially, Elijah worked in industrial plants and was the primary provider for his family. By the mid-1920s, however, just as the Depression was beginning, Elijah experienced more and more difficulty finding work. In addition, the Poole family had grown so that more resources were needed to support them. Two children were born before leaving Georgia, and three others came along in 1925, 1926, and 1929. During this time, periods of Elijah's unemployment became so frequent that the family was forced to stand in soup lines for food. When Elijah was unable to provide for his family, he began to drink. As early as 1926, Clara Poole helped support her family by working as a maid for white Detroit households. Because of her need to care for her small children without the support of her extended family, most of whom were still living in the South, Clara's employment was also precarious. In addition to domestic employment and attending to their children, Clara Poole often took the youngest children with her to ask for assistance and to look for Elijah when he went out drinking during times of unemployment. On occasion she carried him home on her back.[9]

Among new practices and ideas the Pooles encountered in Detroit urban life was a succession of Black religious, quasi-religious, and political movements initiated by and primarily for African Americans. Daddy Grace, Father Divine, the Black Masons, Marcus Garvey's Universal Negro Improvement Association, and the Moorish Science Temple were a few of the organizations assembled there. Amid this religious and ideological ferment, sometime in 1930, W. D. Fard (reputedly an Arab trader) appeared in Detroit's African American communities selling fabrics and other goods and preaching Islam as Black people's real religion. Fard also said that Blacks were a royal people of Mecca, that white persons had evil natures, and that the nature of Black persons was good. In contradiction of orthodox Islam, Fard asserted the impossibility of fellowship between Blacks and whites. When Clara and Elijah Muhammad first heard Fard's teaching, both were attracted to Fard, who also spoke to their material deprivation by de-emphasizing the afterlife and emphasizing human flourishing on earth.[10]

In spite of the racial oppression and poverty they experienced in the South, the difficult life in Detroit was most likely sharpened by the couple's separation from the familiar and slower pace of the rural South, where support and material assistance from friends and relatives were available. The Poole family's desperate situation, exacerbated by Elijah's drinking, probably predisposed both Clara and Elijah for affirmation and a new message of hope they could not find in Detroit's Black churches, and, for that matter, had never so urgently needed to know in the Black Christianity they left in the South. Early on, after hearing one of Fard's lectures, Clara described his teaching as having the potential to "'help my husband.'"[11] Soon both Clara and her husband heard a message in Fard's teachings that related to their current desperation and that spoke to the economic and racial difficulty they left in the South. Perhaps what attracted Clara and Elijah Poole most was the new teachings' repeated validation of their humanity. Southern Black Christianity on occasion may have held out some promise of improved economic situation, as did the Pooles' encounter with what became the Nation of Islam. It is most unlikely, however, that either Clara or Elijah ever encountered in their rural Christianity such a consistent, unabashedly explicit Afrocentric religious expression that spoke clearly against the society's message of white supremacy. The power of this validation of their humanity became the message to which other similarly situated African Americans responded by joining the Nation of Islam. Beyond the NOI, the message found root among the Black masses and stimulated the intensity with which many young Black persons entered civil rights activism and started the Black Power Movement.

Clara and Elijah Poole soon began following Fard, and in 1931, by the birth of their sixth child, Elijah Jr., both had converted to Islam. As the Pooles took a special interest in Islam, Fard seems to have taken a special interest in them. Elijah became a deputy of Fard's with the admonition to "go ahead . . . and start teaching [Islam]" and with Fard's promise to "back [Elijah] up."[12] In 1933 W. D. Fard began using the name W. F. Muhammad (also Wallace Fard Muhammad). Elijah and Clara Poole also took a new surname as a part of their initiation into Islam. Fard required each convert "to write a letter asking for [an] 'original' [Islamic] name; when [converts] received this name, the 'slave name' given to [their] ancestors by the white man was discarded." Initially given the surname Karriem, Elijah Poole's name was changed to Muhammad when he was promoted to Fard's lieutenant and minister. Sometime between 1933 and 1934, Fard Muhammad disappeared from Detroit's Black communities, as unceremoniously as he first appeared. Although there was intense dissension among followers after Fard withdrew, Elijah Muhammad, apparently Fard's choice, eventually emerged as leader of the dominant group.[13] His wife, Clara, played no small part in helping secure this role and its significance.

Muhammad's Role in the Development of the Nation of Islam

The relevance of the Nation of Islam to the Civil Rights Era and especially to the tradition of racial uplift among African Americans derives principally from the role of Black nationalism in ongoing developments of the Movement. The dawning of slogans like "Black is beautiful!" "Black Power!" and "Black Power! Now!" during the Civil Rights Era helped create and name the ripening idea that the Movement was more than agitation for simple racial toleration. Especially among younger activists, calls for full recognition as people and citizens and assertions of the right to access and to participate autonomously in all aspects of civic life reflected the pride, agency, and sometimes the impatience communicated through "Black is beautiful!" and "Black Power!" Race pride and self-determination were central elements of what became NOI teaching. In the first significant book-length study of the NOI, *The Black Muslims in America,* C. Eric Lincoln points out the centrality of self-affirmation and race pride in the group's teachings. "In several important ways, the Muslims tend to strengthen the dignity and self-reliance of the Negro community," Lincoln writes. "They are proving dramatically that a new, positive leadership cadre can emerge among American Negroes at the grass-roots level." Although Lincoln generally casts Black nationalism negatively, he aptly points out its main focus on overcoming racial subordination. Distinguishing "religious" Black nationalism and "political" Black nationalism, Lincoln explains that the "*raison d'être* of both was to devise some means of escaping the implications of being a Negro in a white-dominated society."[14]

Fard's assertion of this possibility was the main appeal of his teaching to initial followers, including Elijah and Clara Poole. In turn, it became the basis of their building an organization for disseminating this "means of escaping" the burdens of the dominant racial view in the United States. Reflecting the perspective on which Delores Williams draws in her Hagar-in-the-wilderness metaphor, Clara once described her efforts as helping communicate "the knowledge that Islam is the only way out of this hell" for Black people "in the wilderness of North America."[15] Among Clara Muhammad's important contributions to the development of the NOI and its message of racial pride were her role in the founding and evolution of NOI Muslim schools (initially called the University of Islam) and her leadership in building the NOI as a religious organization.

The University of Islam/Clara Muhammad Schools

An element of W. D. Fard's work with African Americans in Detroit, developing as part of his small but growing following, was the initial unfolding of specific training for new recruits. Establishing a primary and secondary school system as a Muslim alternative to public schools was central to this training. Clara Muhammad's leadership in developing the Nation of Islam began with her role in formation of what became these private Islamic Schools, initially called the University of Islam.

Fard initiated the University of Islam in 1932. Lincoln asserts that

> within three years, Fard had developed an organization so effective that . . . he had not only set up the temple and established its ritual and worship but also founded the University of Islam (actually, a combined elementary and secondary school), dedicated to "higher mathematics," astronomy and the "ending of spook civilization." He had created the Muslim Girls Training Class which taught young Muslim women the principles of home economics and how to be a proper wife and mother.

> Finally, "fear of trouble with unbelievers, especially with the police, led to the founding of the Fruit of Islam—a military organization for the men who were drilled by captains and taught tactics and the use of firearms." A minister of Islam was now appointed to run the entire organization, aided by a staff of assistant ministers. Each of these men was selected and trained personally by Fard.[16]

As Lincoln points out, the institution evolved as an elementary and secondary school. The term *university* indicated "its curriculum was universal and included instruction in the disciplines considered advanced."[17] In addition to emphasizing strong basic education, a message of racial pride was a significant part of the racial uplift efforts of the University of Islam. During initial development, the University of Islam became instrumental in ushering in "Black is beautiful" and Black Power sentiments, two standpoints that emerged as particularly important to the Civil Rights Era and the ongoing progress of African Americans toward overcoming devastations of racial subjugation. Hakim M. Rashid and Zakiyyah Muhammad say "in their earliest forms [NOI schools] were the ideological predecessors of both the Black Nationalist independent education movement of the 1960s and the current [1990s] Afrocentric education movement."[18] While University of Islam students often excelled in traditional subjects, the emphasis on nationalism has been identified as the primary focus of the NOI schools in the days of Clara and Elijah Muhammad. A 1967 study of the schools asserts the "'main task of the school within the Nation of Islam is to aid students in developing a more satisfying culture and in forming a new identity which refutes the traditional white stereotypes of the Negro.'"[19] Lincoln concurred with this assessment.[20] Establishment of the University of Islam as an institutional means to accomplish this task depended significantly, though not exclusively, on Clara Muhammad.

According to her son, Warith Deen Mohammed, current leader of the Muslim American Society,[21] in spite of her own educational limitations, Clara Muhammad initially directed the school. Clara was the school's first teacher, and the original school met in the Muhammads' home, around her dining-room table, with the six Muhammad children as the first students. In the beginning, Clara's elementary school education and instruction she received from Fard formed the basis of the school's curriculum.

> [Her] own ideas, thoughts, and family history as well as Fard's teachings became sentences to be copied, word groups to be memorized, paragraphs that helped develop penmanship. While textbooks were not available, subjects still included the basics—reading, writing, arithmetic—as well as 'Temple History,' or the founding of the Nation of Islam and the myths about the origins of black people. . . . "It was a curriculum that made a point of ignoring world history as we know it and U.S. history as we know it," added W. D. Mohammed, Clara's fifth son. "And we learned to think," he said, "to have our own thoughts. She'd ask questions and sought our opinions."

As other Nation of Islam members began attending the school, children were separated by gender, a practice emulated in other places. Fard's goal, which the Muhammads took up, was to open a school alongside each NOI temple.[22] As Clara Muhammad reached the limits of her education and as others joined the Nation of Islam, she left off direct teaching and administrative work and became a principal supporter of Muslim schools. Saying she had carried the schools "'as far as she could,'" Clara Muhammad eventually handed over immediate instruction and administration to better-prepared teachers.[23] Before doing so, however, she helped secure their existence by battling for continued operation.

One impediment to continued operation of the first University of Islam was the challenge to Elijah Muhammad's leadership of the Nation of Islam. After Fard left, conflicts about leadership arose within the group. Challenges to Elijah Muhammad's leadership included threats to his life, in response to which he often had to flee Detroit for safety. Sometimes Clara Muhammad accompanied her husband, but more often she stayed behind to hold on to the leadership of the group. Chicago was one of the places to which Elijah Muhammad fled. While there, he recruited new followers, and in 1934 a second University of Islam began.[24]

Another obstacle to continuing existence of the University of Islam was objection of public school officials. During the early 1930s in Detroit, home schooling was illegal. Moreover, in the early decades of the twentieth century, considerable opposition to independent education like Catholic schools remained prominent in some areas. The Detroit school board began almost immediately to challenge the Islamic schools. On April 13, 1934, Elijah Muhammad and other NOI members were arrested and charged with contributing to the delinquency of minors by keeping them out of public schools. While Elijah was in jail, Clara continued operating the school and in at least one instance also was threatened with arrest. During one encounter with police she stood in the doorway of her home and responded, "I will die as dead as this door knob, before I allow my children to attend public school."[25] Eventually Detroit's school board succeeded in closing the school Clara Muhammad ran. It took almost twenty years, but in 1953 Muslim schools legally reopened in Detroit. One of the first reopened schools began on the site of Clara Muhammad's original home school. In April of 1935, a challenge was brought against continuation of the Chicago University of Islam. In this instance, however, after a confrontation in court, the school "remained open."[26]

By 1953, when the Detroit University of Islam recommenced its operation, persons trained in education and curriculum development led NOI schools. One school principal reported that Clara Muhammad supported continued development and redevelopment of the schools by sharing in the teaching of NOI/Islamic dietary dictates and sending money and supplies. She also supported the school by visiting periodically to "'see how the school was doing.'" By this time, her status as first lady of the Nation of Islam not only brought goodwill and her own patronage but also often delivered media attention to the work of Muslim schools. During these visits, Muhammad often offered encouragement, asked about the schools' needs, left contributions, and, when necessary, interceded with her husband to secure necessary funding or supplies. She continued these supportive visits to the schools at least until 1970, two years before her death.[27]

During the 1960s Clara Muhammad frequently attended graduation exercises of University of Islam classes. In some instances she gave the graduation address and generally encouraged students with admonitions to "stay in school and prepare themselves for the tasks ahead."[28] On a 1967 visit to the University of Islam in New York, Clara Muhammad praised the school for offering an alternative to the typically poor quality of public education in inner-city neighborhoods. She remarked that the

> New York Mosque's plan for starting a child's formal education at the age of 2 was 'probably the only one of its kind for black children in America.' The children's alert attitude and their respectful manner would prove 'inspirational' to any black parent who was frustrated by the low standard of education in slum neighborhoods. The pupuls [*sic*] early development is a sound basis upon which to build high school and college education. The school's plan proved that black children have a vast capacity to learn with [*sic*] genuine interest is given to their well-being by parent and teacher alike.[29]

By the time of Clara and Elijah Muhammad's deaths (in 1972 and 1975, respectively), "the University of Islam had become an independent educational system of 41 private parochial schools located throughout the United States." In the late 1970s Elijah Muhammad's son and successor, Warith Deen Mohammed, renamed the University of Islam "the Sister Clara Muhammad Schools." As part of the movement toward orthodox Islam, the schools' curriculum was standardized, continuing to teach "about the African origins of and contributions to civilization," but also attending to a "religious education" consistent with mainstream Islam and in keeping with requirements of the Council of Islamic Schools of North America.[30]

Early Community Activism: Muhammad's Role in the Nation of Islam

As early as 1942 the FBI, through surveillance and informants, listed Clara Muhammad as "among the leaders" of "Allah Temple of Islam . . . telling belief in the Islam religion." The FBI's "investigation of this group revealed that the members are from the lower class Negroes." Many others who followed teachings of Fard were in similar straits as Clara and Elijah Muhammad were when they first heard him.[31] Clara's identification as a leader of the Temple of Islam, apparently an early name for the NOI, derives at least in part from "instructional letters" she sent to temples in Detroit and Chicago, while Elijah was hiding from rivals for leadership following Fard's departure, evading the FBI, or in prison. In a May 16, 1942, search of Temple Number 3 in Milwaukee, Wisconsin, the FBI found letters from Clara sent after Elijah fled to Washington, D.C.[32] While these 1942 records demonstrate Clara Muhammad's early role in the formation of the organization, her leadership in founding and developing the group predates this FBI surveillance; it began almost with the group's inception and continued until her death in 1972.

Accounts vary as to whether it was Clara or Elijah who first heard Fard's teaching and then introduced the other.[33] Whatever the order of their hearing Fard when he appeared in Black Detroit neighborhoods in 1930, both were captivated by the message of racial prominence and material well-being in this lifetime. By 1933 or 1934, when Fard left, he had developed a following, started a school, and begun to put into place other structures to ensure continuation of what became known as the Nation of Islam.

Clara's leadership began almost immediately. In addition to helping found and administer the first school while Fard was still present, her supervision and guidance were essential as Elijah fled dangerous challenges to his position as leader. As early as 1934, when Elijah left Detroit because of opposition to his authority and threats on his life, Clara often remained behind in charge of the family and helping to secure the fledgling group of followers who remained faithful to Elijah. (During the same year, Elijah Muhammad was briefly incarcerated for keeping his children out of public schools.) In late 1935, Elijah Muhammad faced the most difficult of these challenges, with threats on his life and with as many as 75 percent of the members leaving to follow dissenters. He departed for Milwaukee, Wisconsin, leaving minister Malik X to instruct those who remained. In addition to expecting Clara's work with Malik X to keep the organization going, Elijah Muhammad handed "reins over the household to his wife, Clara, who had suffered along with him during the whole succession ordeal."[34] That meant leaving Clara to depend on her own ingenuity and the charity of other Muslims to provide for their seven children in the midst of the Depression. This role of Clara Muhammad in charge of their family and the unsteady Muslim group during its early days persisted intermittently for at least the next ten years.

In 1935, after a few weeks in Milwaukee, where he previously had opened Temple Number 3, Elijah Muhammad went east, making Washington, D.C., into his home base, where he remained partially sequestered from his competitors for about seven years, until 1942. From Washington, he traveled to proselytize in other states and "infrequently" visited his family back in Detroit. By 1939 he opened Temple Number 4 in Washington.[35] As Temple 4 grew, Muhammad's anti-American rhetoric developed and intensified. He began to attract the attention of law enforcement, and on May 8, 1942, Elijah Muhammad, who had announced his conscientious objection to military enrollment, was arrested for failure to register with the newly formed Selective Service Administration.[36] His arrest served as a rallying cry for Muslims, precipitated increased support for Elijah as leader, and, consequently, helped strengthen the organization. Muhammad remained incarcerated for over two months, until his July 23 release. Clara helped raise the five-thousand-dollar bail from Muslim converts and carried the money to Washington in a suitcase.[37]

Clara's rescue of Elijah was indicative of her perseverance during these early years. Elijah Muhammad biographer Claude Clegg III wrote that her "spirituality guided her through the trauma of" difficult financial times when she was rearing the family alone, when the organization was struggling to overcome its divisions, and when Muslims were seeking to overcome attacks by law enforcement. Around the same time of Elijah Muhammad's arrest, leaders of Milwaukee and Detroit temples also were arrested, and on May 16 and 19, respectively, both temples were raided.[38] After posting bond, Elijah and Clara Muhammad left Washington and went to Chicago, which eventually became the headquarters of the Nation of Islam.

During this time and for several years to come, Clara Muhammad continued her role of rearing the family alone and holding together the Nation of Islam during Elijah's absences. While Elijah was in Washington, Clara wrote letters of instruction and encouragement to the temples.[39] After his return to the Midwest, she soon continued this work, since the Chicago respite from difficulties was short. On November 24, 1942, four months after posting bail in Washington, authorities found Elijah guilty of three counts of draft evasion. He also faced eight charges of sedition. On December 18 he was sentenced to five years for the draft evasion conviction. When the Muhammads went to court again in February of 1943, the sedition charges were dropped. Elijah began serving his draft evasion sentence in the Federal Correctional Institute in Milan, Michigan, on July 23, 1943, alongside their son Emmanuel, also convicted of the same charges. The sentencing was not a surprise, and before Elijah began his incarceration, he named Clara "Supreme Secretary" of the

Nation of Islam, formalizing the role she previously had served as leader of the NOI while Elijah was away.[40]

Beginning in 1943, when she was forty-two, and continuing until 1946, Clara Muhammad persisted in rearing their children and overseeing continuation of the Nation of Islam as its Supreme Secretary. Her correspondence became the means through which Elijah obtained news of the temples as well as the conduit for delivering his directives, which sometimes required Clara's interpretation, to the temples. Along with other roles, Clara Muhammad also was a source of inspiration for her husband and son Emmanuel. She copied and mailed verses from the Qur'an to them, in addition to overseeing temple leadership needs and ensuring communication between Elijah and the temples.[41]

As Supreme Secretary, Clara interpreted and oversaw the implementation of Elijah's directives and "intervened during Temple disputes and represented her husband at public engagements within the movement and in the larger society."[42] Moreover, among other NOI activities, Clara took up the difficulties with the FBI. The FBI's surveillance of the Muhammads related directly to the growth and influence of the Nation of Islam. In 1945 FBI agents went to the Muhammads' home in Chicago looking for her second son, Nathaniel, also on draft evasion charges. In a posture akin to Victoria Poinsette's objection to the police, demonstrating her sense of authority and self-worth, Clara refused to cooperate with FBI officers seeking to apprehend her son. An FBI report recounted the agents' encounter with Muhammad:

> Mrs. Clara Muhammad advised that she is the mother of the subject. She stated that the subject left Chicago in February, and that she had since received a telephone call from him, telling her that he was in Detroit, Michigan. Mrs. Muhammad denied that she knew the subject's address in Detroit, and when asked for suggestions as to how he might be located there, she refused to answer, stating that she did not intend to make any such 'guesses.' She stated that if she knew his exact address or nature of employment she would furnish such information, but she insisted that she did not have this information. Mrs. Muhammad denied any knowledge of the subject's purpose for leaving Chicago.
>
> Mrs. Muhammad expressed her unwillingness to discuss the matter at any length. She advised that her husband, Elijah Muhammad, and . . . [name blacked out] were convicted and

> were serving sentences for Selective Service violations. She stated that she and her family, including the subject, are members of the Allah Temple of Islam and are conscientiously opposed to participation in war. . . .
>
> When questioned concerning the subject's activities, employment, and acquaintances, she stated she did not know anything about that and that such information would have to be obtained from the subject. She mentioned that the subject had been disobedient and that she knew little of his affairs. She denied that the subject had contributed to her support or that he has assisted her in purchasing the dwelling house where the family resides and she stated that she wasn't responsible for any 'lies' in subject's Selective Service file in that regard. . . . Mrs. Muhammad stated that she does not have a photograph of the subject.[43]

Muhammad's objection to the ruse of draft evasion and thereby her disbelief of the validity of the charges are evident in her determination to provide the agents as little helpful information as possible.

On August 24, 1946, Elijah Muhammad left prison in Michigan and returned to Chicago. By this time, he had overcome schisms and was clearly identified as the leader of the NOI, thanks in no small measure to his being perceived by Muslims as a martyr persecuted by the FBI.[44] Over the next several years, as Elijah held the reins of the still developing but more solid organization, Clara Muhammad took up the more traditional role for women of the era, supporting her husband by deferring to him and directing her children and others toward his leadership. Thus she began moving into the role as first lady of the Nation of Islam. In keeping with this new role, her son Warith (a.k.a. Wallace), successor to Elijah, recalls that as Elijah's certain ascendancy as NOI leader unfolded, Clara often admonished her children to behave in a manner appropriate to their status. "You are the Messenger's children," Clara said to them, and you "must live a thoroughly ethical Islamic life."[45]

While Clara Muhammad was pioneering in her role as cofounder and a leader of the Nation of Islam and although she spent significant periods having complete responsibility for her family, she helped establish and develop the women's and girls' instructional program advancing the gender stratification that asserted Muslim wives should follow their husbands. The origin of this instruction is said to have come from W. D. Fard, "who was Sister Clara's teacher." Fard's instructions about "the role and responsibilities of a Muslim woman" including "diet, dress, and conduct" originated as part of the effort among initial followers of Islam in Detroit to uplift Black women by attending to issues of dignity and self-respect.[46] The concern for uplift and respect of African American women was no little matter for poor Black women living in cities in the United States, especially during the early and middle decades of the twentieth century. Sociologist Cheryl Townsend Gilkes points out that one effort in Black Christianity to combat denigration of Black women occurred in "sanctified" churches, where the term *sanctification* and the title "saint" served as buttresses against negative stereotypes about Black women's sexuality and value as human beings.[47]

Called "Muslim Girls' Training Classes" (MGT) and "General Civilization Classes" (GCC), the instructional program Clara Muhammad helped establish was a regular part of orientation for women and girls entering the Nation of Islam. As with the Muslim schools, Clara Muhammad laid the groundwork for the program and continued to lead it until others were in place to take over. This included Muhammad's leadership of MGT/GCC for some time after Chicago became NOI headquarters, since "lessons for these classes were sent from Chicago to Muslims in other places."[48]

Designed to inculcate the character of Muslim womanhood in women and girls, MGT and GCC classes were significant in changing the lives of poor women. Contrary to Clara Muhammad's example in the development of the NOI, the training was based on a strict gender hierarchy. Among the duties of Muslim wives and mothers, "in Muslim Girls Training (MGT) classes . . . , female members were informed that they were the key to the success of the black man."[49] While women's equality with men clearly was asserted, the contrary strand that women were "taught to obey their husbands" remained. MGT and GCC classes educated women and girls specifically about domestic skills, family life, and proper public conduct, and asserted that characteristics like "modesty, thrift and service are recommended as their chief concerns."[50]

By the mid-1950s, when the numbers of Muslims were reaching tens of thousands, Clara made public appearances and sometimes spoke in place of her husband. In these instances, however, she consistently presented herself as "the wife of the messenger," and pointed others toward him. This continued through the early 1960s.

An FBI memo, for example, reports that at the "annual convention" of the Nation of Islam in Chicago on February 24, 1961, a Minister Brown "introduced Mrs. Clara Muhammad, the wife of the NOI leader Elijah." Clara is described as announcing "that all present should join in spreading the message of her husband; that the black people in North America should unite to support Elijah who will give them a nation of their own."[51]

In spite of her new role as first lady, Clara's significance as collaborator in leading the Nation of Islam persisted. Once again, from 1963 through 1965, when Elijah was ill and living in Phoenix, Arizona, because of respiratory problems, Clara Muhammad usually was the conduit through which people contacted Elijah, and through which Elijah communicated his wishes to Nation of Islam members.[52] Except for her continued independence in support of Muslim schools, however, Clara's authoritative *public* role in the Nation of Islam became more and more fully that of first lady.

As she engaged this role, Muhammad continued to be a trailblazer. She was "the first black Muslim woman" and had "pioneered the role and identity of African American Muslim women." Although she deferred to Elijah as leader after his incarceration, as she set the pattern for what it meant to be an African American Muslim woman, Clara Muhammad also presented a unique example "in her leadership of a male-dominated organization during its most critical period of existence"[53] and during a time when it was still quite unusual for women in U.S. society to demonstrate such tenacity and authority. Muhammad's management is even more exceptional because of what developed as the role expectation for men and women in the NOI. By the late 1950s, as Lincoln notes, "great emphasis [was] placed upon the husband's responsibility as protector and provider of his family, while women [were] enjoined to be good homemakers and to obey their husbands."[54] This, of course, was considered the ideal situation, and during her tenure of authority among the NOI members, Clara Muhammad moved outside traditional role expectations for women to attend to the needs of the community.

As the decade of the 1960s unfolded, Clara's role as first lady was complicated, if not challenged, by public disclosure of her marital difficulties, including allegations of Elijah's years-long plural infidelities, siring other children, and actual confrontations by his mistresses. In the late spring of 1962, in the midst of this controversy, Clara

Muhammad left the United States to visit her son Akbar, who was studying in Egypt. After about two months in Egypt, she returned, apparently having decided to stay with Elijah.[55] For the remainder of her life Clara Muhammad continued supporting her husband and the Nation of Islam until her death at age 72, in August of 1972.

Muhammad's Religious and Moral Perspectives

Initiated in Southern Black churches and wrought through difficulties of her early married life and evolution of the Nation of Islam, Clara Muhammad's religiosity unfolded as a steady faith in a divinity who provided for her personally and who sought to liberate Black people from the difficulties of "the wilderness of North America."[56] Divine provision for Clara Muhammad meant furnishing food, shelter, and basic necessities for her family during their most difficult encounters with poverty as well as deliverance from the daily confrontation with issues of impoverishment. Divine liberation of Black people included this latter, more comprehensive deliverance from material poverty as well as spiritual and emotional uplift through affirmation of their dignity as human beings. Although Muhammad understood liberation for Black people as coming from God, she also asserted that people participate in their own liberation through individual and communal practices of thrift and self-help and by becoming practicing Muslims as a part of the Nation of Islam, including separation from European Americans. Similar to other Black religious women activists, Clara Muhammad understood her faith as including responsibility to assist in the divine mission by helping others materially, by building the NOI, and by proselytizing for Allah and divine deliverance through the NOI.

Belief in Divine Provision for Life's Necessities

Clara Muhammad's understanding of divine provision is strikingly similar to that of Black Christian women who expect or recount personal rescue and preservation as work of God. Roots of Muhammad's religiosity in Black Christianity seem evident in her portrayal of divine rescue in a "testimony" she recorded in the NOI newspaper *Muhammad Speaks*. In a formula similar to Black church traditions of testifying—in which a deficiency is named and divine activity is identified as being responsible for overcoming difficulty—in late years of her own life, Clara Muhammad wrote that it was "Allah's work" that made possible her family's survival when they could not sustain themselves. "My family and I were at our lowest ebb—in a bad condition," Clara wrote in 1967. "With five children, there were times when we didn't have a piece of bread in the house, nor heat, water or even sufficient wearing apparel. My husband would walk the streets looking for a job daily, but would come home with no job." In addition to describing her family's condition as having a need they could not meet, Muhammad also depicts her sense of responsibility to try to meet the need in a manner similar to practices Cheryl Townsend Gilkes describes in Christian "church and community mothers." Muhammad responded to her family's condition by working when she could, and when this was not possible she determined other means to respond:

> I would go out and try to help him [Elijah provide for the family], but with five small children, I could not work steadily. However, I was successful when I went door to door, asking for work.
>
> The people would question me, and I would tell them the truth. Some of them did not have any work, but they would give me a little money and some gave me food.

In the final lines of the testimony, after describing the need and how it was met, Muhammad praises Allah, even though provision may be seen to have resulted from her own effort and help of others. "This was Allah's work," she wrote, "but I did not know it then. Praise His holy name forever."

In addition to immediate relief from material deprivation, Muhammad described divine provision as removing her family from circumstances of immediate distress about physical survival. In the same article she identifies the bounty of her later years as coming from God: "Now we have plenty of food, clothes and all of the necessities of life." Moreover, Muhammad noted continuing responsibility to attend to others and describes this practice, saying, "We are happy and share it with our brothers and sisters. Sometimes we feed from 35 to 50 people at one time in our home—never without food to spare."[57] For Muhammad, the responsibility to attend to others included rearing her nephew Jamil, making him "feel like one of her own children."[58]

Similar to initial motivations for Baker, Clark, Hamer, and DeLee, Muhammad's impetus to attend to others originated in practical concerns about food, shelter, and quality of life. Years earlier, Muhammad demonstrated this practical attention to neighbors' needs when her family was beginning to engage Muslim practices. According to her son Warith Mohammed, the decision was made (apparently by Elijah) that the time had come for the family to follow Muslim dietary practices more strictly, when Clara recently had purchased pork. Instead of throwing the pork away, Clara gave the meat to a non-Muslim neighbor who also had children to feed.[59]

Belief in Divine Liberation as New Identity and Separation

Clara Muhammad, like her husband, understood Islam as particularly relevant to the plight of Black people in the United States. That is to say, for her, as for Elijah Muhammad, a major significance of Islam was its role in improving and securing the lives of African Americans. Moreover, Muhammad believed that *she and Elijah* were divinely called to respond to the plight of Black people through Islam. "Allah has asked *us* . . . to help solve this problem," she said, asserting Islam as the only way African Americans could overcome their subjugation.

In keeping with the perspective of her husband, Muhammad held that divine liberation of African Americans meant overcoming the false label they had acquired of "so-called negroes." "So-called negroes" was a phrase Elijah Muhammad repeatedly used to classify the status of "American Negroes" as fictitious, a status to be contrasted with what he lifted up as the royal African heritage of Black people. The coincidence of Clara Muhammad's perspective with Elijah's is evident. Clara regularly noted the need for African Americans to awaken from the sleep of their "fictitious identity" and move toward liberation through Islam. In one instance she wrote

> Now I am asking Allah, through the newspaper of His Messenger, to please open the eyes, hearts and ears of our poor blind, deaf and dumb brothers and sisters here in the wilderness of North America—to the knowledge that Islam is the only way out of this hell. I pray daily for my poor people, and I am sincere, brothers and sisters, in trying to help Allah's Messenger in some way.

> Allah has asked us, in His holy words, to help solve this problem: I know we can help because Allah would not have asked this of us if it wasn't possible to do.[60]

Just as she understood Allah's provision in her own life to prescribe her activity in seeking to make life better, Clara Muhammad asserted that divine liberation for African Americans entailed responsibility for persons who would be liberated. Fulfilling this responsibility meant opening their "hearts and minds" to accept Islam and to follow Elijah Muhammad. Even though, Clara said, "Allah has blessed us and thousands of others," joining the Nation of Islam was necessary in order for all African Americans, "every one of the 22 million of us to get their blessings." The fulfillment of this rested on the response of those twenty-two million:

> [Then] we all will be happy. And there will not be a place on our planet Earth for anyone but those who believe.
>
> The Messenger has labored hard for 35 years, trying to open our blind eyes. He does not want a single person destroyed with the wicked. Neither do we, his followers. We all love you.
>
> I have been following him every since he accepted Islam, and I will follow him as long as I live, if it pleases Almighty God, Allah. Praise His holy name forever.
>
> Open up your hearts and minds, and get behind the Honorable Elijah Muhammad, the Messenger of Allah, and Allah will bless you.[61]

Clara held that the blessing of Allah included material deliverance and spiritual and emotional liberation, or changing completely the identity of the "so-called negro."

The predominant means by which Clara Muhammad presented her perspectives about the significance of Islam for Black identity was by her activity in the establishment of the University of Islam (now Sister Clara Muhammad Schools). Through her work initiating and developing the schools, Muhammad institutionalized the teaching of ideas that constantly affirmed Black identity. The significance of this aspect of Nation of Islam education has often been heralded for its importance prior to and during the Civil Rights Era. Blazing a trail for other discussions of Black nationalism and Afrocentrism that followed in the 1960s and beyond, the Nation of Islam schools "placed black people at the center of civilization [and] made them feel good about themselves" at a time when racial oppression and racial violence still were quite acceptable.[62] As early as 1961, Lincoln pointed out the value of this emphasis to Black identity: "The Muslim schools are emphasizing Negro history, Negro achievements and the contributions of Negroes to the world's great cultures and to the development of the American nation. These facts are rarely taught in public schools, and the Muslims may be alone in trying to bring the Negro community to an awareness of its racial heritage."[63] Seeing the significance of this teaching early on, Clara Muhammad integrated religion and Black pride into her moral perspective. Her work in institutionalizing this teaching ensured the continued transmittal of a potent message of uplift related specifically to racial marginalization. In the final analysis, Muhammad presented a religious perspective that, like the earliest emphases in African American Christianity, affirmed the humanity of Black people and Black survival. Muhammad's religious perspective, however, also included an assertion of racial pride and an affirmation of Black nationalism that went beyond most of traditional Black Christianity of her day, promoting one aspect of her thought and racial uplift practice that asserted race pride far beyond the Nation of Islam.

Though she was the first Muslim woman in the Nation of Islam, Clara Muhammad was not alone in her racial uplift and social responsibility work within the Nation of Islam. Like Muhammad, other Muslim women of the 1940s, 1950s, and 1960s understood community uplift work as a part of what it meant to be a Muslim woman. Commenting on the community work of Muslim women in Newark, New Jersey, during the 1960s, Cynthia S'thembile West writes that "whether they were in the home or community, [Muslim women's] work involved some form of educational activism." Describing them in a similar fashion to community workers whom Cheryl Gilkes identifies, West notes that "the neighborhood was considered an extension of the home for Black Muslims." Along with and following Clara Muhammad, in Newark, Philadelphia, New York, Baltimore, Chicago, and other places, "Black Muslim women were part of a social movement that helped black people help themselves."[64]

Gallery of Photographs

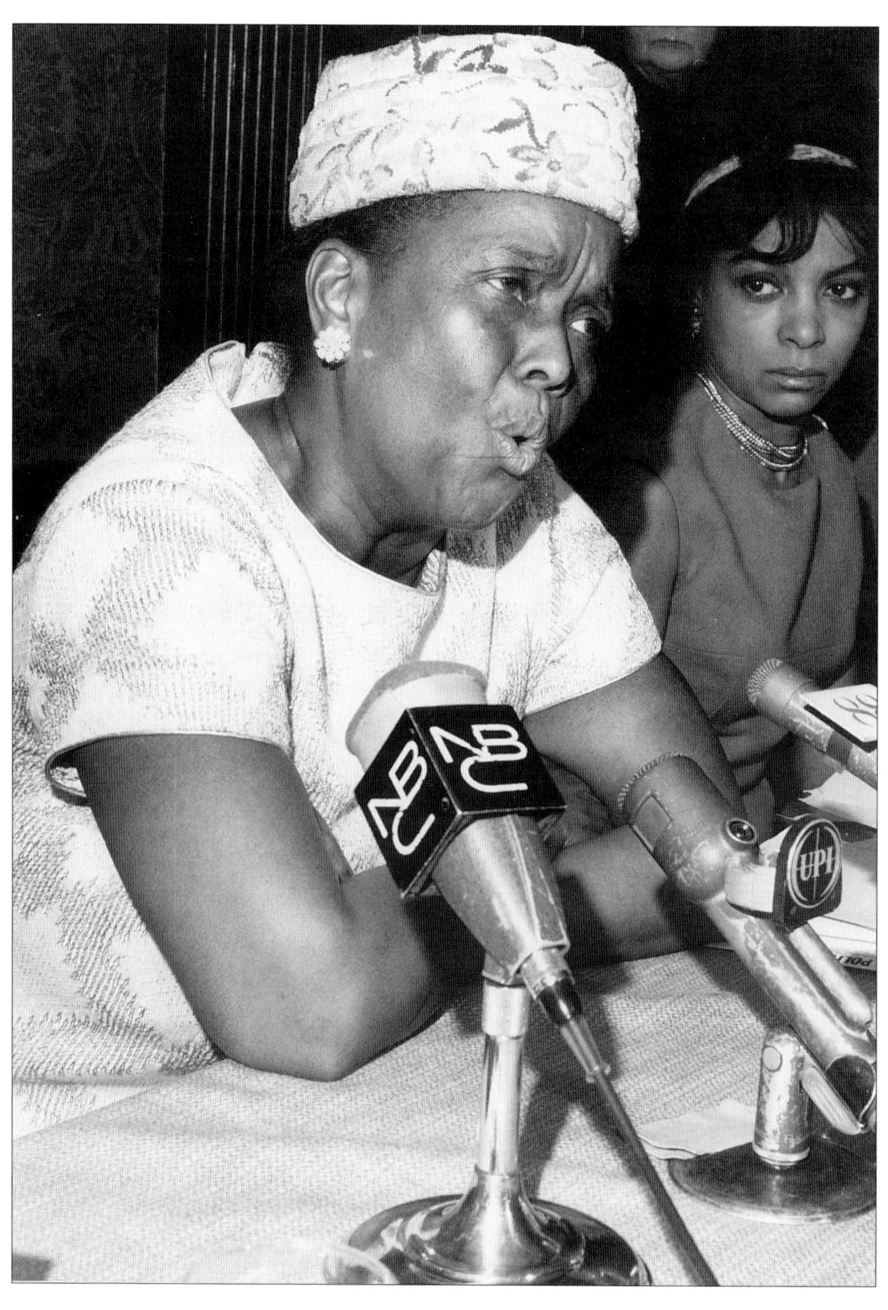

1. *Ella Baker at a news conference on January 3, 1968.*

2. *Septima Poinsette Clark (right) and Rosa Parks at the Highlander Center (date unknown).*

3. *Fannie Lou Hamer (front row, left) and Ella Baker (front row, right), along with other Mississippi Freedom Democratic Party delegates, sing at a rally on the Boardwalk in Atlantic City, New Jersey (August 10, 1964).*

4. *Fannie Lou Hamer marches in a voter registration demonstration outside Forest County Courthouse, Hattiesburg, Mississippi; the hand-lettered sign reads: "Freedom Now, SNCC" (January 22, 1964).*

5. *Victoria Way DeLee (circa 1971).*

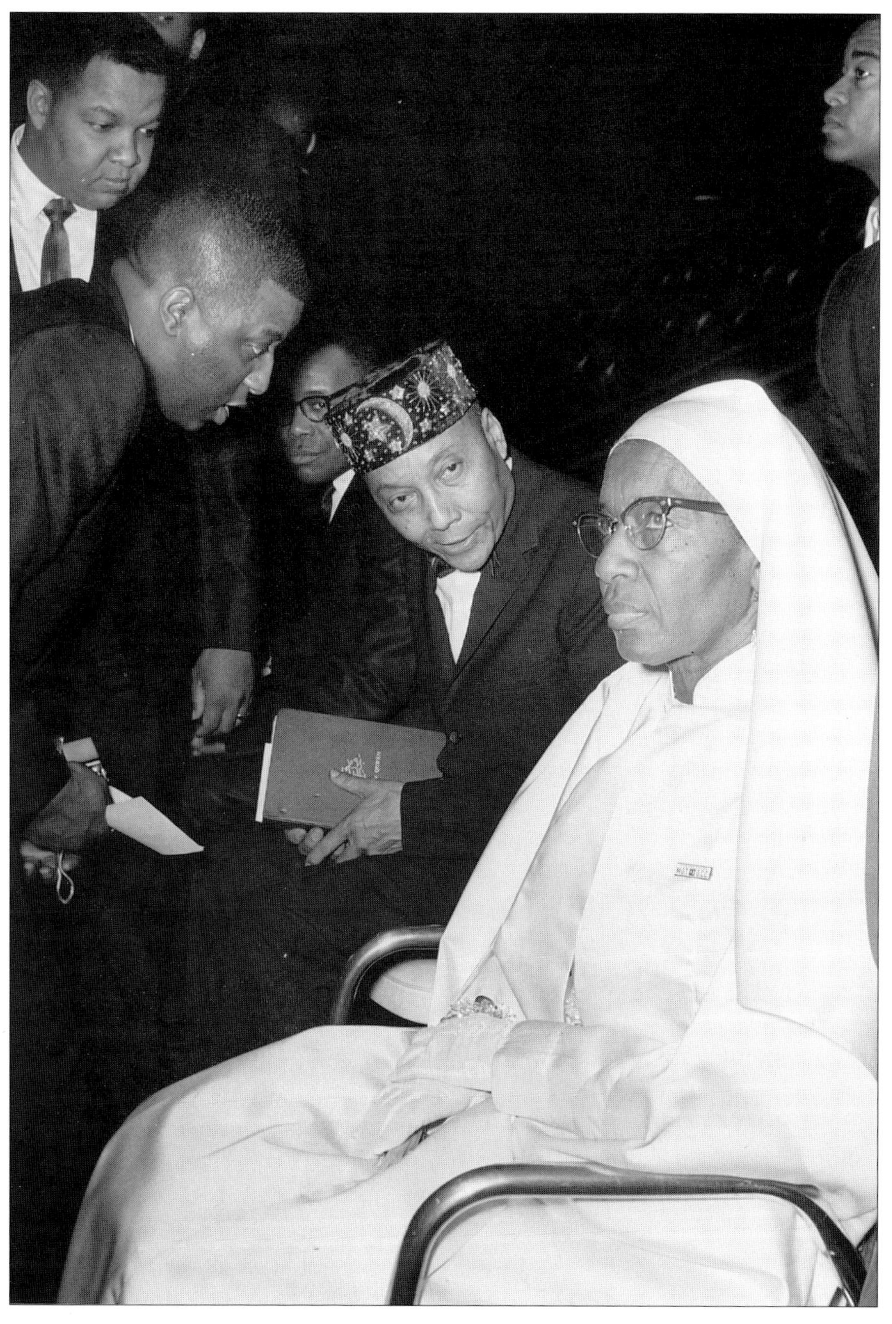

6. *Clara Muhammad with her husband, Elijah (center), at a Nation of Islam conference (date unknown).*

IN UNITY THERE IS STRENGTH

WE SHALL OVERCOME is the song being sung by the group above at the Atlanta Airport last Saturday as a group of 70 Atlanta University students welcomed back to Atlanta from 30-day jail sentences in York, South Carolina, Ruby Doris Smith and Diane Nash. From left to right above are Lonnie C. King, Herschelle Sullivan, Ruby Doris Smith, Mary Ann Smith, and Diane Nash. Miss Smith, a Spelman co-ed, and Miss Nash, from Nashville's Fisk University, were arrested in Rock Hill, South Carolina, after participating in a sit-in demonstration. Photo by Alexander.

7. *Ruby Doris Smith (center), Mary Ann Smith (second from right), and Diane Nash (far right) with two other students, sing together at the Atlanta airport after their return from serving thirty-day jail sentences in South Carolina (clipping from* The Atlanta Inquirer, *March 18, 1961).*

5

"Fire Shut Up in My Bones"

Black Women Students in the Movement

While many Black women activists of the Civil Rights Era interacted with each other, either directly or indirectly, Black women students connected with persons spanning the gamut of civil rights participants. Although a similar assessment may be made of activists like Ella Baker and Septima Clark, who put into place traditions of practice that others followed throughout the Movement, student activists took up veteran community workers' practices first as activists themselves, then as leaders of other students, and finally as leaders of local civil rights participants. Women students' interaction with practices established by others included using an array of protest tactics, especially those focused on carrying forward values of egalitarianism, attention to the least, and asserting race pride and personal agency. By taking up specific traditions of older adult trailblazers focused on organizing, educating, and generally empowering local people, these young adults carried forward values and practices of people like Baker and Clark, whose work both prepared the way and made the connections necessary for students to take the Movement into small towns and rural areas of the South. Often work of student activists made way for people like Hamer and DeLee to step onto the civil rights stage outside of their local communities. Moreover, as members of the generation that ushered in slogans like "Black is beautiful!" and "Black Power!" student activists helped carry forward Clara Muhammad's work to overcome material and emotional denigration caused by racial subordination. Diane Nash and Ruby Doris Smith Robinson were two students whose activism as SNCC workers typified the passion and gamut of interaction in Black women student civil rights activities.

Diane Nash: Passionate Agitation for Positive Quality of Life

Before she moved South, Diane Nash, a high school beauty queen from Chicago, Illinois, anticipated a rather quiet life for herself as she left home and entered college. She enrolled as a freshman at Howard University in Washington, D.C., a mainstay in Black higher education and an ideal place to prepare for a traditional place in upper-class Black life. When she transferred to Fisk University in Nashville, Tennessee, to finish college, however, Nash was appalled to learn that stories her stepfather told her about segregation were true. As she encountered the restrictions and repressions herself, Nash became infuriated and the "rather quiet course"[1] she expected was lost in her zeal to overcome racial repression. For Nash, the fight against segregation was a religious battle to defeat "sin," and to her mind, repentance and change should occur expeditiously. To those who "call for gradualism," Nash wrote, the "answer, it seems to me, is to stop sinning and stop now!"[2] The fervor of this statement became a mark of Nash's activism throughout her civil rights participation. Her focused impatience and clearheaded tenacity made her a leader among student activists in Nashville, a pacesetter in the founding and early evolution of SNCC, and a champion of the 1961 Freedom Rides.

Nash's Moral Formation

Born in 1938 to Leon Nash and Dorothy Bolton Nash, Diane Judith Nash grew up on the south side of Chicago. She was reared a strict Catholic, attending parochial schools throughout her elementary years and transferring to a public high school afterwards. At one time, while she was still a child, Diane considered becoming a nun, but she was discouraged from doing so. Her father grew up in Canton, Mississippi, and, during the great migration of Southern Blacks to the North, moved to Chicago. He served as a clerical worker in the armed forces during World War II and, after he was discharged, studied dentistry. While her husband was away during the war, Dorothy Bolton Nash worked as a keypunch operator in a factory. Because of her mother's work, for the first seven years of Diane's life, she spent days with her grandmother Carrie Bolton, who became quite a strong influence on Diane's sense of herself. After

Leon Nash's military discharge, he and Dorothy separated. Dorothy married John Baker, a Pullman car waiter whose income permitted her to stop working. John Baker's post, a prestigious position among Blacks of the era, provided the family with a relatively comfortable lifestyle among Chicago's Black middle class.[3]

At first sight, it seems improbable that Diane Nash became such a significant and radical Civil Rights Movement participant. Even she once said that she expected her "life to pursue a rather quiet course."[4] This certainly would have been in keeping with the expectation for which she was reared. Her family, feeling themselves models of Negro achievement, was quite patriotic, holding that Black persons could and should be as loyal to the country as whites. In addition to her father, an aunt, two uncles, and her stepfather all served in World War II, and Diane favored a WAC outfit sent to her as a child by her aunt. While opposing the racism of Nazi Germany during the war, Nash's family somehow overlooked racial problems of the United States, thinking America to be freer for Black people than actually was the case. In fact, in Diane Nash's home, conversation about race was suppressed, while identity as Americans was lifted up. In this regard, the life perspective she learned early on, like that taught in many other Black homes, coincided with the ideology of racial uplift that sought to inculcate the Protestant work ethic and Victorian morality among African Americans as an imitation of whites and as the means of moving forward in the United States. Similar to assertions of the ideology of racial uplift, Diane Nash was taught that white people were better off because of hard work and moral goodness.[5] More than anyone else, Diane's maternal grandmother, Carrie Bolton, seems to have inculcated this idea in her.

Reared in Memphis, Tennessee, Carrie Bolton became a maid for a wealthy white physician and his family at age nine. When she began working for them, Bolton was so taken by the material and affective splendor of the family's lifestyle—which differed vastly from her own—that she immediately fell in love with the culture, "ease and grace," and "kindness and consideration" that seemed to pervade her employers' home. Moreover, the physician and his family treated Carrie with some favor. He began to instill in her the idea that she was better than other Black people and that she could and should emulate whites. When she reached adulthood, Carrie moved north and conveyed to her offspring these views about Blackness and whiteness that she absorbed and came to firmly believe. Along with global ideas that cast Blackness negatively and that constructed whiteness positively, Bolton also took in and passed on the specific bias that light skin pigmentation was an advantage, a perspective that typically accompanied these beliefs.

While this identification with whiteness imparted ambiguity and even shame about being Black, at the same time, and perhaps based on the same point of view, Carrie Bolton also taught her granddaughter that she was special. Nash recalls a game she and her grandmother played almost every day when Nash was a child that gave her a positive message about her worth as a person:

> Carrie Bolton would take Diane Nash into her arms, and she would say, "You're more precious to me than anything in the world."
>
> "More precious than one hundred dollars?" the child would say.
>
> "That isn't even close," Carrie Bolton would reply.
>
> "Two hundred dollars?" the child would ask.
>
> "Not even close," the old woman would say.
>
> "More precious than five hundred dollars?"
>
> "Not even close."
>
> And in the end it would turn out that Diane Nash was more precious to this older woman *than all the money in the world.*[6]

The positive ideas imparted in this game, and most certainly in other practices that accompanied it, would account for a strong self-confidence that Nash developed quite early in her life. This confidence, accompanied by moral conviction she derived from her rearing, let Nash respond without a second thought to a newspaper advertisement about a charm school in 1953 and in 1956 enter the local Miss America contest, through the Miss Illinois regional competition. Nash's engaging these practices in the mid-1950s bespeaks a sense of herself that contrasted with Black people's second-class citizenship that was formally and conventionally pervasive across the United States. The same confidence and conviction she demonstrated in these efforts unfolded as personality signatures of her civil rights practice.

Developing self-confidence and moral conviction, particularly on issues of race, could not have occurred for Nash without some complication. Although her grandmother instilled in her grandchild a strong sense of personal worth, Nash got mixed messages about her Blackness. On the one hand, her grandmother commended whiteness as better than Blackness and something to copy. On the other hand, Carrie Bolton's affirmation of her granddaughter's self-worth communicated to Diane that she was a special little "black" girl. In addition to these crossed signals, Nash had experiences during childhood that contradicted Carrie Bolton's message about her being special. One day when she was in elementary school, a nun casually remarked, "You *know* that we love God in our order, because we deal with the least of God's people." Sisters of the Blessed Sacrament, who operated the school Nash attended, only taught African Americans and Native Americans. Over fifty years later, Nash both recalled verbatim the words "least of God's people" and, in keeping with the teaching she received at home to avoid talk about race, remembered that she suppressed thinking and speaking about the sting of the episode. Another painful racial incident Nash remembers is the response of a man at the charm school to which she sought admission. Initially he was quite interested in her, until she gave him her southside Chicago address—a primarily Black area of the city. Upon hearing the address, he asked, "'Are you by any chance colored?'" When she said yes, he replied, "'Dear, we don't have a facility for colored students.'"[7]

In some ways, the mixed messages she received probably predisposed Diane Nash for her civil rights activism. She must have struggled with notions she got from her grandmother about Blackness and at some point decided that she would identify with being Black in a way that her grandmother did not. In addition, her devout Catholic upbringing seems to have combined easily with teachings she received about nonviolent direct action to form clearly in her mind a moral perspective that segregation was sinful and should be strongly opposed. The sense of herself as worthy and the confidence and conviction she developed early in life supported this perspective about segregation and motivated the offense she took at her physical experience of segregation. All of these elements combined and led to Nash's swift and militant entrance into civil rights activism as a student leader.

Nash completed Chicago's Hyde Park High School in 1956 and went initially to Howard University, intending to study law. In 1959, she transferred to Fisk University. At the time she entered college,

Howard and Fisk were among the most prominent historically Black institutions of higher education.

Nash's Entrance into Civil Rights Activities

Diane Nash initially engaged in civil rights practices as a response to being offended and feeling repressed by Southern racial traditions. At the beginning of the school year in 1959, Nash began study at Fisk. In Chicago, Nash's life was less restricted by race, and she was able to explore and enjoy public space more freely. She remembers "really feeling stifled" the fall she went to study at Fisk and recalls herself thinking, "I came to college to grow and expand, and here I am shut in." In addition to the general experience of having limited access to public spaces in town, Nash said, in going south to Fisk she was forced to come to terms with material practices of overt racism. In one instance she said, "I remember I got really outraged" at encountering blatant segregation. "I had a date, and we went to the Tennessee State Fair. The guy was from the South. I started to use the ladies' room, and those were the first signs I had really seen in Nashville, and they were 'white women' and 'colored women,' and I just got furious." Although she had heard stories of segregation from her stepfather about experiences as a waiter on the railroads, it was this firsthand encounter that "really hit me."[8]

> [This] was the first time that I had encountered the blatant segregation that exists in the South. I came then to see the community in sin. Seeing signs designating "white" or "colored," being told "We don't serve niggers in here," and, as happened in one restaurant, being looked in the eye and told, "Go around to the back door where you belong," had a tremendous psychological impact on me. To begin with, I didn't agree with the premise that I was inferior, and I had a difficult time complying with it.[9]

The offense she felt emerged as impatience and intensity, evident in the clear disagreement she expressed about norms with which many Blacks in the South complied. In contrast to her reaction, Nash remembered that her date wondered if "she was truly serious about her anger."[10] As other encounters with segregation occurred, Nash began to ask who was trying to change the way things were. A white exchange student told her of James Lawson's nonviolent direct action workshops being conducted a few blocks off campus, and Nash immediately joined in.

Lawson, who served a year in prison for his refusal as a pacifist to be inducted into the army, was a seminarian at Nashville's Vanderbilt Divinity School and a field representative of the Fellowship of Reconciliation. He had encountered work of Mohandas Gandhi while serving as a Methodist missionary in India. At a local Baptist church in Nashville, Lawson led weekly workshops on nonviolence, preparing for demonstrations and protests against segregated facilities. In the workshops, Nash said,

> we would do things like pretend we were sitting in at lunch counters. We would practice things such as how to protect your head from a severe beating, we would practice other people putting their bodies in between that person and the violence, so that the violence could be more distributed and hopefully no one would get seriously injured. We would practice not striking back if someone struck us.[11]

In addition, Lawson taught Gandhian philosophy and principles of nonviolent civil disobedience, which Nash said "took truth and love very seriously." Workshop participants sometimes conducted lunch counter tests, sending teams into restaurants to request service. When service was withheld, they asked for the manager and discussed the immorality of racial discrimination.[12] Initially, Nash doubted the capacity of nonviolent protests to make a difference. "This stuff is never going to work," she once said, but continued attending because the workshops were "the only game in town" seeking to address segregation. After the first real encounters when she used nonviolence, Nash changed her mind. "A lot of things started making sense to me through the learning of nonviolence as well as the practice of it. And I developed it as a way of life."[13]

Although Nash had participated with Lawson's Nashville workshops since the fall of 1959, the catalyst that helped congeal her changing perspective about nonviolent direct action and that propelled her from the workshops into civil rights leadership occurred the next year in North Carolina. On February 1, 1960, four Black male students from North Carolina A & T College in Greensboro staged a "sit-down protest" of lunch counter segregation at the local Woolworth store. When peers learned of the protest, other students, first from A & T College and then nearby schools, joined in. Soon news about the North Carolina protests spread across the South and then the nation. Having prepared for this very activism, Nash said when Lawson's Nashville group learned of the North Carolina protests, "'we simply made plans to join their effort by sitting in at the same chains.'" The camaraderie snowballed as other students across the South joined in to develop what became the national sit-in movement.[14]

One hundred twenty-four students participated in the first official Nashville movement sit-in on February 13. Although waitresses and customers generally reacted to them with fear, the Nashville students sat continuously for several hours without encountering violence or arrests before returning to campus. A few days later students staged a second Nashville sit-in. Like the first, the second sit-in also occurred without violence and arrests, but Nashville officials began challenging the sit-ins through discussions with local Black clergy, most of whom exhorted students to cancel a third sit-in scheduled for Saturday, February 27. With more than three hundred volunteers prepared to participate, students resisted the ministers' admonitions and carried out the scheduled protest. This time, however, mobs attacked them violently, and the police, arriving at the scene late, immediately arrested protesters.

Since the late fall of 1959, workshop peers had identified Nash as clearheaded, and by the time of the second Nashville sit-in, overcoming her objections, they named her leader of the central committee formed to make decisions for the Nashville movement. Having taken on the role of leader, Nash immediately demonstrated that she *was* both clearheaded and politically astute. Before the third protest, another central committee member, James Bevel, suggested that as leader Nash should avoid being one of the certain arrests anticipated in response to continuing the sit-ins. Bevel reasoned that she should remain outside to arrange bail and recruit other volunteers. Nash understood his reasoning but refused to avoid arrest. Expressing concern about the impression she would convey as a leader, Nash argued that students might think she was afraid if she were not arrested. So on February 27, she was among eighty-one persons taken to jail for disorderly conduct during the third Nashville sit-in. Although students were released on bail the evening of their arrests, the following Monday morning they were tried, found guilty, and fined fifty dollars. Nash's leadership became evident again when she interrupted the smooth procedural disposal of the students' cases by announcing that she and fifteen others would not pay the fine, but—in keeping with principles of civil disobedience—would serve jail time instead. "We feel that if we pay these fines we would be contributing to and supporting injustice and immoral practices that have been performed in arrest and conviction of defendants," Nash stated. With her announcement, students who earlier agreed to pay fines reversed themselves and decided to go to jail as well. Their decision—originating the "jail, no bail" policy later emulated across the South—confounded the city as more protests emerged in response to jailing the students. Nashville's mayor, Ben West, proposed a compromise of releasing students and developing a bi-racial commission to consider desegregation, if students agreed to suspend protests at downtown stores. Days after their release, however, Nash and a few others staged a sit-in at the Greyhound bus station, a venue not covered by the compromise. Surprisingly, they were served without objection, a consequence that is signaled as Nashville's first sit-in victory.[15]

In spite of that victory, the bi-racial committee made no serious recommendations for desegregation. It suggested that every dining area have both a segregated and a desegregated section. For Nash and other students, this recommendation failed completely to address the moral issue their protests represented, so they immediately resumed sit-ins. As tension escalated, segregationists bombed the home of the students' attorney, precipitating a march of more than three thousand people to city hall to meet the mayor. As a leader of the students, Nash walked at the front of the march, placing her in immediate proximity to the mayor upon reaching city hall. When protesters arrived, local minister C. T. Vivian read a prepared statement criticizing the mayor and the city for its moral failure. In his reply Mayor West began doing "the typical thing that politicians do," Nash recalled, "making a political speech." Thinking this a waste of time that was getting nowhere, Nash felt responsible for intervening. "'What can I do? What can I say?'" she remembers saying to herself. As soon as a response occurred to her, Nash took charge of the conversation. "Mayor West," she asked, "do you feel it is wrong to discriminate against a person solely on the basis of their race or color?" The searing moral clarity of the question challenged the mayor, he said later, to respond as a man "and not as a politician." West replied with a nod and simple "yes" affirming the protesters' position. Another student followed Nash's lead and asked the mayor if he was recommending ending segregated dining. West replied that he was. Response to West's answer was immediate: marchers erupted into applause; the city's paper ran a headline the following day, "Integrate Counters—Mayor," stating West's position; and within three weeks Nashville lunch counters were desegregated.[16]

Although this tenacious, quick-witted action became a signature of Nash's civil rights participation, and the immediacy with which she engaged opposition to segregation reflected her certainty that change must occur, the sudden and intense role she took on meant she also contended with fear both as a leader and as a young adult engaged in very dangerous practices. Nash once said:

> After we started, I was consumed with the goal we had set for ourselves, which was desegregating the lunch counters in Nashville—specific lunch counters in Nashville—and also consumed with being scared to death. I remember coming back to the dorm the night they elected me chairperson of the central committee, and I was so afraid I could hardly stand up. I said to myself, "This is Tennessee, and white people down here are *mean*." And I said, "We are going to be coming up against men who are white Southern men who are forty and fifty and sixty years old, who are politicians and judges and owners of businesses, and I am twenty-two years old. What am I *doing*! And how is this little group of students my age going to stand up to these powerful people?"[17]

Although Nash frequently was commended for "'how brave I was for sitting in and marching,'" she said she also "'was . . . wall-to-wall terrified. I can remember sitting in class many times [when] I knew we were going to have a demonstration that afternoon. And the palms of my hands would be so sweaty. I was really afraid.'"[18] Sometimes, Nash said, in the middle of protests or her coordination work, she had to determine ways to overcome fear so she could go on with the work she was doing. Because Nashville papers reported the protests widely, Nash's face was recognizable from frequent newspaper stories. During one campaign, she said, "'I heard one guy in the group of teenagers say, "That's Diane Nash. She was in the paper. She's the one to get." And I realized somebody could stab me or something and not even be seen.'" Nash became "terrified. And so I made a deal with myself. I'd take five minutes during which I'd make a decision that I was going to either put the fear out of my mind and do what I had to do, or I was going to call off the sit-in and resign. I really just couldn't function effectively, as afraid as I was. And I found the courage to put the fear out of my mind and keep functioning."[19]

In addition to calming herself in this specific instance of panic, another important moment in contending with her fear occurred on September 27, when Nash was arrested. In this case she not only struggled with terror she felt about physical danger, including uncertainty about what might occur in jail, but also grappled with the stigma her family attached to going to jail. Former Civil Rights Era reporter David Halberstam argues that when confronted with going to jail, Nash was "dealing with a psychological block more than anything else, the belief that she was crossing a line which she had been raised since childhood never to cross, to be a good girl and stay out of jail, since only bad girls went to jail." In grappling with fear about going to jail, Nash grappled with perspectives inculcated by her grandmother. And once she reached the jail, on one level, Nash confronted the same ideas that captivated Carrie Bolton about her Black identity:

> The two white male cops who were doing the fingerprinting . . . looked at her light skin and talked to her as if she were different from the others. Perhaps they thought she was white. They made disparaging remarks about the other blacks, about the way they looked and smelled, and about the thickness of one boy's lips. One of the students said he was a minister and the two cops then made fun of black preachers. They were in some crude way trying to let her know that she had a chance to be like them, a chance to be on their side. To her surprise she felt her fear turn into growing anger. Who, she thought, were these two white cops to judge her? And in that instant she understood completely why she was doing this, that this country forced you to make decisions about color that you did not want to make. Suddenly, after all these years she knew how black she was. It was not her idea to judge people on color; it was America and Tennessee and Nashville which had decided to judge her on color and the color of her friends. She gave them her fingerprints and walked away from the desk more sure than ever of what she was doing and why she was doing it.[20]

The change that occurred in this moment strengthened Nash and clarified for her the meaning of the practice in which she was engaged. About one year after this encounter with incarceration, another, longer experience in jail advanced Nash's evolution and made clear for her the necessity to transcend values and ideas about race that pervaded the nation and that were taught to her as a child.

Nash's Civil Rights Participation

Along with the Nashville protests, sit-ins by students across the South captured the attention of the nation. Among persons marveling at the students' energy was Ella Baker, who at the time still was affiliated with the SCLC. Baker convinced the SCLC board to sponsor a conference for sit-in leaders over Easter weekend (April 16–18, 1960) at her alma mater, Shaw University, in Raleigh, North Carolina. Understanding the significance of their energy and single-minded enthusiasm, Baker encouraged students to form an organization independent of the SCLC, the NAACP, and CORE. Students followed Baker's counsel and established themselves as the Student Nonviolent Coordinating Committee (SNCC). Because the Nashville group had spent time studying principles of nonviolent direct action, because they were in many ways more articulate than other students who attended the conference, and because their group was larger than any other delegation, Nashville became preferred as the locale from which the first SNCC chairperson would emerge. Nash, who clearly articulated the Nashville perspective, was favored as the time for selecting a chair approached. She was not chosen, however, and Marion Barry, another Nashville delegate, was selected instead. The election apparently occurred while Nash was out of the room. Accounts vary as to whether this occurred because of jockeying to avoid selecting a woman or because of Nash's own reluctance.[21]

The new organization adopted a statement of purpose that was deeply influenced by religious perspectives developed by the Nashville movement. Establishing nonviolent direct action as its practice and prioritizing religion as a rationale for activism, the statement reads:

> We affirm the philosophical or religious ideal of nonviolence as the foundation of our purpose, the presupposition of our faith, and the manner of our action. Nonviolence as it grows from the

> Judaic-Christian tradition seeks a social order of justice permeated by love. Integration of human endeavor represents the crucial first step towards such a society.
>
> Through nonviolence, courage displaces fear; love transforms hate. Acceptance dissipates prejudice; hope ends despair. Peace dominates war; faith reconciles doubt. Mutual regard cancels enmity. Justice for all overthrows injustice. The redemptive community supersedes systems of gross social immorality.
>
> Love is the central motif of nonviolence. Love is the force by which God binds man to Himself and man to man. Such love goes to the extreme; it remains loving and forgiving even in the midst of hostility. It matches the capacity of evil to inflict suffering with an even more enduring capacity to absorb evil, and all the while persisting in love.
>
> By appealing to conscience and standing on the moral nature of human existence, nonviolence nurtures the atmosphere in which reconciliation and justice become actual possibilities.[22]

Although Lawson primarily is credited with writing the statement, a handwritten paper titled "Non-Violence Speaks to the Movement," by Nash and another Fisk student, Peggi Alexander, recommended ways SNCC should approach its work.[23]

After the Raleigh conference, SNCC decided to meet regularly. Nash attended SNCC's first gathering, May 13–14, and the fall conference, October 14–16, both of which were held in Atlanta. At the fall conference, Nash was among sit-in participants who led workshops.[24] During a February 1961 Atlanta steering committee meeting, SNCC participants made a decision that began to identify the group as a permanent and significant civil rights organization. On January 31, a CORE field secretary and nine students sat in at a lunch counter in Rock Hill, South Carolina. When arrested the group determined to continue their protest by serving full jail sentences. Upon learning of the decision, SNCC steering committee members took its first formal action as an organization and unanimously decided to support the Rock Hill group. Four persons volunteered to join Rock Hill protesters by serving jail sentences as well: Charles Jones from Johnson C. Smith University in North Carolina, Charles Sherrod of Virginia Union College, Mary Ann Smith of Morris Brown College in Atlanta (who was replaced by her sister, Ruby Doris Smith from Spelman College in Atlanta), and Diane Nash.[25]

The thirty days in Rock Hill's jail proved to be life-changing for Nash. She began to shift her perspective about people entirely. She encountered women in jail who were not students and began to think of them differently. Nash learned firsthand of the sometimes desperate circumstances of the women's lives that caused them to adapt and act in ways that she would not ordinarily consider reasonable. "For the first few days" in jail, Nash said, "the heat was intense in the cell. Breathing was difficult. . . . We couldn't understand why the women in the cell hesitated to ask that a window be opened or the heat be turned down. It turned out that it was because they were so often cold in their own homes, and had come to value heat so highly, that they were willing to suffer from it if they could just have it."[26] Nash came to understand these women—whom she had been taught were "bad" and whom she should avoid—as the same as other persons who "worried about their children like all the other women she knew." Moreover, "there was a lack of meanness to them which surprised her."[27]

While in the Rock Hill jail, Nash had ample opportunity for study and deliberation. She was reassured by reading the autobiography of Gandhi, who also "had been arrested for disturbing the peace," and the Acts of the Apostles. Nash reflected on the work she was engaged in and determined to become even more committed to it. Soon after her release from jail, Nash left college to work full-time as a civil rights activist. "'The Chaucer classes,' she said, 'became unbearable after Rock Hill.'" Moreover, Nash had become frustrated with the lack of support and reprimands for her work by authorities at Fisk. She took a job working for both SNCC and the local SCLC chapter. Making about twenty-five dollars a week, Nash rented a room at the Nashville YWCA, having determined that "'I'll be doing this for the rest of my life.'"[28] It was not long before Nash's full-time civil rights activism propelled her into national leadership, as she became fully engaged in carrying forward the Freedom Rides, the next major protest of the Civil Rights Movement.

Initiated as a project of CORE to test interstate travel desegregation, the original Freedom Riders left Washington, D.C., headed for New Orleans, Louisiana, on Thursday, May 4, 1961. They traveled with little difficulty through Virginia and North Carolina, but were beaten by a mob waiting at the Greyhound bus terminal in Rock Hill,

South Carolina. Upon leaving Rock Hill, buses traveled through Georgia without event, but on May 14 (Mother's Day), as riders crossed into Alabama, they were surrounded by a mob just outside Anniston, Alabama. Bus tires were slashed, and the bus was bombed. After a short hospitalization, the Riders tried to continue to Louisiana by bus, but could not do so.

Diane Nash and members of the Nashville movement heard about the bombing of the Freedom Riders in a radio news broadcast on Sunday. Nash insisted the Nashville movement must continue the Rides, saying she felt "'as though *we* had been attacked,'" and "demanded that they take immediate action to support the Ride."[29] On Monday morning, when they heard that the Freedom Riders, nudged by the Kennedy administration, which asked for a "cooling-off period," had decided to give up on the Ride, Nash telephoned CORE leader James Farmer, coordinator of the Rides, to determine if he objected to Nashville activists continuing the protest. Farmer warned Nash that what she was considering was practically suicidal. "'We fully realize that,'" Nash replied with some annoyance, "'but we can't let them stop us with violence. If we do, the movement is dead. Whenever we start a drive, all they will have to do is roll in the violence and we will turn over and play dead.'"[30] Farmer finally agreed, and from that moment on, Nash became coordinator of the Freedom Rides. Consulting with Nashville students as well as other SNCC participants, especially those nearby in Atlanta, Nash began immediately recruiting volunteers to recommence the Rides.

Farmer was not the only one who thought carrying on the Freedom Rides was too dangerous. As she prepared for continuing, Nash contacted Reverend Fred Shuttlesworth, a Birmingham activist, to request support for Riders. "Do you know that the [other] Freedom Riders were almost killed here?" Shuttlesworth asked. Nash replied that she did and succeeded in garnering his support. She also phoned Martin Luther King Jr. in Atlanta, urging his participation because of the attention it would bring. When King refused, she decided to try to persuade him in person. Accompanied by another Nashville group member, she drove to Atlanta, but in spite of their extended pleas, King and those around him affirmed his decision not to participate because of the inevitability of violence and, as they saw it, the likelihood of King's death should he participate. Back in Nashville, clergy supporting the Nashville movement also thought it too dangerous to take over the Rides and discouraged their continuation. Along with John Lewis, Nash argued the students' perspective that the Rides must continue. In the end, students decided to go forward.

On the very solemn evening before they left, twenty people wrote out and signed wills or wrote letters with messages to loved ones, some including directions on what should happen to their belongings. The next morning, Nash said, "Some of the students gave me sealed letters to be mailed in case they were killed. That's how prepared they were for death."[31]

The new Riders left Nashville around six o'clock on Wednesday morning, May 16, heading for Birmingham to pick up where the protest had stopped. "My own role," Nash said later, "was to stay at the telephone, to keep contact with Birmingham, to hear from the riders as often as they could call, to make arrangements ahead in Montgomery, to keep the Justice Department advised—in short, to coordinate."[32] Keeping in touch was a most important role in view of the real possibility of violence. To her credit as a leader, in spite of a slim budget, Nash had earlier installed an emergency phone line that would remain open for activists to always have a way to get in touch with the Nashville headquarters.

As Riders approached Birmingham, Sheriff Bull Connor flagged down and boarded the bus. He instructed the driver to go to the bus station, where he separated Freedom Riders from the other bus passengers and took them to jail. Freedom Riders spent Wednesday night and part of Thursday night in Birmingham jail. Then at about 1:00 A.M. on Friday, May 19, Connor roused the Riders and drove them to the Tennessee–Alabama border. Arriving at about 3:00 A.M., Connor dropped the students off in a wooded area of the rural town of Ardmore, Alabama. Fortunately, they were near a Black home, whose residents fed riders and permitted them to call Nash, who sent cars to pick them up and return to Birmingham. Returning to Birmingham later Friday morning, Riders went first to Shuttlesworth's home and then back to the Birmingham bus station, where they joined reinforcements who had traveled to Birmingham by train and plane.

As coordinator of the renewed Freedom Rides, Nash also spurned attempts by Kennedy administration representatives to discourage continuation of the Rides. When Nash and other students' determination became clear, Kennedy Justice Department officials negotiated with Alabama Governor John Patterson for safe passage of Riders through the state. About 8:30 A.M. on Saturday, May 20, Riders boarded a bus escorted by state police to Montgomery. Arriving in Montgomery around 11:30, student Riders, the press, and a Justice Department official were attacked by a mob. This was probably the most frightening time of the entire ride for Nash.[33] With assistance from police nowhere to be found, the confrontation turned especially bloody. Nash said:

> We listed all the names of the persons who had left Nashville and began trying to account for them. We would ask the students as they called in, 'When did you last see _____?' The reports we got that morning were: John Lewis was bleeding profusely from the head; another student seemed unconscious; Jim Swerg had been cornered by about sixteen or seventeen men and was being beaten. They had lead pipes, knives, and guns. In a relatively short time, however, we were able to account for all of the students. Miraculously, no one was dead.[34]

As the story continued making news, King, Abernathy, C. T. Vivian, Shuttlesworth, more news media, and Diane Nash all headed to Montgomery. Most Freedom Riders spent Saturday night in the hospital. Sunday evening, May 21, at a mass meeting at Montgomery's First Baptist Church, where Nash, King, and others gathered, a white mob surrounded the church, threatening violence. The group sought help from Washington, but around 4:00 A.M., Monday, May 22, the Alabama National Guard dispersed the mob, to circumvent Attorney General Robert Kennedy's threat to bring in federal troops.

During the meeting at church, Nash became upset that King and his followers had come in and were taking over. She conflicted with and prevailed over King, who recommended discontinuing the Rides at the continuing request of Attorney General Robert Kennedy for a "cooling-off period." On Monday, May 22, tensions continued to rise between Movement groups, as SCLC and CORE seemed to be usurping the students. King again declined the invitation to join the Rides. On Wednesday, May 24, 1961, Riders ate a "desegregated breakfast" at the bus terminal and left Montgomery to go to Jackson, Mississippi. Alabama officials escorted them to the Mississippi state line where Mississippi law enforcement took over. Arriving safely in Jackson, Mississippi, Riders were arrested for breach of the peace and refusing to obey police when they attempted to use segregated restrooms.

Nash drove with a Mississippi attorney to Jackson, where she found no real infrastructure of civil rights activism for support. She did get help from Medgar Evers, a state NAACP leader, who let her use his phone and office. Basically, however, she was alone. Freedom Riders were convicted, fined two hundred dollars, and given suspended sixty-day jail sentences, which they refused, deciding on the "jail, no bail" tactic to draw attention to the protest.[35]

As Riders served jail sentences, U.S. Attorney General Robert Kennedy and other Justice Department officials called a meeting with a group of civil rights activists in early June to discuss focusing on voter registration instead of direct action. Diane Nash and several other SNCC leaders were among those invited. "'It was direct and clear that money would be made available from foundations for SNCC to do voter registration . . . thousands of dollars,'" Nash said later. Nash was skeptical of the offer, saying that accepting the scheme would mean the federal government was "'in control of the Southern black movement. And I knew that if they were making thousands and thousands of dollars available, then we were in real danger of that happening.'" Although no one attending the meeting "'responded directly to the overture,'" afterwards, when some leaders in SNCC began to declare their approval, Nash objected strenuously. "'It wasn't that I did not want to do voter registration, . . . but that I did not want the voter registration to become SNCC's major reason for being. I didn't want it to be under the control of the Kennedys."[36]

More than thirty years later legal scholar Lani Guinier asserted a related concern when she wrote that the focus almost exclusively on voting rights and later on "black electoral success . . . supplanted the more transformative and inclusionary vision of the original civil rights activists." According to Guinier, focus on enfranchisement and on Black electoral success reflected a significant narrowing of the civil rights vision. Focus on voter registration suggested that the broad range of social rights and civic recognition are accomplished through acquiring the right to exercise the franchise. This obfuscated and eclipsed the meaning and potency of the broad range of protest practices that, while not themselves offering a final response to the large civil rights vision, consistently called attention to a variety of specific places in society where the traditions of domination and marginalization were maintained. Focus on Black electoral success represented an even narrower perspective by deflecting attention away from the significance of full participation of formally excluded persons as a guiding norm toward the election of Black representatives as a goal. This obstructed potential attention to values like civic responsibility and participation as accompanying enfranchisement rights and, more importantly, as a significant part of the broad civil rights vision of full inclusion and participatory democracy.[37]

In June, July, and August of 1961, the SNCC executive committee met monthly to hash out its direction. During the August meeting at Highlander Folk School, a standoff emerged between students who preferred to continue direct action and students who preferred to take up voter registration. Diane Nash led the group preferring direct action, who also suspected that the Kennedy administration's call for "cooling off" was an effort to dampen SNCC students' militant stance. In the end, Ella Baker helped avert a split in the organization by suggesting that SNCC develop two foci: one on direct action, which Diane Nash was selected to direct, and a second on voter registration, which Charles Jones was selected to coordinate.[38]

During the fall of 1961, Nash married James Bevel, who had decided to stay in Mississippi after serving a sentence for his Freedom Ride arrest. By early 1962, a group of SNCC workers shared a rented house in Jackson, including newlyweds James and Diane Nash Bevel. Initially, the Bevels lived and worked in Mississippi, traveling about the state to meet with Black people in small groups and encourage them to seek to change conditions in their lives. It was during this period that Nash helped organize the Ruleville meeting in which James Bevel preached and Fannie Lou Hamer joined the movement.[39]

Among other work the Bevels completed in Mississippi was teaching high school students techniques of nonviolence, for which Diane Nash Bevel was arrested in May of 1962. She was charged with "contributing to the delinquency of minors." Tried and convicted in Jackson, Nash was sentenced to two years in jail. Expecting their first child in a few months, Nash refused bail and refused to appeal the conviction.

> We in the nonviolent movement have been talking about jail without bail for two years or more. The time has come for us to mean what we say and stop posting bond. . . . This will be a black baby born in Mississippi, and thus wherever he is born he will be in prison. I believe that if I go to jail now it may help hasten that day when my child and all children will be free—not only on the day of their birth but for all their lives.

Embarrassed by the prospect of Nash delivering in jail, Mississippi officials released her after a short time in prison. On August 5, 1962, the Bevels welcomed their daughter Sherrylynn.[40]

While they continued working in Mississippi, James Bevel took employment with the SCLC, whose local Nashville staff Nash had already joined. The Bevels eventually moved nearer to SCLC headquarters in Atlanta, from which they worked as a home base across the South. In September 1963, they were working on a voter registration drive in Edenton, North Carolina, when news broke of the Sixteenth Street Baptist Church bombing in Birmingham, Alabama. Four little girls—Addie Mae Collins, Denise McNair, Carole Robertson, and Cynthia Wesley—were killed while preparing for Sunday school. When they learned of the bombing, Nash said later that she and her husband "cried . . . because in many ways we felt like our own children had been killed. We knew that the activity of the civil rights movement had been involved in generating a kind of energy that brought out this kind of hostility." Nash says the pain she and James Bevel experienced at learning of the girls' death caused them both to consider using violence in retaliation "as a real option." The second option they considered, and which they chose, was to substantially increase enfranchisement of African Americans in Alabama. "We deliberately made a choice," Nash said. "We promised ourselves and each other that if it took twenty years, or as long as it took, we weren't going to stop working on it, trying until Alabama blacks had the right to vote. So we drew up that day an initial strategy draft for a movement in Alabama designed to get the right to vote." The Bevels presented their plan to the SCLC, which did not immediately get on board, but the couple maintained their commitment to the plan. "'We knew,' said Diane, 'that if [James] proceeded to do the organizing and we developed the Alabama movement to a certain point, that the people in Alabama would ask Martin to come over. And he couldn't say no. And that's exactly what happened.'" After the birth of their son, Douglass, in May of 1964, James Bevel went ahead to begin work and find residence for the family in Selma, Alabama. Diane Nash Bevel followed in the fall.[41]

By this time, Nash was becoming a behind-the-scenes worker. She continued to lead important work like canvassing and organizing for Selma protests, but she had primary responsibility for their two small children. As a result, James Bevel took center stage as a visible leader and speaker during the Selma protests, depending in no small way on the background work of Diane Nash Bevel. The Bevels' work resulted in dramatic events and changes in Selma, eventually leading to the confrontation at Edmund Pettus Bridge and the now famous Selma to Montgomery march led by Martin Luther King Jr. By the time of the march in 1965, however, Diane Nash had separated from James Bevel and moved back to Chicago with their children.[42] After the dissolution of her marriage and her move to Chicago, Nash supported her family with jobs that accorded with her beliefs. She prioritized taking good care of and giving strong support to her children. In late 1966 Nash traveled to North Vietnam with a group of American women as part of the peace movement. She maintained her commitment to nonviolence, writing in an article upon her return from Vietnam, "I am against the war because I am against using murder as a solution to human problems."[43]

Nash's divorce from James Bevel was finalized in 1968. Throughout the 1970s and 1980s and into the 1990s, she worked as a writer, did tenant and general housing advocacy work, and completed other social service work. She returned to college to complete her degree in 1989.[44]

Nash's Religious and Moral Perspectives

Diane Nash's understanding of the meaning of the Civil Rights Movement was substantially religious. As an activist, she described the situation in explicitly religious language as a problem of social "sin" that could only be "redeemed" by "radical love." This religious reading of segregation and of the social context emanated from her organic understanding of human relationship as one of mutuality from which social life, social problems, and social progress arise. From her religious perspective and her understanding of relationship derived her quite militant practice to change society in accord with her beliefs.

Perhaps the most potent aspect of Nash's religious understanding of civil rights activism issued from the several ways she saw mutuality as operating in human relationships. First, Nash understood the normal relationship of human beings to one another as relations of mutual worth. She argued that the essence of the problem of racism was the failure of white Americans to acknowledge the mutual humanity shared with Black Americans. Moreover, Nash held, this problem was not exclusive to race relationships in the United States, but also applied to other countries wherever racism prevents persons from recognizing human mutuality. After one of her arrests, she wrote:

> I believe that when men come to believe in their own dignity and in the worth of their own freedom, and when they can acknowledge God and the dignity that is within every man, then Berlin and Jackson will not be problems. . . . If the policeman had acknowledged the God within each of the students with whom I was arrested last night, would he have put us in jail? Or would he have gone into the store we were picketing and tried to persuade the manager to hire Negroes and to treat all people fairly?

Nash asserted that the origin of civil rights protests was Black persons' assertion of their dignity against the statutes and conventions that denied human mutuality, and, therefore, the dignity of African Americans as human beings: "The Negro is seeking to take advantage of the opportunities that society offers, the same opportunities that others take for granted, such as a cup of coffee at Woolworth's, a good job, an evening at the movies, and dignity. Persons favoring segregation often refer to the rights of man, but they never mention the rights of Negro men." Nash asserted that protests in which she and others participated sought to awaken in society the mutuality that she understood as constitutive not only of human relationship but also of democracy. Until that awakening, she said, civil rights protests needed to continue. "The problem . . . centers around the questions of truth, honesty, justice, and democracy. What is needed is concern for human rights—not just white human rights. Until such time as this realization comes, Freedom Rides and similar such southwide projects are necessary."[45] In addition to asserting the need for white persons to recognize their mutual humanity with Black Americans, Nash also held—along with other practitioners of nonviolent direct action—that behavior of civil rights activists during protests should reflect acknowledgment of this mutuality as well. "In our nonviolent workshops, we had decided to be respectful of the opposition, and try to keep issues geared towards desegregation, not get sidetracked. The first sit-in we had was really funny, because the waitresses were so nervous. . . . One in particular, she was so nervous, she picked up dishes and she dropped one, and she'd pick up another one, and she'd drop it. It was really funny, and we were sitting there trying not to laugh, because we thought that laughing would be insulting and we didn't want to create that kind of atmosphere."[46]

Another aspect of mutuality for Nash was the view that persons participating together in a social context share certain benefits and deficits that derive from that context. In the case of a racially segregated society, the deficits include living in fear, loss of communication, and a negative parochialism and ignorance. "Segregation has its destructive effect upon the segregator" as well as upon those who are segregated, Nash asserted. "The most outstanding of these effects perhaps is fear." Nash characterized the fear produced by segregation as a "needless fear" since it is "fear of the unknown." In defense against the unknown, the pervasiveness of fear produced the system of "Jim Crow [which] fosters ignorance. The white person is denied the educational opportunities of exchange with people of a race other than his own." In addition to ignorance arising from the lack of contact through reciprocal exchange, Nash maintained that violence practiced and consented to by segregationists was itself the manifestation of ignorance that derived from the absence of mutual exchange. This is evident in the hatred on the "faces of whites in newspaper pictures of the mob," she said. Moreover, the "white hoodlum element is often provoked and egged on by the management or by onlookers; this is the type of degradation into which the segregator unfortunately slips." In addition to fear and ignorance, another mutual social deficit deriving from segregation is the constant necessity for duplicity. The duplicity encourages whites to act dishonestly toward Blacks in business relations, and it compels Blacks to deceive whites in conversations about social relationships. In general, Nash said, segregation "fosters dishonesty between the races."

> It makes people lie to each other. It allows white merchants to accept the customers' money, but to give them unequal service, as at the Greyhound and Trailway bus lines, where all customers pay the same fares but some are not free to use all the facilities in the terminals and at restaurants where rest stops are made. Fares are equal, but service is not. The system forces the Negro maid to tell her employer that everything is all right and that she's satisfied, but when she is among her friends she talks about the injustice of the system.

Nash identified the most ubiquitous mutual deficit stemming from segregation to be generally limited social and economic development. Such slow social progress results from a segregated society's "not allowing all its citizens to produce and contribute to the limit of their capacities." In these cases, "the entire city, or region, or country, will suffer, as can be seen in the South's slow progress in industrial, political, and other areas today and in the weakening of American influences abroad as a result of race hatred." "Worst of all," the torpid intellectual and moral effect on people is seen in deficiencies that mutually accrue to members of segregated societies. This is evident, she wrote, in "the stagnancy of thought and character—of both whites and Negroes—which is the result of the rationalization that is necessary in order that the oppressed and oppressor may live with a system of slavery and human abasement."[47]

The final experience of mutuality that Nash explores is the organic mutuality of groups that make up a society. For Black people in the case of segregation, this means living in poverty and without common social rights and functioning in a role of inferiority and subjugation to make possible the benefits enjoyed by whites. Nash held that restrictions in "housing, school, jobs" reflect the segregator's need for "a built-in lower economic class . . . employed in the most menial capacities and . . . paid the lowest wages."

> Segregation reaches into every aspect of life to oppress the Negro and to rob him of his dignity in the South. The very fact that he is forced to be separated obviously implies his inferiority. Therefore the phrase "separate but equal" denies itself. The things non-black Americans take for granted, such as a movie and dinner date for college students, or a coffee-break downtown, are usually denied the black American in the South. Sometimes he may obtain these services if he wishes to compromise his dignity.

> He might, for example, attend a downtown movie if he would enter through the alley entrance and climb to the balcony to be seated.

Such oppression that "extends to every area of life . . . has a real effect upon the Negro." In her analysis of the organic mutuality of social groups, Nash asserted African Americans bear an additional negative burden of being the class on whose lack of full life the system exists. Echoing W. E. B. Du Bois's description of double-consciousness, Nash described the emotional duality that Black people experience: "An organism must make some type of adjustment to its environment. The Negro, however, continues to deny consciously to himself, and to his children, that he is inferior. Yet each time he uses a 'colored' facility, he testifies to his own inferiority. Many of the values that result from this dual self-concept are amazing to note."[48] For Nash, this situation that denies mutuality of persons living in social relationship is a circumstance of radical moral evil, or sin.

When she moved to Nashville in 1959, Nash "came then to see the community in sin." Nash described as symbols of sin the "signs designating 'white' or 'colored,' being told, 'We don't serve niggers in here,' and, as happened in one restaurant, being looked in the eye and told, 'Go around to the back door where you belong.'" Nash understood "sin" as affecting the entire society. In addition, she did not characterize sin as limited to practices or behaviors but as the nature of life that persisted in a society where human mutuality is not enacted. The flawed nature of social life, the relations of duplicity, the emotional duality of oppressed persons all represent for Nash "this stage of sin" encountered in Nashville, "when I first came there in September, 1959." She also argued that sin involves actions or failure to act. She said "that white and Negro Americans are committing sin every day that they hate each other and every day that they allow an evil system to exist without doing all they can to rectify it as soon as they can." Recognizing this social sin is contrary to "acknowledg[ing] the God within men," that allows one to call for a "'cooling off period,' or plead for gradualism" in the face of actions trying to correct the problem.[49] For Nash, the response to what she identified as "radical evil" was militant practice of "radical love."

As a college student and an initial member of SNCC, Diane Nash shared with peers involved in the Civil Rights Movement an intense and militant perspective about social change. Her tenacious persistence in working with the initial protests in Nashville, from sit-ins to boycotts, reflected Nash's militant stance. This was seen again in her interaction with various groups, including the Justice Department, who repeatedly attempted to dissuade Nash from continuing the Freedom Rides. Convinced that halting the Freedom Rides would cause an extreme slowdown in Civil Rights Movement victories, Nash adamantly refused to stop the Rides. Her intense action in these instances reflects both what she might describe as her practice of radical love and her impatience that change she felt should have occurred "a long time ago . . . after the Civil War" should occur now without delay.[50] Gradualism, according to Nash, was unsuccessful in overcoming the moral problem of society. "No person or country can have a clear conscience and a noble mien with such a sin on its conscience," she argued. "I'm interested now in the people who call for gradualism. The answer, it seems to me, is to stop sinning and stop now! How long must we wait? It's been a century. How gradual can you get?" For Nash, the militancy with which the "sin" of segregation should be opposed required nothing less than willingness to give one's life. Asserting this as the reason for the position she took on continuing the Freedom Rides, Nash said, "Mob violence must not stop men's striving toward right. Freedom Rides and other such actions must not be stopped until our nation is really free."[51]

This militant perspective and the radical activity in which Nash participated reflected her commitment to nonviolence as the means by which the moral problem of segregation could be overcome. As she saw it, the movement of nonviolent direct action was a movement seeking mutual change for mutual benefit by means of love. "We used nonviolence as an expression of love and respect of the opposition, while noting that a *person* is never the enemy," Nash said. "The enemy is always attitudes, such as racism or sexism; political systems that are unjust; economic systems that are unjust—some kind of system or attitude that oppresses."[52] Against those who felt nonviolent protests were immoral means to achieve the goal of overcoming segregation, Nash asserted to the contrary that using nonviolent direct action was a loving means to achieve the goal since it reflected the rejection of violence and willingness to suffer to achieve the desired end.

> The students have chosen non-violence as a technique; there is no reason why they couldn't have taken up guns. It [use of non-violence] was a responsible choice, I think. We have decided that if there is to be suffering in this revolution (which is really what the movement is—a revolution), we will take the suffering upon ourselves and never inflict it upon our fellow man, because we respect him and recognize the God within him. . . . I think we need to understand that this is a question of real love of man and love of God. Is there such a thing as moderate love of God or moderate disdain for sin? I think we need radical good to combat radical evil. Consider the South. It can be the answer for the free world; it can be the pivot. The problem there is a vital challenge for truth; for respect for man. In a word, it is a question of dignity.[53]

The "nonviolent movement," Nash wrote, "(1) is based upon and motivated by love; (2) attempts to serve God and mankind; (3) strives toward what we call the beloved community. This is religion. This is applied religion." Asserting work of the Civil Rights Movement as religious work, Nash stated, "I think it is the work of our Church."[54]

Nash identified five stages of nonviolent direct action as including the following:

> The first step was investigation . . . where we really did all the necessary research and analysis to totally understand the problem. The second phase was education, where we educated our own constituency to what we had found out in our research.
>
> The third stage was negotiation, where you really approached the opposition, let them know your position, and tried to come to a solution. The fourth stage was demonstration. The purpose of demonstrations was to focus the attention of the community on the issue, and on the injustice. And the last stage was resistance, where you really withdraw your support from the oppressive system. And during this stage would take place things like boycotts, work stoppages, and nonsupport of the system.[55]

As with her characterization of the social problem of segregation using religious language, Nash did not equivocate in her understanding that the work of "love" practiced through nonviolence was religious work of "conversion" or "redemption." Moreover, the conversion she anticipated was change that occurred both in persons and in society. "The purpose of any nonviolent demonstration is to focus the attention of people on how evil segregation really is and then to change their hearts," she said.[56] "The purpose of the sit-ins and the Freedom Rides and any other such actions, as I see it is to bring about a climate in which all men are respected as men, in which there is appreciation of the dignity of man and in which each individual is free to grow and produce to his fullest capacity. We of the movement often refer to this goal as the concept of the *redeemed* or the 'beloved' community."[57]

Nash's characterization of the society of mutuality ("in which all men are respected as men") as a "redeemed" community reflects her particular interpretation of the "beloved community" so often referred to by civil rights participants. Nash's use of *redeemed* captures the religious idea. Furthermore, in keeping with one distinctively Christian understanding of redemption, Nash's use of *redeemed* intimates a crucifixion metaphor, identifying the suffering by civil rights activists through nonviolent direct action as redemptive activity, demonstrating, like Christ, "radical love." The redemption did not result from seeking suffering, as some understand the Christian symbol of crucifixion. The suffering issued from the retaliatory violence that arose as a result of opposing systems of sin.

In addition to invoking the Christian image of crucifixion, Nash also used redemption to lift up the social responsibility theme of Black religious women's activism. The expectation that one participates in redeeming society as religious duty reflects Nash's assertion that oppressed persons should take responsibility for precipitating change. Continuing her assertion that persons in societies live in an organic mutuality, Nash said that nonviolent direct action anticipates persons' "recognizing that oppression always requires participation of the oppressed." With this recognition comes responsibility. If love is the means one chooses, taking responsibility means that "rather than doing harm to the oppressor, another way to go is to identify your part in your own oppression, and then withdraw your cooperation from the system of oppression, and guarantee if the oppressed withdraw their cooperation from their own oppression, the system of oppression cannot work." Taking on this responsibility is empowering, since, "when you do identify your own responsibility in an oppressive situation, . . . it puts you in a position of power. Because then you are able to withdraw your participation and therefore end the system."[58] Moving beyond the tradition among some Black religious women of interpreting only one side of religious social responsibility, Nash maintained her emphasis on mutuality by asserting the obligation to change oppression in a society as a responsibility of all members of the society.

> Problems lie not so much in our action as in our inaction. We have upon ourselves as individuals in a democracy the political, economic, sociological, and spiritual responsibilities of our country. I'm wondering now if we in the United States are really remembering that this must be a government "of the people" and "by the people" as well as "for the people." Are we really appreciating the fact that if you and I do not meet these responsibilities then our government cannot survive as a democracy?[59]

In her assertion that democracy persists through persons' taking up this responsibility, Nash's perspective corresponds with explicit concerns articulated by Ella Baker and Septima Clark, both of whom sought to increase participation of all persons in systems that govern their lives.

Nash's significant role as a female student leader meant she was among persons blazing a trail that became the path of the modern women's movement in the United States. Mid-twentieth-century statements about the status of women derived from the accumulated experiences of civil rights participants like Diane Nash.[60] In spite of, or perhaps because of, Nash's role as a trailblazer, throughout her civil rights participation she encountered difficulty because of her gender. Except for the period of her local leadership in the Nashville movement, this gender difficulty was the case from early on in her participation with SNCC and the SCLC. When the first chair of SNCC was elected at its founding meeting in Raleigh, the vote was held when Nash was out of the room. Some people, including John Lewis, felt this was a deliberate action designed to select a man instead of a woman.[61] As her role in the movement grew and she interacted with Martin Luther King Jr. and the SCLC during her leadership of the continuing Freedom Rides, Nash encountered a trivialization of her role similar to that described by Baker and Clark. When Nash and her husband began to work primarily for the SCLC, Nash's role became even more diminished. Although being a mother of two young children during this period affected this change, it was not the only factor. As theologian Jacquelyn Grant points out, the diminishing of Nash's activity related directly to its being celebrated as "backbone" (read background) work.[62] At the SCLC Nash continued to contribute meaningfully to projects she and James Bevel worked on together. Andrew Young observed:

> No small measure of what we saw as Jim's brilliance was due to Diane's rational thinking and influence. The preachers of SCLC were not advocates for women's equality at this stage of our moral and political development, and Diane was not on the SCLC payroll. As in the traditional church structure, a preacher's wife might direct the choir, run the Sunday school, and chair the women's fellowship without any compensation but her husband's salary. It is not to our credit that we followed that model with Diane.[63]

Recalling norms of the time, Nash said that men were expected to hold leadership positions and that she often preferred not to "take out-front positions." Reflecting on gender relations in SNCC, she said that on the basis of her work and relations with people, she developed a reputation that made it necessary for men in SNCC to acknowledge her leadership and take her seriously. "I ran into some real problems in terms of being the only woman at the stage where we were just setting SNCC up as an organization."

> It was really rough not being just one of the guys. They did tend to look at me that way. However, they had to tolerate me because I had such a strong local base in Nashville, and at that time I had gotten probably more publicity than any other student in the movement and had been on the cover of *Jet* magazine a couple of times and things like that. . . .
>
> Even though they disagreed a lot of times, they tolerated me because they didn't want me to say that these guys just really aren't okay. I had a real good image because I took truth and love seriously, the basic tenets of non-violence. And people who knew me and worked with me knew that and so my word would tend to be taken seriously. I was taken seriously by a lot of people. That's what helped me. . . . [Otherwise] they'd have wiped me out.[64]

Reflecting on her work, Nash said she is "very satisfied" with her role as a catalyst for changes in society: "'The Voting Rights Act resulted from Selma, and all those black officials got elected. It's a satisfaction that has to do with the fact that—this isn't modest, but—with the fact that my living has made a difference on the planet. And I love that. I really do.'"[65]

Ruby Doris Smith Robinson: Building Community and Sustaining Community Protest

Ruby Doris Smith Robinson, once identified as the "heartbeat"[66] of the Student Nonviolent Coordinating Committee (SNCC), lived less than six months past her twenty-fifth birthday in 1967. Because she died so young, because she did not see late evolutions of the Civil Rights Movement, and because she left no significant writing or telling of her story, Ruby Doris Smith Robinson often is minimized in or completely absent from accounts of the Movement. Students of SNCC history know Robinson's story better, but even in some versions of that history, Robinson's role is significantly hidden. Robinson became involved with SNCC in 1961 as an extension of activism she engaged in as a student at Atlanta's Spelman College through the student-led Atlanta Committee on Appeal for Human Rights. In the spring of 1963, she became a full-time staff member in SNCC's Atlanta headquarters. Beginning in 1963 and 1964, SNCC's most intensely active period, and continuing throughout her life, Robinson was the no-nonsense office and program manager who tried to help channel student energies demonstrated through protests into hard work and discipline on behalf of the Black struggle, especially to seek to empower marginalized local people in rural communities, particularly in the South.[67]

Similar to Diane Nash with the renewed Freedom Rides, during SNCC's most active period Robinson was the lifeline to SNCC fieldworkers across the South. Because she was committed to and consumed by "enabling" the cutting-edge social change work SNCC inspired and carried out, much of Robinson's role and voice became obscured by the time and attention she paid to nuts and bolts of keeping SNCC and its workers going. In this regard, Robinson did what Gilkes says many Black women community activists do: build up and keep organizations running, often in the shadow of male "leaders." Still, Robinson became SNCC's highest-ranking and most authoritative woman (some even say it was she who ran SNCC, while James Forman was formally executive secretary), but because of her lack of significant formal status until near the end of her own life and the demise of SNCC as an active organization, the work she did is easily identified with the important practices often designated as "women's work."[68]

Robinson grew up participating in traditional Black church customs at West Mitchell Colored (later Christian) Methodist Episcopal Church, near the Atlanta University Center in Georgia. When she entered civil rights activism, Robinson affirmed Movement practices as corresponding with her Christian beliefs. Among these were convictions she had developed about siding with and seeking to empower persons who seemed most marginalized. As SNCC and Robinson became more radical, she articulated connections to Christianity less literally. What became clear and remained consistent in Robinson's work, however, was a keen sensitivity to the disenfranchised on whose behalf she worked. Robinson developed this concern as a schoolgirl and maintained it throughout her life. Perhaps in some sense this accounts for her immediate and intense concern for addressing quality-of-life problems caused by racism. She became convinced that SNCC was a vehicle for addressing these problems and exhausted her time and energy to this end, including consistently demonstrating sensitivity to emotional and material needs of SNCC volunteers and staff so they could carry out the organization's work. Even as SNCC began to change and collapse, Robinson maintained allegiance to the organization, and, perhaps more than any of her peer leaders of SNCC near its end, persisted in her devotion to SNCC's original program of changing conditions for African Americans by empowering local people.

Religious and Moral Influences in Robinson's Early Life

Ruby Doris Smith was born April 25, 1942, in Atlanta, Georgia. She was the second child and second daughter in John and Alice Banks Smith's family of seven children. John Thomas Smith was born in the rural farming community of Ashburn, Georgia. He left Ashburn on foot headed for Atlanta at age fifteen, taking odd jobs to provide for himself on the way. When he reached Atlanta, Smith earned a living through various business ventures, eventually establishing a comfortable life as a mover after he met and married Alice Banks. Following their marriage, the Smiths bought a home with room to open a neighborhood grocery store, and another room for Mrs. Smith to operate a hair salon. In addition to various other entrepreneurial ventures, at one time John Smith managed a gospel group. He eventually became a Baptist minister and established his own church.[69]

Because of his religious beliefs, Mr. Smith was quite strict. He "refused to allow dancing in the house" and tried to keep a close, protective watch on his children. This strict religiosity became a point of tension between John Smith and his daughter Ruby. Older sister Catherine described their father as the "domineering-type . . . [who] had strong religious beliefs. He wouldn't let her go to dances, parties—couldn't go out on late dates and all this. [He was] very strict about everything." Because of her father's strictness, during her senior year in high school Ruby Doris left home to live with her maternal aunt Ruby O'Neal, for whom she had been named.[70] In addition to demonstrating objection to her father's austerity, Ruby Doris's leaving home reflected the willfulness that became a striking characteristic of her personality as a child and marked so much of her leadership as a young adult activist. The rift between father and daughter was later mended, though Ruby's civil rights activism during college made the truce an uneasy one. Despite her father's severity, biographer Cynthia Fleming says Robinson enjoyed many ordinary amusements of childhood. She had supportive parents who gave their children pleasures routine to the Black life of which they were a part. They went on frequent family outings like picnics and boat rides, and, as was traditional for many Black families of the era, regularly attended and participated in church life.[71]

Much of the routine pleasures in the Smith children's lives derived from the role of their mother. Born in 1912 to a family of sharecroppers in Barnsville, Georgia, Alice Banks lost her mother to tuberculosis when she was eight years old. Among the last things her mother, a "skilled seamstress," did was to make new dresses for two of her daughters, Alice and Ruby, to wear to her burial. As Barnsville economic prospects were dismal, the Banks children looked to Atlanta for a better future. In 1928 sixteen-year-old Alice followed her elder sister Annie to Atlanta. Alice completed beauty school, took a job as a beautician, and (like Septima Clark) immediately began sending money home to help her family. Alice also completed work for her high school diploma some time later. She met and married Smith in 1939.[72]

Though both her parents were religious, Ruby Doris seems to have been more deeply influenced in her social and moral perspectives by her mother. Alice Smith dedicated herself to her family's development and harmonious interaction. Wanting her children to become educated and well-rounded, Mrs. Smith encouraged concentration on their studies and, from funds she made styling hair, paid for extracurricular activities like ballet and piano lessons. As the Smith children developed, Ruby Doris became quite independent. Recalling her daughter's self-reliance that became evident early on, Mrs. Smith said, "Once she was clear, she was going to do it whether it was what you wanted or not." Among other times, this was evident when older sister Mary Ann started kindergarten at a church-sponsored school. Three-year-old Ruby Doris contended she must go along, and by age four she entered first grade. Because of Ruby Doris's independence, in addition to encouraging her children's development, Alice Smith used "energy and skill" to lessen friction between the strong-willed daughter and her husband. The necessity of managing the friction continued into Ruby's young adulthood; when she was a college co-ed, Mr. Smith "felt that his daughter's political decisions placed her life and future in needless jeopardy."[73]

In this latter case, Alice Smith may have felt some sympathy for her daughter's posture. Ruby Doris's civil rights participation was a kind of extension of Mrs. Smith's own activism. "She has so much social conscience," Robinson once said of her mother. When asked how her mother influenced her, she cited Mrs. Smith's practice of providing information and resources to help Black men who were fleeing the brutality of Southern work gangs. "Well, my mother always kept a suit of men's clothes in the house and a package of things—a little silver money, matches, names and telephones, maybe of certain preachers around the South who would help" the men escaping the chain gang.

> When I was little—our house was on the escape route for Negro men on the prison chain gangs. You know, Negroes used to be really brutalized on the chain gangs not so long ago, and they escaped when they could. It's still pretty bad for Negro men in prison. . . .

> Once or twice I remember a lotta commotion in the house and whisperin' and a strange man in the kitchen in the middle of the night.
>
> She took a big risk. Didn't matter what he did or who he was—he was a Negro man off the chain gang and if they caught him, they'd beat him to death. So she helped him escape.
>
> But my daddy was very angry about it. He was afraid we'd all be killed if they caught us.[74]

In an uncanny foreshadowing of her own premature death, during this interview Robinson also said of her mother, "she's a strong woman and she *could* influence my son if I'm not with him enough."[75]

Throughout elementary and high school, Ruby Doris followed through on her mother's desire that her children be well-rounded. She participated in programs at school, at church, and in the community. In high school she was active with the yearbook staff and student council and track, basketball, and tennis teams, and she served as a majorette. She also excelled at schoolwork, which came easily to her. At church, Ruby Doris participated in youth and college choirs and the youth group. In 1956, she was an alternate delegate to the Christian Methodist Episcopal National Youth Conference in Memphis, Tennessee.[76]

With her independent spirit and opportunities to participate in many activities as a child, Ruby Doris Smith became quite an extrovert. She also developed a matter-of-fact, take-care-of-business personality, coupled with (perhaps owing to her mother's example) a deep sensitivity for outsiders. "Ruby had a sense of fairness and a sympathy for the underdog that were an important part of the essence of her personality," biographer Cynthia Fleming writes.

This was most evident in her loyal friendship toward Brenda Jefferson, a "painfully shy and insecure" neighbor who often was teased and left out by other children because she had a learning disability. Throughout Jefferson's difficulty with schoolwork and peers, Ruby "was always there," Jefferson said. "She always tried to help me." Ruby Doris's help included "support and understanding" as well as pragmatism. In one instance,

> [when] Brenda left her lunch in a classroom while . . . rehearsing for a school play [someone ate it]. The same thing happened the day after. On the third day, Brenda's stomach fluttered with

> nervous anticipation as she slowly opened the door and walked to the desk where she had left her lunch. Once again, it was gone. . . . At this point, Brenda consulted Ruby Doris, who immediately devised a plan. The next day, Ruby sprinkled a liberal amount of hot sauce on Brenda's sandwich, and then Brenda left her lunch in the customary place. That was the last lunch that disappeared.[77]

On another occasion, when they were high school freshmen, Smith convinced Jefferson to enter the campus queen competition. Ruby appointed herself Brenda's campaign manager and often made speeches on her behalf, resulting in Brenda's election as first runner-up.[78]

In addition to sensitivity she felt for her friend Brenda, during her adolescence Smith began to develop a nascent consciousness about racial issues. When she was thirteen, she watched reports of the Montgomery Bus Boycott on television and recalled being impressed by seeing elderly people walking and walking. Robinson recalled the scenes later as having contributed to her own political activism.[79] The reports may have helped her decide on race work as a career for herself. Her sister Catherine remembers Ruby saying as an adolescent, "'I know what my life and mission is. . . . It's to set the black people free. . . . I will never rest until it happens. . . . I will die for that cause.'"[80]

Robinson's Civil Rights Activism

When she enrolled at Spelman College in 1959, contrasting sharply with what Diane Nash encountered at Fisk, Smith entered an atmosphere that encouraged student participation in social justice activism. As early as 1957 Spelman College students accompanied their white history professor Howard Zinn in attempts to integrate the gallery at the Georgia General Assembly. Other faculty and NAACP leaders also encouraged Spelman students to get involved in social changes.[81] In February of 1960, when she saw reports of the Greensboro sit-ins, Smith said she "began to think right away about it happening in Atlanta, but I wasn't ready to act on my own." Just over a month later, shortly after Nashville students joined in, student government leaders representing Black colleges and seminaries of the Atlanta University Center published "An Appeal for Human Rights" in the *Atlanta Constitution,* stating that they intended "to use every legal and non-violent means at our disposal to secure full citizenship rights as members of this great Democracy." Student body officers representing the six Atlanta University Center schools signed the document, including Ruby Doris's sister Mary Ann, secretary of the Morris Brown College Student Government.[82]

After organizing themselves as the Atlanta Committee on Appeal for Human Rights, students planned their first sit-in for March 16. "When the student committee was formed in the Atlanta University Center," Smith said, "I told my sister [Mary Ann], who was on the Student Council at Morris Brown College, to put me on the list. And when two hundred students were selected for the first demonstration, I was among them." Two hundred Black students fanned out into various protest locations. Smith "went through the food line in the restaurant at the State Capitol with six other students, but when we got to the cashier, she wouldn't take our money. She ran upstairs to get the governor. The Lieutenant Governor came down and told us to leave. We didn't, and went to the county jail." Arrested and "charged with breaking the peace, intimidating restaurant owners, refusing to leave the premises, and conspiracy," Ruby Doris Smith was one of the seventy-seven students, including thirteen from Spelman, taken to the Fulton County Jail. Bail was posted, and students were released.[83] Later that spring, over Easter weekend, April 14–16, in Raleigh, North Carolina, Ella Baker organized the meeting at Shaw University that ended in the birth of SNCC. Because she was a member of the Atlanta Committee on Appeal for Human Rights steering committee, Mary Ann Smith attended the gathering, but Ruby Doris did not.

When the school year ended and many students left Atlanta for the summer, no other massive protests occurred until the fall. Still, demonstrations of the preceding spring initiated ongoing movement activism among students in Atlanta. A few students who remained in Atlanta for the summer broadened their protests to boycotting local supermarkets that would not hire Black clerks. Other protests included sit-ins in city hall and city, state, and county cafeterias.

Once she became engaged in civil rights practices, Ruby Doris Smith seems to have decided to turn totally toward the work. Like many other college students of the era, as Diane Nash said, school either lost its relevance or became secondary. Mary Ann observed that Ruby Doris "'went off on a rocket . . . in terms of total commitment.'"[84]

When the Atlanta student movement got started, Ruby Doris began almost immediately to demonstrate her tenacious commitment to it, even though she was not a member of the group's steering committee. Two Atlanta movement colleagues recalled: "There was a core group . . . who were there for the hard planning, and Ruby Doris was always there. I mean she was always there. And I'm not even sure whether she was officially on the executive committee or not. But she was the kind of person who would be there if something had to be done. She would get an assignment whether she was on the committee or not."[85] During the summer of 1960, Ruby Doris continued to recruit volunteers for boycotts. At times she was the lone person marching with a sign in front of a store.

After an August 4–6, 1960, SCLC workshop on nonviolence, twenty-five Atlanta University Center students staged kneel-ins at local churches on August 7. Ruby Doris Smith, now a Spelman sophomore, attempted to attend the Sunday morning worship at Atlanta's First Baptist Church. Ushers barred her entrance, but Smith "pulled up a chair in the lobby and joined in the singing and worship service."[86] Smith's reaction to being barred from church is one of her earliest articulations of beliefs that motivated her participation in the protests: "When I was refused admission to the Church, I was stunned at first by the reaction of ushers." Reflecting the idealism of an eighteen-year-old, which was so important to stimulating ongoing work of many students of SNCC, Smith said:

> I feel that segregation is basically a moral problem, and for this reason, I feel that Church is one institution where the problem can be "thrashed out." I think the kneel-in movement is an appeal to the consciences of Christians, who are primarily "good" people. Even if we were not admitted to worship, as was true in my case, I think that the attempt in itself was a success, because the minds and hearts of the people who turned us [a]way were undoubtedly stirred.[87]

When students returned to school in the fall, they began picketing all over Atlanta's downtown. Ruby Doris marched with colleagues in an October 19 protest of lunch counter segregation. Joined by Martin Luther King Jr., who was arrested at a department store, this protest prompted city officials to begin negotiating with students. After the mayor's failure to get merchants to compromise, students continued demonstrations in November.[88]

In the meantime, SNCC had begun holding regular meetings in Atlanta since its April founding, beginning with its first official meeting on May 13–14, 1960. A conference on direct action was held October 14–16, with another gathering in late November.[89] Mary Ann Smith, but not her sister Ruby Doris, attended each of these events as SNCC began to work out its identity. Replacing Lonnie King, an Atlanta Committee on Appeal for Human Rights steering committee member who could not attend a February 3–6, 1961, gathering, Ruby Doris joined Mary Ann in attending SNCC's next meeting, which proved to be a defining moment in the organization's history. At that meeting, SNCC leaders heard about arrests of students from Friendship Junior College in Rock Hill, South Carolina, for attempting to integrate lunch counters. Taking the first significant action since its founding, SNCC decided to send four members to Rock Hill in support of student protesters there, who would serve the thirty-day jail sentences as part of their protests instead of posting bail. SNCC had decided to initiate the "jail, no bail" tactic at its October meeting. The four students selected to go were Diane Nash, Charles Jones, Charles Sherrod, and Mary Ann Smith.[90]

Although Mary Ann had participated in SNCC's founding conference and was a member of the original Atlanta Committee on Appeal for Human Rights, as time approached to leave for Rock Hill, she became less excited about the prospect of being arrested and spending time in jail. Her sister Ruby Doris became more excited. In the end, Ruby Doris talked Mary Ann out of the trip so she could go.[91] "I went home that night to explain to my mother," Ruby Doris later recalled. "She couldn't understand why I had to go away—why I had to go to Rock Hill." Although Ruby Doris explained to her mother why she "must" go, since Mrs. Smith was very familiar with her daughter's tenacity, the explanation may have served Ruby more than her mother. "I think they felt so helpless with her," Mary Ann said of her sister years later. "What ever she's going to do, she's going to do."[92] In spite of Ruby's explanation and other times when their parents felt uncertain about Ruby's activism, Mary Ann said that "for the most part [their parents] were supportive" of their daughters' Civil Rights Movement participation. This did not negate the elder Smiths' concern for their daughters' safety, however. Lonnie King, a leader of the Atlanta student movement reported that Mrs. Smith once told him, "'You've got both of my girls in this thing and I hope it works out.'"[93]

Rock Hill marked Ruby Doris Smith's full-time entry into civil rights activism. During the thirty-days of incarceration, she said, "'I came to think of myself as an individual, as opposed to what whites might have thought of me as a person.'" While there she read, sang, and held frequent discussions with her cellmates. This included spending time talking with women imprisoned for other reasons and discussing with co-protester Diane Nash ways to end segregation.[94]

With these other cellmates, Smith and co-protester Diane Nash discussed the Civil Rights Movement and use of nonviolent direct action. "'The other prisoners couldn't believe that we could leave whenever we wanted,' Ruby Doris said. 'By the time we left,' she said, 'they were firm believers in the movement.'" With Nash, Smith discussed strategies for continuing the work against racial discrimination. According to Nash, the two women "'analyzed extensively the situation of segregation and how to get out of it.'"[95] Smith and Nash conducted their own scripture reading and prayer, connecting the Rock Hill sit-ins to Christian faith, and local religious leaders who supported the students regularly visited Smith, Nash, and other protesters.[96]

In addition to engaging with persons and circumstances of her immediate context at the Rock Hill jail, Ruby Doris related civil rights practices of other persons in Rock Hill to protests she had engaged in back in Atlanta. She asked her sister Mary Ann to "keep me abreast of negotiations" about segregation with merchants in Atlanta. She also reported to Mary Ann political reactions to protests against segregation in Rock Hill. "'The officials here are getting "stiff" on picketing,'" Ruby Doris wrote to her sister. "'The tension is *high* downtown. Whenever [picketers] go down, a crowd of hoodlums gather around and eventually they begin to "fight" (or beat up someone). The police come to [the] rescue after the incident gets out of hand—only to arrest the picketers.'"[97] The relationship of student demonstrations in Atlanta to other protests across the South and around the country was the origin of Ruby Doris's Rock Hill arrest. This connection that she saw in SNCC's work and with which she immediately became engaged by volunteering to go to Rock Hill was one that significantly determined the unfolding of Smith's role in SNCC.

Having time to contemplate the Movement while in jail, Smith later said that while there she determined some things she would do to continue the work of the Civil Rights Movement. In 1966 journalist Phyl Garland reported her saying that in Rock Hill she made several "idealistic commitments to herself," including to continue "challenging the system in ways that are sometimes dramatic, but more often mundane—making certain SNCC functions properly by running the office, keeping track of bills, conceiving fund-raising projects and, when possible, going out into the field."[98] This characterization of the work she would do as a SNCC staff member covered quite precisely the role she came to play in the organization.

By the end of her Rock Hill sentence, Smith had become consumed with work for the Movement. Less than two months after her release from the Rock Hill jail, she became involved with continuation of the Freedom Rides that Diane Nash had orchestrated in May. Smith was the only non-Nashville person to join the initial replacement Freedom Riders in Alabama.[99] In some sense, Smith's participation as a replacement Rider derived from her being geographically situated in Atlanta. Historian Howard Zinn records that when "news came that the Riders could not go on by bus, that they were flying to New Orleans, an excited discussion went on over long distance between Nashville and Atlanta, the two centers where SNCC had its strongest contingents. The Ride, they decided, should continue." Diane Nash began organizing the successors to the original Riders. Once the decision was made to continue the Ride, Ruby Doris Smith began looking for ways to travel so she could join the Nashville group. This proved to be difficult since many Black persons who supported the Movement in Atlanta thought it a perilous undertaking and tried to convince her not to go. Eventually Smith was able to raise needed funds and on May 18, 1961, she flew to Birmingham, Alabama, to join the other SNCC Riders. Before leaving Atlanta, however, Smith significantly helped advance the renewal of the Rides by telephoning "all the SNCC affiliates at campuses across the South to mobilize support."[100] Arriving alone in Alabama, the first thing Smith did was go to meet the others. She recounted the difficulty of trying to get a driver to take the group to Montgomery, the next leg of the Freedom Rides.

> When I got to Birmingham I went to the bus terminal and joined the seventeen from Nashville. We waited all night trying to get a bus to Montgomery. Every time we got on a bus the driver said

> no, he wouldn't risk his life. The terminal kept crowding up with passengers who were stranded because the buses wouldn't go on. The Justice Department then promised Diane that the driver of the 4:00 a.m. bus would go on to Montgomery. But when he arrived he came off the bus and said to us: "I have only one life to give, and I'm not going to give it to NAACP or CORE!"[101]

Because of an agreement between the Kennedy administration and the governor of Alabama, the driver returned and took them on to Montgomery on Saturday, May 20. But the difficulty of continuing the Rides became even greater in Montgomery. Smith recalled that police protection suddenly fell away once they reached Montgomery. A mob that had gathered first beat the CBS cameraman who was filming the activities. Then, as Riders disembarked, the crowd "started beating everyone," Smith said. "I saw John Lewis beaten, blood coming out of his mouth. People were running from all over. Everyone of the fellows was hit. Some of them tried to take refuge in the post office, but they were turned out. . . . We saw some of the fellows on the ground, John Lewis lying there, blood streaming from his head." Both police and medical attention were slow to arrive, Smith reported.[102] Miraculously, no one was killed, although several Riders, news personnel, and a U.S. Justice Department official stayed at least one night in the hospital. Riders spent four difficult days in Montgomery before heading on to Mississippi, the final leg of the Ride. Once they arrived, all Freedom Riders were arrested on May 24 for attempting to use white restrooms in the Jackson, Mississippi, bus terminal.[103]

As with the Rock Hill arrest, Ruby Doris and others decided to serve the jail sentence as part of their protest. Writing to her hometown paper, the *Atlanta Inquirer,* Smith said she had "'no intention of leaving' before her sentence expires on August 11." Her days were occupied (in similar fashion to the Rock Hill sentence) with activities that included scripture reading, singing, writing letters, visits from local clergy, and ballet and Spanish lessons. As news of the revived Freedom Rides spread, other people from around the country came to join their efforts, so in Mississippi, unlike the Rock Hill experience, Smith had many more protesters around her. Diane Nash, who coordinated the renewed Freedom Rides, did not go to jail in Mississippi.

In a letter dated June 19, 1961, Smith wrote that she was accompanied by "25 female riders" separated by race. In jail, she joked "separate-but-equal" did apply, since "accommodations for all are the same." Through the newspaper, Smith encouraged her hometown to support the protesters, asking that they send "stationery, stamps, and novels to read" and even a "little fruit or candy . . . because so far Atlanta, to my knowledge, has made no contributions." She reported that protesters shared "whatever we get." Smith also passed along what news she had of other Atlantans who were there with her. Conditions in Mississippi were "filthy" and overcrowded, Smith said. At one point she shared a cell for four persons with thirteen other women. Smith quipped that she longed to be back in Rock Hill.[104]

Ruby Doris served a two-month term in the Hinds County jail and in Mississippi's Parchman Penitentiary. Looking through the windows at Parchman, she said, "they could see the men prisoners going out to work in the fields every morning. 'There were fifty, sixty Negro men in striped uniforms, guarded by a white man on a white horse. It reminded you of slavery.'"[105] This sight of Black men in the ubiquitous striped uniforms of Southern work gangs perhaps also reminded Smith of her mother's assisting men escaping chain gangs. Seeing again the relationship of her work to her mother's activism likely affirmed the position she had taken and what she was doing.

After release from prison, Smith worked with SNCC's summer voter registration project in McComb, Mississippi. In this voter registration work, she canvassed door to door trying to get people to register to vote. That summer Smith also participated in Albany, Georgia, demonstrations.[106] In the fall, she attended SNCC's three-week training seminar on social change at Fisk University. This was the same session at which Fannie Lou Hamer first became involved with SNCC after escaping threats to her life in Sunflower County, Mississippi. One argument at the session developed around SNCC's response to youth who threw rocks during demonstrations. Smith said she found it understandable that Blacks would strike back. Moreover, demonstrating the practicality for which she became well known, Smith reminded colleagues that even though nonviolence was a principle of the Movement, many Black people armed themselves.

> "We have to understand this thing seriously, that we represent our community sure enough," she said, "but we only represent a

> small segment of our community when we come to talk about nonviolence, you know. The over-whelming majority of our people are not believing in nonviolence and we know that. So if we are going to make this a mass movement like we say, we have to understand that."[107]

According to former SNCC worker Bernice Johnson Reagon, Smith's comments point to the heart of the incidents and discussion that initiated SNCC's view of "nonviolence as a tactic rather than a way of life, a philosophical difference between their [SNCC's] policies and those of Martin Luther King, Jr."[108]

By the beginning of the school term, Smith, who spent more of her sophomore year demonstrating and working for SNCC than in school, had to reapply for admission to Spelman. Her application for readmission included recommendation letters from Ella Baker, Martin Luther King Jr., John Lewis, and James Forman. The Spelman administration readmitted her, though reluctantly. Perhaps more than any other factor supporting her application was Spelman faculty and administration's prevailing sympathy for her efforts.[109] Spelman officials in general took responsibility for their students, Chaplain Norman Rates said. After the first arrests of Spelman students following the earliest Atlanta University Center protests, the school was contacted and made arrangements to post bail. "'Spelman had a special relationship with the law in Atlanta,' Rates explained. 'Whenever a Spelman girl got into trouble with the law, the institution took responsibility for her.'"[110] In addition to this general support of students, Spelman faculty also supported the cause. Some of the earliest Spelman student protests were led or encouraged by faculty. Other faculty gave special attention to helping students cover work they missed. History professor Clarence A. Bacote particularly remembered supporting Ruby Doris Smith in this way: "When I discovered her sincerity, I decided a young woman like this deserves all of the help you can give her. So, what I did was to have conferences with her. I would give special tutoring. Tell her what she missed and suggesting things she should read."[111]

Spelman's readmission of Smith affirmed her convictions and activism. She withdrew from and returned to school again later; eventually, taking course overloads and with scholarship support from SNCC, the National Council of Negro Women, and the American Baptist Home Mission Societies, Smith continued her activism and graduated in 1965.[112]

Smith continued her relationship with SNCC, and, in keeping with a commitment she made to herself in the Rock Hill jail, she began volunteering to complete needed tasks at SNCC's offices. During the summer of 1962 she worked on SNCC projects in Cairo, Illinois, and in the spring of 1963 she again withdrew from Spelman to work for SNCC full-time. She became a staff member of SNCC as a result of her consistent volunteering at the office. In April of 1963 she coordinated SNCC's third annual conference in Atlanta. Although Smith completed fieldwork in Tennessee, Mississippi, Georgia, and South Carolina, her most significant work for SNCC was in managing programs and general administration. Her formal duties eventually included bookkeeping, personnel management, and coordinating programs of college students working in the South.[113]

By the summer of 1964 Smith's management role was crucial. That year SNCC joined CORE, the SCLC, and the NAACP in the Council of Federated Organizations, which organized the massive voter registration project in Mississippi that became known as Freedom Summer. Large numbers of volunteers were recruited to fan out across Mississippi, going into some of the most rural and isolated places to register Black voters. Because volunteers provided their own livelihood while in Mississippi, it was difficult for Southern Blacks to participate. "Every volunteer was told that he or she must have five hundred dollars," SNCC executive secretary James Forman recalled. Expressing a concern similar to Diane Nash's when she opposed the Kennedy administration's offer to support voter registration drives, Smith felt that Black people should direct the Movement's programs. She "made a concerted drive to recruit some black people from the South, given the limitations of funds," Forman said.

After Freedom Summer, along with Forman, Smith questioned the wisdom of bringing in a large number of new, untrained white volunteers who had not undergone security checks to immediately join SNCC's staff. Smith's concern was intensified, Reagon says, by her apprehension about the organization's "ability to survive under the combined pressure of the influx of white volunteers and the involvement with other civil rights groups in an umbrella organization." Although both Forman and Smith expressed concern to move more slowly, the additional eighty-five persons were added to SNCC's staff.[114]

During Freedom Summer Smith "organized student recruits, met the day-to-day needs of the field staff, and responded to emergencies." She also managed the Sojourner Motor Fleet of cars needed to transport persons in rural areas as part of the registration drive. The Sojourner Motor Fleet, which grew to more than one hundred cars, provided transportation for field-workers and voter registrants across eight states. By summer's end Smith's role had enlarged to include overseeing daily organizational programs, devising and making immediate decisions about policy as the need arose, and continuing to provide support and direction for SNCC field staff after Freedom Summer.[115] She worked with the staff to respond to volunteer applications, often including coordinating housing and eating arrangements, writing, for example, to one Chicago applicant that although SNCC housing was full, the organization would assist with arrangements in the city.[116] At other times Smith corresponded with donors. She thanked them for contributions, added their names to SNCC's mailing list (if they so desired), and encouraged their continued support.[117]

Smith also helped secure resource persons for SNCC training projects. In late 1962 she wrote to a journalist asking for assistance "in the area of communications," saying because of the "vast resources that you possess . . . we know that your knowledge would indeed serve as an asset to our program."[118] Other correspondences from Smith helped coordinate work with students on campuses across the country, and interpreted the nature of SNCC work to potential applicants. Though Smith saw the value of white students to SNCC work, she spoke (and wrote) frankly about safety, strategic issues, and when and where Blacks and whites best served SNCC's overall purposes. In response to a communication seeking a place for white field-workers, Smith wrote:

> In reference to your letter of May 13 . . . there are absolutely no openings to work in SNCC projects in Mississippi for whites. And, only a few Negroes are needed there (special research project for next year).
>
> Also, I would like to point out that most of SNCC's projects are long-range. This means that persons willing to work should thing [*sic*] in terms of at least 6 months to a year. In some areas, it has

> taken this long to really become organized in the community. Thirdly, in most of the areas in which SNCC is now working the presence of whites would serve only as a catalyst for violence and fear among the people. For this reason, openings for white persons are scarce. Such is especially true if they only want to work for a few months. . . . We have an orientation session each year. . . . Field secretaries in a given area have the authority to hire Field Workers who are mostly local people. Once they receive a sufficient amount of sophistication, they become field secretaries. . . .[119]

Smith also interpreted and helped manage SNCC's relationship with other organizations. She wrote on one occasion that because of the perception that the NAACP seemed "resentful toward other organizations coming in to work" it seemed "unwise" for SNCC to move into the community, since "it has been our policy in the past to try and cooperate when possible with other groups and to respect their rights in a given community as long as they kept the program moving."[120] After Freedom Summer Smith joined nine other SNCC staff, including Fannie Lou Hamer, on a trip to Africa sponsored by entertainer Harry Belafonte to help them overcome the exhaustion of the summer's work.

Upon her return from Africa, Smith began urging SNCC to develop relationships with African countries.[121] In 1964 Smith returned to school at Spelman, and in November she married Clifford Robinson, a mechanic for SNCC's Sojourner Motor Fleet. The couple had one son, Kenneth Toure, named after Sékou Touré, the President of Guinea, which Ruby Doris had visited in 1964.[122]

By this time Ruby Doris Smith Robinson had become a nucleus around which much of SNCC's activity revolved. "Ruby Doris dominated SNCC," recalled former SNCC staff person Joyce Ladner. "We'd have a little joke, is it Jim [Forman, SNCC's executive secretary] running SNCC or Ruby Doris?"[123] No woman ever chaired SNCC, but Robinson did succeed Forman as executive secretary several years after Freedom Summer, as SNCC was entering its decline.

From early on in SNCC's most active work, Robinson was an influential and respected staff member. A part of her influence derived directly from the pivotal role she played during Freedom Summer and beyond as the primary connection between field staff and SNCC, which was in some sense the main link between field staff and the outside world. Former SNCC worker Judy Richardson declared that Robinson "really was their lifeline if they were in the field. They would talk to Ruby more than they would talk to Foreman [*sic*]. If they needed something, I think the sense was . . . Foreman was essential to the organization, but he was not necessarily the field person. Ruby was the field person; Ruby was the organizer, a field kind of organizer." Consequently, Richardson said, "when Ruby Doris spoke, people listened. . . . The guys had a great, great deal of respect for . . . Ruby Doris."[124] Robinson's significant role in SNCC likely did not derive from her position at all: she originally joined SNCC's staff as an administrative assistant. Her influence, then, came from the way she took charge of circumstances and opportunities as she sought to ensure the organization's viability. Often this meant improvising as she addressed personnel and interpersonal issues. Another former SNCC staff member, Jean Wheeler Smith, commented that "everybody had incredible respect" for Ruby Doris, who "seemed to run the place." She recalled Ruby Doris once taking her to task for wasting time:

> One day I was sitting around the office in Atlanta, I think I was drinking Cokes and flirting or something, and Ruby came over to me and said, "Get up and go get your license. If you want to go"—I wanted to go to some project—"you can't expect someone's going to drive you there," so it was Ruby who made me go get a license.[125]

Ruby Doris once identified herself as a kind of bookkeeper. "In this organization I'm sort of the coordinator of finances. I decide what we can spend for what and usually I have to tell them that we can't afford it no matter what it is!"[126] While coordinating finances was among the tasks to which she attended, Robinson, like Ella Baker, carved out and cultivated a role for herself as manager of an organization that left an important mark on the evolution of the Civil Rights Movement. Forman, who "supervised" Robinson in that role, described her as his coworker whose contributions were invaluable.

> Ruby and I worked very closely and she was enormously efficient, hard-working, committed. But Ruby was far more, both to me and to the organization, than just a vital prop in the administrative structure. She had brilliant ideas—ideas always more

> advanced than those of many others in SNCC. Her political perceptions and understanding of people were amazingly sharp. She acted as a mentor of mine in many ways. SNCC staff members became angered by Ruby's actions sometimes; she often had to make unpopular decisions about paychecks, cars, and other resources, and stick to them.[127]

Although Robinson wielded considerable power in the organization, for the majority of her tenure with SNCC that power did not relate to her formal position. Moreover, while several other women held relatively important roles as leaders of SNCC field projects (leading in much higher percentages than in any other civil rights organization), gender continued to be a factor that limited women's possibilities within SNCC. During Freedom Summer Robinson led a women's group in discussing the movement's failure to achieve gender equality, and she participated with a group of women who conducted a sit-in of Forman's office to protest the limitations placed on women's roles in SNCC.[128] Although Forman was himself a target of that sit-in, he also observed that Robinson sometimes "endured vicious attacks" as she tried to develop more structure in SNCC operations. Some people who attacked Robinson "embodied male chauvinism in fighting her attempts as executive secretary to impose a sense of organizational responsibility and self-discipline, trying to justify themselves by the fact that their critic was a woman."[129]

Robinson's actions within SNCC showed clearly that she was opposed to limiting people's responsibilities and roles on the basis of gender. At a Waveland, Mississippi, retreat in November following Freedom Summer, SNCC staff considered various position papers written in advance to help focus discussions on issues central to continuing social change.[130] One paper submitted by an anonymous person (or persons) focused on the role of women in the Movement. Robinson, who by this time wielded weighty influence, ensured that the paper receive attention by presenting it herself. This paper, titled "Women in the Movement," is generally, and likely accurately, attributed to a group of white women. It has become a source of some tension since historians and feminists have identified it as an important document of the women's movement. That Robinson's role as a leader of women's challenges to male dominance in SNCC predated the paper is not disputed. Tension and some confusion arise from failure to communicate the evolution of the paper as a statement by white women reflecting their disenfranchisement from leadership in white groups like the Southern Students Organizing Committee (SSOC) and Students for a Democratic Society (SDS), the tradition of Black women's serving more prominently in available leadership opportunities in SNCC, and the then current and heated debate about expelling all whites from SNCC. Although Robinson affirmed the paper and supported its implications by reading it at SNCC's Waveland meeting, the feminist literary history of the document belies the reason that it originated, as Casey Haden recalls, from a group that was "white and related to Literacy House conversations about women . . . [who] were all white." The paper reflects the quite potent and emotional concern of these women, many of whom were outcasts from white society because of their affiliation with SNCC and the Civil Rights Movement. Unfortunately, what evolved in the paper was the initial concern of this group for the role of "[white] women in the Movement," as, with both the expelling of white workers and the demise of SNCC, they saw the world and the work for which they had made sacrifices begin both to erode and to exclude them.[131]

Black women's leadership in SNCC was more frequent and pronounced than that of white women. This accounts for some tension about the paper and around the role of women in SNCC. Another source of tension was the sexual interactions of white women and Black men arising in the intense interracial collaboration of SNCC's work. Yet another source of tension was the increased questioning among some more recent African American SNCC workers of whites' participation in the organization. White women in SNCC shared concerns about gender with Robinson and other Black women; however, the rise of discussions about women's roles within SNCC and within the Civil Rights Movement occurred alongside increased assertions of Black pride, which eventually evolved into concern for sociostructural change. This change was invoked, among other ways, by the slogan "Black Power." As tensions evolved within SNCC around the role of white people in the movement, white women who expressed concerns about gender restrictions reflected the narrowing of their participation that resulted from racial tensions as well. This may account for some white feminists' depictions of

Robinson as opposed to women's issues; these depictions neglect early perspectives she asserted on gender discrimination and overlook her main commitment to the development of SNCC as a vehicle for changing the circumstances of all African Americans.[132] On the other hand, attempts to determine in Robinson's gender concerns complete congruity with concerns raised by white women overlook the significant factor that Robinson's role and perspective as a Black woman leader in SNCC was not compromised by concerns about race as were white women's, notwithstanding the patriarchy evident in the organization.

Robinson, who supported the Black Power slogan as a rallying cry of the Black masses for significant social change,[133] saw as the signal issue the development of leaders of either gender to enhance SNCC's work. Responding to a query about women's work in SNCC in a 1966 interview, Robinson said, "'Of people in the field, about 20 percent are women,'" but, pointing to her concern above all things that SNCC's work on behalf of Black people continue and grow, she asserted that "'we need more *people,* not necessarily men or women.'"[134]

In observations about gender not directly related to interactions within SNCC, Robinson contended with the complications of negotiating marriage, a career, and motherhood. With some regret about the need for her mother to attend her son, Robinson said,

> I know what it suggests when I say that my mother is keeping him while my husband and I work—that we're living the same old matriarchal style. But nowadays all these grandmothers can say that they're bringing up their grandchildren so the parents can work in the Movement and it sounds better. . . . Well, I've found out that there's no answer, really, for a woman who works in a career and has children. Like, my baby knows who his mother is, I think, but it's his grandmother who's giving him the food and that means something very special. He's getting more of her . . . nature than he is of mine.[135]

She identified the legacy of racism that sometimes presented Black women opportunities not available to Black men, echoing Victoria DeLee and expressing in some measure a traditional perspective about male leadership. In discussing options, particularly in employment, that determined Black women's roles as providers for their families,

Robinson related civil rights activism to changes needed to overcome imbalances that sometimes made Black women's income opportunities primary to Black family survival. Referring to circumstances like those of Clara Muhammad's early adult life, Robinson said:

> In the past, Negro women had to assert themselves so the family could survive. . . . Fortunately, more men are becoming involved with the movement and the day might come when women aren't needed for this type of work. But I don't believe the Negro man will be able to assume his full role until the struggle has progressed to a point that can't even be foreseen—maybe in the next century or so.[136]

Robinson's apparent regret that the situation existed reflected what seems to be a contradiction. (Her choices can be compared to those of Clara Muhammad, who made significant contributions to the Nation of Islam before taking the less visible role of first lady.) In view of normative gender perspectives during the 1960s when she was an activist and the 1940s and 1950s when she was growing up, however, Robinson's perspective fit what was common in social life.

On May 16, 1966, Ruby Doris Smith Robinson was elected to succeed James Forman as executive secretary of SNCC. In this achievement, she ascended to the highest formal position of any woman in a major civil rights organization. Twenty-four-year-old Robinson had worked with SNCC for more than five years. She was well respected and had proven herself a steady and effective leader.[137] Unfortunately, as she rose to the post, SNCC as an organization and civil rights activism as a social movement were beginning to fall apart. In June after her election, Robinson joined many other SNCC staff in supporting the emergence of the Black Power slogan.[138] The rise of the cry for Black Power became a difficulty for SNCC, however.

On the one hand, Black Power made SNCC the target of federal inquiry. By November 1966 it was being investigated for tax evasion by the Internal Revenue Service. Robinson was in the thick of this investigation, which many in SNCC perceived as harassment. Forman said that through Robinson's correspondences with the IRS, SNCC "indicated in many letters, SNCC was willing to pay any taxes it might legitimately owe." Forman recalled being

> with Ruby Doris Robinson on several occasions when she had confrontations with the bureau [of Internal Revenue], and,

> together, we argued that we would give them our records of receipts and disbursements—we were willing to cooperate to that extent, although we knew that the whole investigation was part of a harassment campaign—but we would not turn over any information concerning our donors.[139]

As a result of the popularity of the Black Power slogan, SNCC apparently became a suspicious organization to the IRS.

On the other hand, the slogan, which struck a chord with the Black masses, signaled within SNCC the culmination of the debate that had unfolded both about the role of whites in the Movement and about the nature of SNCC as an organization. Concerns about the role of whites in the Black struggle had been brewing for several years, as questions emerged about deference toward whites, paternalism, and autonomous formation of African American leaders. Moreover, there was developing among some of SNCC's new leaders and workers a shift away from its original character of identifying with and empowering local people and toward separation from local communities and identifying as a kind of pacesetter group.[140] Forman said this derived from class conflict motivated by "middle-class, egoistic individualism."[141]

Perhaps exacerbated by the IRS investigation, both internal tensions reached their peak at the December 1966 SNCC staff retreat in upstate New York. At that retreat in a close vote, SNCC decided to expel whites from decision-making capacities in the organization. Moreover, the undercurrent opposition to the leadership and even participation by local people fully surfaced. During the meeting, Forman wrote, some "Black staffers were making such comments as 'Mrs. Hamer is no longer relevant' or 'Mrs. Hamer isn't at our level of development.'"[142] Different perspectives among Black SNCC staffers about the place of whites in the Movement reflected something of an "old" versus "new" split, as did the perspective about the significance of local people.

As a longtime member of SNCC, Robinson remained committed to the organization's original character as a group seeking to empower local people by working in solidarity with them. As early as 1964 she had made clear her understanding of SNCC's role as one that should focus on "blacks concerned 'with the basic necessities of life,'" which, she said, meant SNCC should determine creative ways to make "'basic changes in the power structure'" to the advantage of poor Black people. Robinson kept concerns for local people before SNCC's decision-making body. At an April 1965 SNCC Executive Committee meeting in Holly Springs, Mississippi, Robinson reported that community workers in Cambridge, Maryland, were concerned that SNCC volunteers were beginning to "stifle community growth." Her pointing out the concern resulted in a determination to "investigate all problems and spend time doing work on the matter." At the same meeting, Robinson changed the venue of SNCC workshops scheduled for Washington, D.C. SNCC should "have people come to [the] south for workshops," Robinson said, because of the "convenience for local people."[143] Robinson maintained this focus on local people as a priority throughout her work with SNCC. Biographer Fleming writes that "one of her main interests was helping local people in Deep South areas who were faced with economic reprisals because of their assistance to SNCC field staff operating in their communities. . . . She knew that they were the backbone of the struggle, and she was determined to help them." One of the ways Robinson did this was to help coordinate and distribute donations SNCC solicited.[144]

Robinson's pragmatism determined her position on white staff in SNCC. While she supported the Black Power slogan and Black nationalist position, by this time, as one of the longest tenured members of SNCC who had worked with white staff throughout that period, Robinson had developed a perspective that one coworker said "'wasn't anti-white, [but] was pro-black.'"[145] She did go through a time of an intense adversarial position on whites, especially white women, as she sorted through the complications that resulted from initial intimidation of local Black folk by whites, concerns she had about developing Black leadership, and complications in personnel and interpersonal relations deriving from sexual relations between Black men and white women. However, Robinson said, this changed, when "I realized what I was doing to myself. I was losing my self-respect and even losing my looks. I finally had to work myself out of it. I had to find a new sense of my own dignity, and what I really had to do was start *seeing* all over again, in a new way. . . . That's one thing Negroes are trying to do now—to *see* differently. That's hard!"[146] Moreover, Robinson's pragmatism and her focus on making a meaningful difference in all people's lives made her critical of SNCC staffers who focused on the Black/white question to the neglect of substantial programming. One SNCC Atlanta office colleague said that "Robinson 'maintained a strong nationalist line' but insisted that staff members demonstrate a willingness to work rather than 'sit around talking about white people.'"[147]

Robinson's concern for local people and for SNCC's program and character and her practical approach to the issue of white participation in SNCC are also reflected in her position on unilateral public statements made by then current SNCC chairperson Stokely Carmichael (a.k.a. Kwame Toure), who has often been seen as the architect of the Black Power slogan. "At one point," James Forman writes, "Ruby Doris Robinson introduced a motion to silence him for six months; she felt that his statements favoring armed struggle and other violent acts brought down too much heat on the field organizers and general repression on black people. Ruby Doris believed we should organize quietly for armed struggle rather than preach it constantly and openly. But this motion was tabled after much discussion."[148] The acrimonious battle at the New York retreat ended by limiting white participation and altering SNCC's character. About a month later, in January 1967, while on a fundraising trip back in New York, Robinson fell ill. She was eventually diagnosed with terminal cancer and died on October 7.

Robinson's Religious and Moral Perspectives

Religious and moral perspectives shaped in Robinson's childhood appear to have pervaded her activism and standpoint throughout her civil rights work. Early in life she demonstrated sensitivity for the most vulnerable. The example set by Robinson's mother, which she recalled as influencing her, and Robinson's friendship with Brenda Jefferson both point to this concern for the weak as an important value since her youth. In addition, as a college student entering the Civil Rights Movement, Robinson asserted convictions that coincided with her own Christian upbringing and with the general tenor of the early Civil Rights Movement. "I feel that segregation is basically a moral problem," Robinson said, "and for this reason, I feel that Church is one institution where the problem can be 'thrashed out.'" Moreover, she counted on nonviolent protests to stir the minds and "appeal to the consciences of Christians."[149] Like Diane Nash, Robinson also used explicitly religious language to characterize segregation, saying it was an "evil" system that Christians must oppose. As Robinson's early activism proceeded, she continued to express belief in the need for moral persuasion through nonviolent protests, and she began to articulate the position that her activism was a part of the work that she must do. In a letter to Brenda Jefferson from jail in Rock Hill, Robinson wrote:

> I feel, however, that because of my convictions this is the only thing that I could do. I know that this sacrifice is small when compared with the cause which motivated me to do it. I also realize that this is the only way that one can truly express the philosophy of non-violence—the willingness to suffer and accept the punishment of society rather than obey the evil of a system like segregation.[150]

Perhaps these early assertions by Robinson express an idealism that corresponded with her youth. Biographer Fleming writes that as she was dying of cancer, Robinson returned to her religious roots, requesting her sisters to "sing Christian songs for her" and "to read the Psalms to her, along with some of the other scriptures."[151] As Robinson's encounters as an activist increased and her own more mature perspectives unfolded, however, she used explicitly religious language less frequently, but continued her moral opposition to the system of segregation that disenfranchised African Americans with religious fervor. Moreover, according to Reagon's assertion, Robinson's perspective evolved to consider nonviolence as a tactic rather than a philosophy.

As she matured as an activist, Robinson spoke in more political language and began to develop an economic analysis of the circumstances of African Americans. In spite of her changing language and analysis, however, throughout Robinson's short life, the value that remained consistent was her concern for the weak and vulnerable. She saw this in SNCC's early character and remained faithful to it. Examples of this concern are evident throughout Robinson's work with SNCC. One of the earliest is her 1964 opposition to enlarging the SNCC staff. At the October 1964 staff meeting after Freedom Summer, when many volunteers wanted to stay in the South and work for SNCC, Forman and Robinson opposed the tremendous push to include them. Their opposition was based on an understanding of SNCC's commitment to empowering local, rural, often uneducated people. As Forman later recalled, the conflict at the meeting was part of

> a fundamental struggle . . . to shift the power of decision making in SNCC from a rural, Southern, black base to a Northern, middle-class, interracial base. That shift received a momentous boost when the October, 1964, staff meeting voted to put an additional eighty-five persons on staff—most of them middle-class and Northern, many of them white.
>
> This proposal was made at the meeting by a number of staff members for various reasons, including the need they felt for more personnel on their projects with certain kinds of "technical and linguistic skills."

This focus on "technical and linguistic skills" was obviously contradictory to the practices of empowering local rural Black people. Many of these people, though tremendously gifted, were poor, illiterate, and untrained. This movement that Forman identifies as a "fundamental" shift signaled a turn toward the traditional perspective about locals as unworthy of significant attention and even expendable. The irony of this position is that it represented the pervasive attitude that Black people, particularly in the South, sought to overcome and transform through civil rights participation. Among other things this was a stark departure from what had been considered a primary goal of SNCC—empowering local people. "Ruby Doris Robinson and I led the fight against the proposal to put the eighty-five people on staff," Forman says. Unfortunately, their position lost.[152]

Robinson in some sense may be said to have sought to maintain a connection between the original character of SNCC and its later development and work. She expressed a continuing concern for being in solidarity with local people as a means of improving the lives of Black people generally in the United States. Similar to Ella Baker, she thought enhancing the lives and capacities of the most marginalized people was the means of determining positive social change. Robinson's persistent commitment to the most oppressed, Forman wrote, characterized her as "one of the few genuine revolutionaries in the black liberation movement."[153]

Nash and Robinson: Young Visionary Activists

Diane Nash and Ruby Doris Smith Robinson made similar contributions to the Civil Rights Movement. Both women were forerunners in the wave of student participation that gave the Movement a significant shot in the arm. Both helped determine the principles guiding SNCC's activity. In this latter contribution, one may be said to have built on the other. In this regard, their contributions, though integrally related, were different. Nash was present from the original organizing meeting for SNCC and its early days of trying to create and actualize an identity. In addition, Nash helped determine several of SNCC's early programmatic activities and even sought to secure direct action as a permanent aspect of SNCC's programs. Robinson, who was a participant in SNCC's early protests, became involved in programming but eventually became most important because of her work within the administration. Just as Nash was clearly committed to the need for direct action, Robinson clearly saw as essential securing the administrative and interpersonal infrastructure of the organization. Both were concerned about egalitarianism among SNCC workers as well as in society. Both sought to carry the Movement to the masses and acted to do so with intensity. While Nash helped form SNCC's identity in its initial organizational stages, Robinson sought to safeguard this identity as SNCC matured. One distinction between the two women may be the evolution of their roles in the Movement. While Nash persisted in activism after marriage and the birth of her children, for a time her role waned because of her husband's activism and her domestic responsibilities. On the other hand, Robinson also married and became a mother, but her role in the Movement evolved in a manner similar to that of Ella Baker and Septima Clark, continuing at a level of intensity throughout her short life. While many religious women activists took charge of situations around them in order to attend to issues confronting their communities, Robinson, similar to Baker and Clark before her, made community activism her professional career. As did Clark and Baker, Robinson completed invaluable volunteer work that eventually evolved into paid employment with a major civil rights organization. In this regard, Robinson followed her foremothers, especially Baker, in self-consciously carving out and cultivating a role for herself in the Movement. Though their positions were circumscribed by gender perspectives of the era, each ultimately held formal leadership positions in civil rights organizations: Ella Baker was Director of Branches for the NAACP and then served as Acting Executive Director of the SCLC; Septima Clark was Director of Workshops for the Highlander Folk School and later became Director of Education for the SCLC; and, finally, Ruby Doris Smith Robinson initially was Office Administrator and Personnel Director of SNCC until she was named Executive Secretary, the highest post any woman held in a major civil rights organization.

As younger activists who benefited from the accomplishments of people before them, Diane Nash and Ruby Doris Smith Robinson envisioned profound changes in the quality of Black life. Both women worked with a kind of fervor—and perhaps abandon—that helped secure the significance of SNCC as a civil rights organization and, more important, made SNCC an agent that factored significantly in bringing about 1960s social change.

6

Testimony, Witness, and Civic Life

The Meaning of Black Women's Civil Rights Participation

Testifying and Witnessing

Thousands of Black women became involved in civil rights activism as a means of continuing their ordinary efforts to live faithfully. Their civil rights work reflected everyday practices of witnessing and testifying through which they brought their religious faith and devotion into public life. The ease with which many women understood civil rights practices as extensions of their religious practice often meant they did not consider questions about appropriate relations of religion and politics that frequently encumber religious people considering engagement in public life. For these women the question was not whether but how they should testify about and witness to their faith in meaningful ways.

Both testifying and witnessing presuppose an encounter with God—the former issuing as speaking about God's work and the latter reflecting behavioral response to God's activity and presence. As conventional practices of some Black religious traditions in the United States, testimony may be understood as preceding witness. Testimony occurs because one, in the vernacular of the tradition, "has to tell somebody." The speech about what God has done arises from the power of an encounter with God that makes it impossible "to keep it to myself." Subsequent to the encounter motivating testimony as speech is the expectation of living in ways that reflect having had the encounter—adjusting or changing one's behavior. As Ella Baker said, for example, "I took the position that you were supposed to change after baptism." Consequently, she tried "to control my temper. I had a high temper. . . . And so this was my way of demonstrating my change, by trying to control my temper."[1] Victoria DeLee also asserted a compulsion to change following her powerful encounter with the divine through preaching. Recalling the event, she said that she "had . . . planned on killin' . . . some white people just like they had kill all them Black people. . . . And when that preacher preached that sermon that Sunday, I got converted to myself right in that church, right there."[2] After consultation with her grandmother, who advised DeLee to seek forgiveness and to "love the white people," DeLee prayed for a change of heart "to love white folks."[3] The changes to which Baker and DeLee refer indicate both an inner disposition and an outer practice that correlate testimony (telling about an encounter with God) and witness (living in ways that reflect one's encounter with God).

In the correlation of testimony and witness with Black religious women's civil rights activism is connection of the faith claim—that one has had an encounter with God—to practical activity. The assertion of having an encounter with God—generally understood as an internal personal experience—coincides with the Christian conception of God's spirit being active within a person. The speech of testimony (claiming experience of such an encounter through speech) and the activity of witness also affirm the concept of divine presence within people, asserting that God within a person makes a difference in what she does when she brings the God within to bear on how she interprets, understands, and relates to the world around her. Moreover, assertion of a divine presence within that inspires an external witness presupposes an internal locus of authority giving direction and courage to confront what may even seem to be insurmountable challenges, anticipating that God will "make a way out of no way."

For women of this tradition, the encounter about which testimony occurs and that arouses witness inspires more than simple personally pious acts of controlling one's temper or not hating one's enemies. Practices of personal piety are only a beginning. Real witness occurs in how one persistently lives in relating to others and to structures in social life, including how one uses one's agency to help those in greatest need. This may more properly be understood as a spirituality rather than a personal piety, when spirituality is understood as a way of responding to divine encounter by living in ways that affirm one's understanding of divine norms and by living in opposition to practices that challenge or are in conflict with those norms. In contexts like that of the Civil Rights Era where socio-cultural conventions and traditions ordinarily opposed flourishing for African Americans, spirituality as a way of life meant living against the grain, living in conflict with and as a challenge to the status quo. Here, spirituality is understood as a way of life, whereas personal piety relates more to religious ritual. While piety as a means of facilitating encounter and relationship with the divine generally is understood as essential to theistic spirituality, piety may also be understood as the whole of religious practice with no meaning for social life. This contrasts with assertion of spirituality as ordinarily relating to other persons and to the world in particular ways.

In addition to changes in their personal lives, these women assert that having an encounter with God means making a connection between their professions of faith and what they do every day. That is to say, being faithful means living in ways that bring the meaning of professions of faith into systems, institutions, and conventions of social life. Recalling as an adult practices taught to her during childhood, Ella Baker said her life's work reflected what she understood as the "Christian concept of sharing with others. . . . Then, there were people who 'stood for something,' as I call it. Your relationship to human beings was more important than your relationship to the amount of money that you made."[4] Like Baker, Septima Clark—who some may certainly characterize as a pious individual and as a church-oriented woman—also saw being a Christian as more than personal piety. In addition to practices of religious devotion, Clark sought to change social life through her citizenship education work, which she also declared was her effort to "possess and . . . attain . . . the spirit of" Jesus by "striving with every energy, working . . . in the true spirit of fellowship to lift [the unfortunate] to a higher level of attainment and appreciation and enjoyment of life."[5] Fannie Lou Hamer concurred with this emphasis on relating to others and to social life, asserting that "we can't separate Christ from freedom and freedom from Christ. The first words of Jesus' public ministry was Luke 4:18, where freedom is the central theme. . . . We serve God by serving our fellow man."[6] Similarly, Victoria DeLee said that in her activism she was responding to what she felt was God calling her to "help those who can't help themselves."[7] Many women student activists, no less than the older adults, also affirmed engaging and embodying faith. Reflecting on the sit-ins and Freedom Rides, Diane Nash wrote that the "nonviolent movement (1) is based upon and motivated by love; (2) attempts to serve God and mankind; (3) strives toward what we call the beloved community. This is religion. This is applied religion." Asserting that the work of the Civil Rights Movement was religious, Nash said, "I think it is the work of our Church."[8] Explaining her own participation in sit-ins and kneel-ins, Ruby Doris Smith observed "that segregation is basically a moral problem, and for this reason, I feel that Church is one institution where the problem can be 'thrashed out.'" Moreover, Smith felt such Christian religious practice should be universal and said she counted on nonviolent protests to stir the minds and "appeal to the consciences of Christians."[9] In another religious tradition, Clara Muhammad also asserted that in her practice of Islam she was responding to God's call to help her "brothers and sisters here in the wilderness of North America." Presenting her belief that God calls people to respond to problems, Muhammad continued, "Allah has asked us, in His holy words, to help solve this problem: I know we can help because Allah would not have asked this of us if it wasn't possible to do."[10] All these women both lived with conviction and lived out convictions that derived from their self-understanding as religious persons. Those convictions were values they held and a related vision of social life that they sought to bring into existence through their practices as civil rights participants.

Values and Virtues: Models and Practices in Black Religious Women's Activism

Practices in these women's lives reflected values they held and their vision for society. Though the specific practices they undertook to realize their vision differed, they shared several values that they sought to bring to common social life. Consonance of the women's values may be attributable to their participation in Black religious traditions of racial uplift and social responsibility. Seeking to overcome ongoing distresses in Black life deriving from racism and attempting to alter society's formal and conventional sources of distress particularly, but not only in Black life, these seven women affirmed Black religious values of survival, freedom, and universal human flourishing. Although they shared values and held a common vision, the women engaged different contexts and practices. For example, Baker and Clark's education levels and previous work experience contributed to their relatively settled lifestyles during the Civil Rights Era, presenting them more opportunity to consider patient, deliberate behind-the-scenes[11] action. DeLee, Hamer, and Muhammad lived in contexts of difficulty and desperation, in which there was urgency to act, precipitating their front-line activism. As college students Nash and Robinson did not have settled lifestyles, careers, or even many years of experience. This allowed their fervent engagement with Civil Rights Movement issues, including the impatient intensity of their work. Based on their social locations, including but not limited to their ages, education levels, economic situations, and primary vocations, the women undertook means and practices appropriate and available to them as they sought to live out shared values and to realize a common social vision.

Three values all of these women shared were the importance of human mutuality, the necessity of responding to the most marginalized, and the multidimensional requirement of responsibility. Most of them asserted the importance of human mutuality, since their work to overcome subordination of African Americans related directly to this value. For Baker, mutuality meant persons respecting and recognizing each other as human beings through equal treatment. Pointing out the natural expectation of mutuality and pointing to the disposition on which she sought to build in her organizing work, Baker said, "No human being relishes being spit upon like an animal. . . . Natural resistance is already there."[12] Baker's perspective on mutuality motivated her lifelong work to help people develop the means of acting on their own behalf to improve their situations in life. Hamer and DeLee asserted the value of human mutuality through the urgency with which they acted in seeking to defeat extreme injustices of Southern rural farming and sharecropping communities. Both Hamer and DeLee began their activism as a means of overcoming persistent and severe subordination they and their communities faced. "We had wondered," Hamer said, as she recalled students' practices of treating rural Southern Blacks as equals and with dignity, "if there was anybody human enough to see us as human beings instead of animals."[13] The significance of human mutuality as a value she sought to realize was perhaps most fully articulated by Diane Nash. "I believe that when men come to believe in their own dignity and in the worth of their own freedom," she said, "and when they can acknowledge God and the dignity that is within every man, then Berlin and Jackson will not be problems." Nash held that mutuality not only meant reciprocal recognition of persons, but also induced integrity in relationship, since the lack of mutuality in the system of segregation "fosters dishonesty between the races [and] makes people lie to each other."[14] Although the assertion of human mutuality was a basic component of national creeds, the predominant absence of practices of mutuality in interpersonal and social relationships of Blacks and whites made assertion and affirmation of this value essential in each of these women's work.

The necessity of responding to the most marginalized related intrinsically to the value of human mutuality. Because the absence of human mutuality is most fully experienced by and most intensely affects those persons for whom the benefits of social life are remote, the women asserted that responding to the most marginalized was necessary to affirming the value of human mutuality. Baker's emphasis on organizing was the means by which she sought to empower local people—those most easily oppressed or ignored by social norms—to take charge of their own lives and thereby wrest or elicit respect. "The major job," Baker said of her organizing work, "was getting people to understand that they had something within their power that they could use, and it could only be used if they understood what was happening and how group action could counter" oppression.[15] Clark saw attending to the least fortunate as Christian duty and as the logical means of ameliorating the quality of life in the entire society.

> I am convinced that the advancement of our lowly ones to the opportunities of first class citizenship also will lift to a better life those who now enjoy a higher status.[16]

> Christians can never be content with token progress by a fortunate few. They must continually remain sensitive to the will of God for the redemption of 'the saints of rank and file. . . .' The Citizenship Education Program is attempting to provide an opportunity for these people to help themselves and their neighbors.[17]

For Muhammad, Hamer, and DeLee, who acutely experienced rural and urban poverty, racial violence, and oppression firsthand, the necessity of responding to the most marginalized initially emerged as attending to their own distressed communities through determined and urgent responses to survive and thrive in "the wilderness of North America," "see that things were changed," and "fix it" for their communities. Among student civil rights participants, Robinson sought to keep alive the emphasis on responding to the most marginalized as she consistently advocated that SNCC employ mostly local people. Robinson maintained this value even as her own life and the life of SNCC waned. By that time it meant many in SNCC viewed her as out of step with the organization's evolution.

Encouraging a form of civic responsibility that fosters reciprocity and egalitarianism, these women asserted the perspective that individuals in more favorable social positions have a responsibility to help elevate those in least favored positions. Their notion of responsibility was multidimensional, however. On the one hand, through their work and words, they pointed to the need for those who were able to attend to the "least." On the other hand, they also maintained that all people shared responsibility for improving society through their own actions and agency. For Baker, this meant individuals should use their inherent resources to alter circumstances in their lives. "My basic sense of it," she said, "has always been to get people to understand that in the long run they themselves are the only protection they have against violence or injustice. . . . People have to be made to understand that they cannot look for salvation anywhere but to themselves."[18] In a similar vein, while Clark worked to equip local leaders who could instruct others in citizenship education, she also argued that people who would benefit from the program should be agents of their own improvement by taking actions to ensure that they are "advancing themselves through study of the ABC's of learning."[19] Both Baker and Clark advocated helping people to help themselves and emphasized developing local leaders to do this. As leaders, initially in their local communities, Hamer and DeLee promoted the idea of individuals' responsibility in their own actions as agents. "God wants us to take a stand," Hamer once said. "We can stand by registering to vote—go to the court to register to vote."[20] Nash also emphasized multidimensional responsibility. Arguing that love was the motive of civil rights activities, Nash said that for those seeking to overcome the problems of racial subordination, taking responsibility means "that rather than doing harm to the oppressor, another way to go is to identify your part in your own oppression, and then withdraw your cooperation from the system of oppression." Taking on this responsibility is empowering since, "when you do identify your own responsibility in an oppressive situation, then it puts you in a position of power. Because then you are able to withdraw your participation and therefore end the system."[21]

Identifying these three values evident in Black religious women's civil rights activism is an initial stage in analyzing and theorizing about their work. Theories and analyses serve useful purposes when they give back to communities accurate interpretations and reflections that enable refinement, clarification, and extensions of their practices. If we recall the characterizations of Black religious women's thought and activism by four womanist theologians, it is possible to determine the resonance of their conceptions with what these seven women did and said. Katie Cannon says Black women's morality reflects practice of and passing on particular virtues to ensure physical and emotional survival, human dignity, and fullness of life. Delores Williams explicates Black religious women's collaboration with God to determine survival/quality-of-life practice. Jacquelyn Grant argues that Black women's religious hope calls them to develop survival strategies and to attend to needs of the least. Cheryl Townsend Gilkes asserts that Black religious women's community activism reflects attention to community-building and community-sustaining work. The resonance of these scholars' analyses with Black religious women's activism lifts up the significance of their and others' work for society and potentially extends the women's practices by identifying their importance to Black communities and the wider society.

As participants in the tradition of Black religious women's activism, these women's civil rights work, like the activity of their predecessors, changed moral societal norms. One aspect of the moral import of their work is the legacy of character traits they carried as they conducted their civil rights activism. Such character traits often are referred to as virtues because they emerge as exceptional features of personality for which individuals are admired and respected and, more importantly, through which people contribute to the common good. Emerging in what Delores Williams calls a "wilderness" context and arising as what Cannon calls "coping mechanisms related to their own cultural circumstances," virtues of these Black religious women activists evolved as appropriate responses to their interpretations of divine guidance to help people survive systems of oppression and experience freedom and flourishing in their everyday lives.[22] Three virtues they embodied were innovation, taking charge, and hope.

As a personality trait that contributes to the common good, innovation emerged as the impetus to create new practices, organizations, and systems; to improvise; and to act in ways that were appropriate to conditions the women encountered to realize values they held. Sometimes innovation unfolded as a necessary response to exclusion from existing channels of social participation. At other times innovation issued as imagining and creating appropriate means to realize in social life values the women held. Baker's emphasis on organizing and Clark's development of the citizenship education program are examples of innovation wherein they conceived and established structures and systems to respond to immediate goals and to pass on possibilities beyond the immediate context. Robinson's work developing and attending to the day-to-day structure of SNCC also was innovative as she entered the life of a fledgling organization and helped secure it by devising and establishing systems of practice to sustain it. Nash's continuation of the Freedom Rides and Hamer's and DeLee's taking on the role and responsibility of leaders all included improvisation while promoting their visions for social life. Muhammad's work is shot through with innovation as she cofounded and helped organize and build the Nation of Islam. Not only did she help create an organization, new practices, and systems of thought but she also left Christianity, re-created herself as a Muslim woman, and helped thousands of others to imagine the world differently and convert to Islam as a response to difficulties of being Black in the United States.

Another constant in these women's lives was taking charge of their lives and contexts. That is to say, frequently these women reasoned and acted outside traditional boundaries as they determined the means to direct the vitalities of the Movement toward particular ends. This included living out a faith they had made their own and not becoming discouraged, overwhelmed, or doubtful when religious institutions or leaders failed. They also improvised, built on, and broke with religious traditions when necessary. In most instances their taking charge resulted from the necessity of determining how to move beyond the predominant and repressive social policies and conventions as they sought to change society. They reinterpreted religious traditions cleverly, imaginatively, and resourcefully, including bringing accessible and practical interpretations to Scripture. They all promoted lively, engaged interaction with religious traditions that broke with static and unfruitful practices of much of church life, determining with Hamer that "if I had to choose today between the church and these young people—and I was brought up in the church and I'm not against the church—I'd choose these young people."[23] In looking at the work of students who came to Mississippi as the work of Christian love, Hamer asserted that practices of Christianity are not limited to religious institutions and in fact go beyond them. By engaging in those practices as an indigenous local leader, Hamer took charge of her own life and influenced the perspectives and actions of others.

In other instances taking charge entailed going against the norms associated with persons, especially other women, from similar social locations. These women activists recognized the status of African Americans as legislatively and conventionally subjugated people in U.S. society and confronted their own diminished status as women within U.S. society and Black religious culture. While their practices of witness emerged in the context of subjugation, they did not succumb to an identity of victimization. In fact, through faith they felt empowered to transform their immediate contexts and society beyond their geographically proximate communities. As a schoolteacher, Clark's unorthodox method of using local language, ideas, and objects empowered and affirmed her students and accomplished the objective of enabling literacy. Moreover, Clark did not conform to expected behavior of doing only what she was told. She thought for herself and decided to act against strictures others tried to place on her. Neither Clark nor Baker fit easily into expected norms of women of their era, since both were single for most of their lives, traveled extensively, and confidently took charge of major aspects of the Civil Rights Movement. As sharecroppers and rural women with limited literacy, Hamer and DeLee used wit to break outside and move far beyond traditional life experiences of their peers to become influential community leaders and political figures. Each of these women helped change social life by taking charge of her own life and by taking hold of opportunities to lead and influence others.

A third virtue exhibited by these religious Black women civil rights participants was hope. They all had hope that a new vision of society was possible and worked to realize that vision. On the one hand, that hope reflected an established theological conviction anticipating the realization of faith through God's fulfilling God's promises. Hamer demonstrated this outlook in her assessment of changes that occurred in Mississippi as a result of student activism across the state:

> We Negroes had hoped and we had faith to hope, though we didn't know what we had hoped for. When the people came to Mississippi in 1964, to us it was the result of all our faith—all we had always hoped for. Our prayers and all we had lived for day after day hadn't been in vain. In 1964 the faith that we had hoped for started to be translated into action. Now we have action, and we're doing something that will not only free the Black man in Mississippi but hopefully will free the white one as well.[24]

Most of these women probably agreed with Hamer's view that their hoped-for vision of a new society depended primarily on God fulfilling God's promises.

On the other hand, people like Baker maintained some connection to this tradition of theological hope while also perceiving hope as realizing divinely created potential through individuals' organizing and acting on their own behalf. "People have to be made to understand that they cannot look for salvation anywhere but to themselves," Baker said.[25] "I just don't see anything to be substituted for having people understand their position and understand their potential power and how to use it. This can only be done, as I see it, through the long route, almost, of actually organizing people in small groups and parlaying those into larger groups."[26] Baker saw hope arising from what God empowers people to do for themselves.[27] Baker easily articulated her perspective that social change resulted in large measure from people using what she identified as their "God-given" potential and agency. Although Clark, Hamer, DeLee, Muhammad, Nash, and Robinson did not articulate this view, their views did resonate with Baker's since they all expected that their work and the activity of communities in which they worked would make a difference in social life. Through practice of these three virtues—innovation, taking charge, and hope—and others related to them, religious women civil rights activists helped push our society closer to the ideals of its creeds.

Black Religious Women and Public Life

The legacy of the Civil Rights Movement, which broadened social participation in the United States, continues to be felt today. This persists in spite of political, legislative, and conventional efforts to roll back or sidetrack moral and political changes aimed at truly democratizing interactions of all people. Much of the contemporary understanding of the meaning of freedom in the United States sprang from the broad vision of the Civil Rights Era. The shape of the Movement and the widespread influence that it had and continues to have relate directly to the important role of many women who organized, strategized, and collaborated in seeking to live in ways that reflected their religious values and to realize their vision of a good society. While these women may be seen as initially focusing on circumstances of African Americans, the social and moral import of work they did for common life in the United States reached far beyond Black communities and deepened, lifted, and heartened others' conceptions of liberty and justice.

It cannot be denied that many legislative and judicial advances during the Civil Rights Era and beyond were based in religious values. The 1964 Civil Rights Act, the 1965 Voting Rights Act, the 1966 Supreme Court decision affirming constitutionality of the Voting Rights Act, and the 1988 Federal Fair Housing Act, among other federal, state, and local initiatives, derived from values like those expressed by these Black women civil rights activists. Such legislation and judicial decisions sought broadly to address the oppression of African Americans on the basis of race, and, embracing expanded views deriving from the Civil Rights Era, included prohibitions on discrimination based on gender, age, religion, ability, national origin, and other conventional means of exclusion.

The religious language of love may more appropriately express the values enacted in these women's practices. Love may be identified with recognizing, valuing, and respecting persons by seeking their flourishing as human beings, including attending to material well-being, affirming human mutuality through increasing opportunities for all to participate, empowering people to fully realize their potential, and affirming as beneficial the gifts that each person brings to human society. This emphasis on love as a means of attending to human flourishing through practices of organizing, teaching, protesting, advocating, and agitating pervaded these religious Black women's civic participation. In addition to actual social changes that derived from their activism, these women's practices of witness and testimony and the broad Civil Rights Movement vision continue to be reminders of the norm of prioritizing the value of human personality and relationship over values of commodification, consumption, and separation. These women's persistent practices of organizing, teaching, and agitating bore witness to their understandings of human mutuality and relationship as divine gifts and to their understanding of divine calling to affirm human community. By testifying about and witnessing to the value of human community, they brought to public debate a norm of relatedness that challenged the notion of individual rights as a value that trumps every other value confronting it. As moral practice, the significance of witnessing and testifying, like that of other resources from religious communities, lies in the possibility and hope these practices bring to common civic life. Witness and testimony are means of embodying and practicing particular virtues. Witness and testimony both carry religious values and practices into the public square and identify and pass on values that help form others as religious persons, who also reproduce the values through their influence on the perspectives and work of those following in the tradition.

Notes

Chapter 1: Religion and Public Life

1. For an exploration of the role of religious institutions as providing "safe space" in the lives of African Americans, see Peter Paris's discussion of the Black "surrogate world" in *The Social Teaching of the Black Churches* (Philadelphia: Fortress Press, 1985) and C. Eric Lincoln and Larry Mamiya's discussion of the "black sacred cosmos" in *The Black Church in the African American Experience* (Durham: Duke University Press, 1990).

2. See, for example, Taylor Branch, *Parting the Waters: America in the King Years, 1954–1963* (New York: Simon & Schuster, 1988), and idem, *Pillar of Fire: America in the King Years, 1963–1965* (New York: Simon & Schuster, 1998); David J. Garrow, *Bearing the Cross: Martin Luther King, Jr. and the Southern Christian Leadership Conference* (New York: Vintage, 1988); Aldon Morris, *The Origins of the Civil Rights Movement: Black Communities Organizing for Change* (New York: Free Press, 1984); Belinda Robnett, *How Long? How Long? African-American Women in the Struggle for Civil Rights* (New York: Oxford University Press, 1997).

3. These works include Zita Allen, *Black Women Leaders of the Civil Rights Movement* (New York: Franklin Watts, 1996); Cynthia Griggs Fleming, *Soon We Will Not Cry: The Liberation of Ruby Doris Smith Robinson* (Lanham, Md.: Rowman and Littlefield, 1998); Joanne Grant, *Ella Baker: Freedom Bound* (New York: Wiley and Sons, 1998); Chana Kai Lee, *For Freedom's Sake: The Life of Fannie Lou Hamer* (Urbana: University of Illinois Press, 1999); Robnett, *How Long? How Long?;* Bettye Collier-Thomas and V. P. Franklin, eds., *Sisters in the Struggle: African American Women in the Civil Rights–Black Power Movement* (New York: New York University Press, 2001); Lynne Olson, *Freedom's Daughters: The Unsung Heroines of the Civil Rights Movement from 1830 to 1970* (New York: Scribner's, 2001); Constance Curry et al., *Deep in Our Hearts: Nine White Women in the Freedom Movement* (Athens: University of Georgia Press, 2000).

4. See Charles Marsh, *God's Long Summer: Stories of Faith and Civil Rights* (Princeton: Princeton University Press, 1997). Marsh examines the

theological perspectives of five persons active during the Civil Rights Movement, exploring religion as motivation of both support for *and* opposition to the movement.

5. For a discussion of survival and liberation themes in black religion, see Gayraud Wilmore, *Black Religion and Black Radicalism: An Interpretation of the Religious History of Afro-American People* (New York: Orbis, 1986), 220–41, and Lincoln and Mamiya, *The Black Church,* 199–212. Also see Cornel West, *Prophesy Deliverance! An Afro-American Revolutionary Christianity* (Philadelphia: Westminster, 1982). West's categories "priestly" and "prophetic" correlate with survival and liberation characterizations, respectively. Of the priestly stream in Black religion, West says it regards "quotidian components," whereas the prophetic stream is visionary and contributes to "every individual regardless of class, country, caste, race, or sex [having] the opportunity to fulfill his or her potentialities." The "prophetic Christian tradition," West says, "must insist upon both this worldly *liberation* and otherworldly salvation as the proper loci of Christianity" (16, emphasis added). On survival and affirmation of life, see Eugene Genovese, *Roll, Jordan, Roll: The World the Slaves Made* (New York: Pantheon, 1974), 212–13.

6. Lincoln and Mamiya, *The Black Church,* 4-5; Wilmore, *Black Religion and Black Radicalism,* 234; West, *Prophesy Deliverance,* 18; Albert Raboteau, *Slave Religion: The "Invisible Institution" in the Antebellum South* (Oxford: Oxford University Press, 1978), 309ff.

7. Lincoln and Mamiya, *The Black Church,* 201–4ff.; Wilmore, *Black Religion and Black Radicalism,* 221–33; West, *Prophesy Deliverance,* 16–18; Raboteau, *Slave Religion,* 309; Paris, *The Social Teaching of the Black Churches,* 87.

8. Kevin K. Gaines, *Uplifting the Race: Black Leadership, Politics, and Culture in the Twentieth Century* (Chapel Hill: University of North Carolina Press, 1996), 4, 5–9 passim. Also see Evelyn Brooks Higginbotham, *Righteous Discontent: The Women's Movement in the Black Baptist Church, 1880–1920* (Cambridge, Mass.: Harvard University Press, 1993), 19–21, 185ff.

9. Gaines, *Uplifting the Race,* 2. Also see Higginbotham, *Righteous Discontent,* 211. Higginbotham identifies this version of racial uplift as "'race work' or responsibility to the collective cause of African Americans."

10. Wilmore, *Black Religion and Black Radicalism,* 82, 92, 228–29; Gaines, *Uplifting the Race,* 31. My distinction between racial uplift "ideology" and racial uplift "practices" derives from the contrasts Gaines makes.

11. Andrew Billingsley, *Mighty like a River: The Black Church and Social Reform* (New York: Oxford University Press, 1999), asserts that the "com-

munity outreach" role of Black churches, responding to various issues in Black communities, "happened before, is happening now in some places and in some form, and might well happen in the future on an even grander scale."

12. Joyce A. Ladner, "'Black Women as Do-ers': The Social Responsibility of Black Women" in *Sage: A Scholarly Journal on Black Women* 4:1 (summer 1989): 87, 88.

13. Paris, *The Social Teaching of the Black Churches,* 15. Also see Wilmore, *Black Religion and Black Radicalism,* 229ff.; and West, *Prophesy Deliverance,* 18. It should be noted that Paris and Wilmore describe universal human flourishing as a constituent of Black religious belief, while West associates this perspective with the whole of "prophetic Christianity." It is clear, however, that all three are referring to what some might describe as "essential" Christianity.

14. Dorothy Sterling, *We Are Your Sisters: Black Women in the Nineteenth Century* (New York: Norton, 1984), 151, 265; Higginbotham, *Righteous Discontent,* 124.

15. See Alice Walker, *In Search of Our Mothers' Gardens: Womanist Prose* (San Diego: Harvest, 1983), xi–xii.

16. Delores S. Williams, s.v. "Theology, Womanist," in Letty M. Russell and J. Shannon Clarkson, eds., *Dictionary of Feminist Theologies* (Louisville: Westminster John Knox, 1996), 299–301.

17. Katie Geneva Cannon, "The Emergence of Black Feminist Consciousness," in Letty M. Russell, ed., *Feminist Interpretation of the Bible* (Philadelphia: Westminster, 1985), 30; Katie Geneva Cannon, *Black Womanist Ethics* (Atlanta: Scholars Press, 1988), 4.

18. Katie Geneva Cannon, "Resources for a Constructive Ethic in the Life and Work of Zora Neale Hurston," *Journal of Feminist Studies in Religion* 1 (spring 1985): 40.

19. Ibid., 39–40. Cannon's use of *unctuousness* reflects a Black colloquial expression indicating audacity and courage.

20. Cannon, *Black Womanist Ethics,* 99–105; Cannon, "Resources for a Constructive Ethic in the Life and Work of Zora Neale Hurston," 39–40, 46; Cannon, "Moral Wisdom in the Black Women's Literary Tradition," in Larry L. Rasmussen, ed., *The Annual of the Society of Christian Ethics* (Vancouver: The Society of Christian Ethics, 1984), 176–77.

21. Cannon, *Black Womanist Ethics,* 125–42.

22. Ibid., 143–45.

23. Katie Geneva Cannon, "'The Wounds of Jesus': Justification of Goodness in the Face of Manifold Evil," in *Katie's Canon: Womanism and the Soul of the Black Community* (New York: Continuum, 1995), 109–10;

Cannon, "Womanist Interpretation and Preaching in the Black Church," in *Katie's Canon.*

24. The narratives of Hagar and Ishmael are found in Genesis 16 and Gen 20:1-20.

25. Delores S. Williams, *Sisters in the Wilderness: The Challenge of Womanist God-Talk* (New York: Orbis, 1993), 108.

26. Ibid., 22.

27. Ibid., 206; Williams, "Womanist Theology: Black Women's Voices" in Leon Howell and Vivian Lindemayer, eds., *Ethics in the Present Tense: Readings in Christianity and Crisis, 1966–1991* (New York: Friendship, 1991), 67.

28. Williams, *Sisters in the Wilderness,* 60.

29. Ibid., xiii.

30. Ibid., 196.

31. Jacquelyn Grant, *White Women's Christ and Black Women's Jesus: Feminist Christology and Womanist Response* (American Academy of Religion 64; Atlanta: Scholars, 1989), 197.

32. Jacquelyn Grant, "Black Theology and the Black Woman," in Gayraud S. Wilmore and James Cone, eds., *Black Theology: A Documentary History* (Maryknoll, N.Y.: Orbis, 1979), 423–24.

33. Jacquelyn Grant, "Womanist Theology: Black Women's Experience as a Source for Doing Theology," in James H. Cone and Gayraud S. Wilmore, eds., *Black Theology, a Documentary History, Volume 2: 1980–1992* (Maryknoll, N.Y.: Orbis, 1992), 45.

34. Ibid., 205, 212.

35. Grant, "Black Theology and the Black Woman," 427, 430.

36. Cheryl Townsend Gilkes, "'If It Wasn't for the Women . . .': African American Women, Community Work, and Social Change," in Maxine Baca Zinn and Bonnie Thornton Dill, eds., *Women of Color in U.S. Society* (Philadelphia: Temple University Press, 1994), 231, 239, 242; idem, "The Roles of Church and Community Mothers: Ambivalent American Sexism or Fragmented African Familyhood?" *Journal of Feminist Studies in Religion* 2 (spring 1986): 42–43.

37. Cheryl Townsend Gilkes, "'Together and in Harness': Women's Traditions in the Sanctified Church," *Signs: Journal of Women in Culture and Society* 10:4 (1985): 679, 687.

38. Cheryl Townsend Gilkes, "The Role of Women in the Sanctified Church," *Journal of Religious Thought* 43:1 (spring/summer 1986): 35.

39. Cheryl Townsend Gilkes, "Going Up for the Oppressed: The Career Mobility of Black Women Community Workers," *Journal of Social Issues* 39 (fall 1983): 119.

40. Cheryl Townsend Gilkes, "Successful Rebellious Professionals: The Black Woman's Professional Identity and Community Commitment," *Psychology of Women Quarterly* 6 (spring 1982): 296; Gilkes, "Building in Many Places: Multiple Commitments and Ideologies in Black Women's Community Work," in Ann Bookman and Sandra Morgan, eds., *Women and the Politics of Empowerment* (Philadelphia: Temple University Press, 1988), 53–56; Gilkes, "Going Up for the Oppressed," 117.

41. Gilkes, "Building in Many Places," 69, 75.

42. Ibid., 74.

43. Gilkes, "'If It Wasn't for the Women,'" 238.

44. Williams, *Sisters in the Wilderness,* 170.

45. Cannon, "'The Wounds of Jesus,'" 109.

46. Gilkes, "Going Up for the Oppressed," 119.

47. Grant, "Black Theology and the Black Woman," 430.

48. See, for example, Lincoln and Mamiya, *The Black Church,* xix.

49. Thomas Hoyt Jr., "Testimony," in Dorothy C. Bass, ed., *Practicing Our Faith: A Way of Life for a Searching People* (San Francisco: Jossey-Bass, 1997), 92, 94.

50. See, for example, Riggins R. Earl Jr., *Dark Symbols, Obscure Signs: God, Self and Community in the Slave Mind* (New York: Orbis, 1993), 52ff.; Will Coleman, *Tribal Talk: Black Theology, Hermeneutics, and African/American Ways of "Telling the Story"* (University Park: Pennsylvania State University Press, 2000), 141ff. passim; and Albert J. Raboteau, "Introduction," and Paul Radin, "Status, Fantasy, and the Christian Dogma," in Clifton H. Johnson, ed., *God Struck Me Dead: Voices of Ex-Slaves* (Cleveland: Pilgrim, 1993), xix–xxv and vii–xii.

51. Hoyt, "Testimony," 92, 102.

52. Ibid., 93–94.

53. Ibid., 101.

54. Olive Gilbert and Frances W. Titus, *The Narrative of Sojourner Truth* (New York: Arno, 1968, 1878), 18, 42–43; Nell Irvin Painter, *Sojourner Truth: A Life, a Symbol* (New York: Norton, 1996), 4, 11, 112. Painter notes an alternative spelling of the last name as Van Wagenen.

55. Gilbert and Titus, *The Narrative,* 17–19.

56. Ibid., 27–28.

57. Ibid., 29–37; Painter, *Sojourner Truth,* 18.

58. Gilbert and Titus, *The Narrative,* 41–43; Painter, *Sojourner Truth,* 25.

59. Gilbert and Titus, *The Narrative,* 45–54; Painter, *Sojourner Truth,* 33–34.

60. Painter, *Sojourner Truth,* 25; Gilbert and Titus, *The Narrative,* 65–67.

61. See discussion on pp. 13–14 and note 50 above.

62. Gilbert and Titus, *The Narrative,* 73–76.

63. Ibid., 79–87; Painter, *Sojourner Truth,* 39ff.

64. Her reference is to the biblical cities Sodom and Gomorrah, which were destroyed by God. The scripture to which she refers is Gen. 18:16—19:29.

65. Gilbert and Titus, *The Narrative,* 100–101; Painter, *Sojourner Truth,* 5, 73.

66. Gilbert and Titus, *The Narrative,* 115–16.

67. Painter, *Sojourner Truth,* 82, 88; Gilbert and Titus, *The Narrative,* 109–15.

68. Gilbert and Titus, *The Narrative,* 115–23; Painter, *Sojourner Truth,* 88–100.

69. Painter, *Sojourner Truth,* 103, 110–12.

70. Ibid., 114, 116–17.

71. Nell Irvin Painter, "Sojourner Truth," in Darlene Clark Hine, ed., *Black Women in America: An Historical Encyclopedia,* vol. 2 (New York: Carlson, 1993), 1174–75.

72. Painter, *Sojourner Truth,* 125–26, 167–68; Gilbert and Titus, *The Narrative,* 133–35.

73. Elizabeth Cady Stanton, Susan B. Anthony, and Matilda Joslyn Gage, eds., *History of Woman Suffrage,* vol. 1 (New York: Fowler and Wells, 1881), 567–68.

74. Painter, *Sojourner Truth,* 180; Gilbert and Titus, *The Narrative,* 140–41.

75. Painter, "Sojourner Truth," 175.

76. Gilbert and Titus, *The Narrative,* 60; Painter, *Sojourner Truth,* 24. Truth's solitary sanctuary is an interesting parallel to the brush arbor worship spaces of slaves, particularly in the South, who often went by stealth at night to meeting places apart from the supervision of plantation owners and overseers. See Coleman, *Tribal Talk,* 51, 90.

77. Gilbert and Titus, *The Narrative,* 108–9.

78. Ibid., 101, 152.

79. Ibid., 100; Painter, *Sojourner Truth,* 73.

80. Gilbert and Titus, *The Narrative,* 109.

81. Reputedly the largest African American denomination, the National Baptist Convention formed in 1895 when state and local associations of independent Baptist churches united. Independent Black Baptist congregations emerged as African Americans of the antebellum and postbellum era withdrew from white congregations to organize their own churches. See Albert J. Raboteau, *Canaan Land: A Religious History of African Americans* (New York: Oxford University, 1999), 68ff.

82. Within traditions of Black community activism, there evolved a widespread expectation that Black persons with means would seek to improve the overall circumstances of Black people, or would seek to do, as it came to be called, "race work." This evolved as an expectation that all Black persons, and especially educated and/or economically advantaged African Americans, would participate in "race work" or "racial uplift work." Historian Evelyn Brooks Higginbotham defines *race work* as "responsibility to the collective cause of African Americans." Persons who regularly took up this work often were called *race leaders*. Cheryl Townsend Gilkes notes that these persons were often also called "race men" or "race women." See Higginbotham, *Righteous Discontent,* 211, and Gilkes, "Building in Many Places," 54.

83. Juanita Fletcher, "Nannie Helen Burroughs," in Barbara Sicherman and Carol Hurd Green, eds., *Notable American Women, The Modern Period: A Biographical Dictionary* (Cambridge, Mass.: Belknap, 1980), 125; Higginbotham, *Righteous Discontent,* 158; and Opal V. Easter, *Nannie Helen Burroughs* (New York: Garland, 1995), 25, 27.

84. Easter, *Nannie Helen Burroughs,* 26–27; Higginbotham, *Righteous Discontent,* 156.

85. See Higginbotham, *Righteous Discontent,* esp. chap. 5.

86. Easter, *Nannie Helen Burroughs,* 27–28; Higginbotham, *Righteous Discontent,* 150.

87. Easter, *Nannie Helen Burroughs,* 58.

88. Evelyn Brooks, "Religion, Politics, and Gender: The Leadership of Nannie Helen Burroughs," *The Journal of Religious Thought* 44:2 (winter/spring 1988): 10.

89. Higginbotham, *Righteous Discontent,* 212–13.

90. Fletcher, "Nannie Helen Burroughs," 126–27; Easter, *Nannie Helen Burroughs,* 64–65.

91. Easter, *Nannie Helen Burroughs,* 62.

92. Marcia Riggs notes this cross-boundary work as mediatory practice of Black club women. See Marcia Riggs, *Awake, Arise, and Act: A Womanist Call for Black Liberation* (Cleveland: Pilgrim, 1994), esp. chap. 5.

93. Higginbotham, *Righteous Discontent,* 151–52.

94. Higginbotham, *Righteous Discontent,* 218–19; Easter, *Nannie Helen Burroughs,* 100–102.

95. Easter, *Nannie Helen Burroughs,* 127.

96. Ibid., 37–38, 116. Emphasis added in first quotation.

97. Higginbotham, *Righteous Discontent,* 216, 292–93 n. 113.

98. Ibid., 150, 152.

99. Ibid., 160; Easter, *Nannie Helen Burroughs,* 29ff.

100. Higginbotham, *Righteous Discontent,* 160; Easter, *Nannie Helen Burroughs,* 29.

101. Higginbotham, *Righteous Discontent,* 163.

102. Nannie Helen Burroughs, *What Do You Think?* (Washington, D.C.: n.p., n.d. [circa 1950]), 8–9.

103. Ibid., 31.

104. Ibid., 21, 24.

105. Higginbotham, *Righteous Discontent,* 176.

106. Burroughs, *What Do You Think?* 36–37.

107. Nannie Helen Burroughs, *New and Old Paths to Fertile Fields* (Washington, D.C.: Women's Convention Auxiliary to the National Baptist Convention, n.d.), 5, 7–8.

108. Burroughs, *New and Old Paths;* Easter, *Nannie Helen Burroughs,* 73.

109. Easter, *Nannie Helen Burroughs,* 60.

110. Ibid., 42.

111. Ibid., 60.

112. Brooks, "Religion, Politics, and Gender," 17; Higginbotham, *Righteous Discontent,* 24.

113. Burroughs, *New and Old Paths,* 45.

114. Nannie Helen Burroughs, "Unload Your Uncle Toms," in Gerda Lerner, ed., *Black Women in White America: A Documentary History* (New York: Vintage, 1973), 551–53. The scripture to which she refers here is Josh. 1:2.

115. Easter, *Nannie Helen Burroughs,* 73. The scripture to which she refers is Titus 1:6.

116. Ibid., 133. The scripture to which she refers is John 5:8.

117. Ibid., 138–39. The scriptures to which she refers are Acts 17:26, Matt. 23:8, and Gen. 9:19-27.

118. Ibid., 134.

119. Higginbotham, *Righteous Discontent,* 175.

120. Easter, *Nannie Helen Burroughs,* 107.

121. Ibid., 97.

Chapter 2: Continuing the Traditions

1. For reference to Baker as mother, see Aldon Morris, *The Origins of the Civil Rights Movement: Black Communities Organizing for Change* (New York: Free Press, 1984), 233. In the title and text of her master's thesis, "Midwifery and Grassroots Politics: Ella Jo Baker and Her Philosophy of Community Development," Vanessa Lynn Davis identifies Baker as a midwife of the movement (Vanderbilt University, Nashville, Tennessee, 1992).

2. Barbara Ransby's fine article, "Behind-the-Scenes View of a Behind-the-Scenes Organizer: The Roots of Ella Baker's Political Passion," begins to explore the connection of Baker's civil rights activism to religious faith and

the influence of Baker's Baptist missionary mother. However, Ransby leaves out the significant influence of Baker's Baptist minister grandfather (whose religious practice focused primarily on empowering the community of African Americans in which he lived) and does not engage the religious values and ideas embedded in Baker's speeches, writing, and work. See Ransby's article in Bettye Collier-Thomas and V. P. Franklin, eds., *Sisters in the Struggle: African American Women in the Civil Rights–Black Power Movement* (New York: New York University Press, 2001).

3. Joanne Grant, *Ella Baker: Freedom Bound* (New York: Wiley and Sons, 1998), 13–18; Barbara Ransby, "Ella Josephine Baker," in Darlene Clark Hine, ed., *Black Women in America: An Historical Encyclopedia,* vol. 1 (New York: Carlson, 1993), 70–71.

4. Grant, *Ella Baker,* 19.

5. Barbara Ransby, "Ella J. Baker and the Black Radical Tradition" (Ph.D. dissertation, University of Michigan, Ann Arbor, 1996), 37.

6. Grant, *Ella Baker,* 14-17; Charles Payne, "Ella Baker and Models of Social Change," *Signs: Journal of Women in Culture and Society* 14 (summer 1989): 886; Ellen Cantarow and Susan O'Malley, *Moving the Mountain: Women Working for Social Change* (Old Westbury, N.Y.: Feminist Press, 1980), 57–58.

7. Grant, *Ella Baker,* 16–17.

8. Cantarow and O'Malley, *Moving the Mountain,* 59.

9. Ibid., 59–60.

10. Grant, *Ella Baker,* 18, 19.

11. Payne, "Ella Baker and Models of Social Change," 887; Cantarow and O'Malley, *Moving the Mountain,* 55; Joan Curl Elliott, "Ella Baker," in Jessie Carney Smith, ed., *Notable Black American Women* (Detroit: Gale Research, 1992), 40.

12. Grant, *Ella Baker,* 17.

13. Payne, "Ella Baker and Models of Social Change," 886.

14. Cantarow and O'Malley, *Moving the Mountain,* 57–58.

15. Grant, *Ella Baker,* 1, 7, 12.

16. Ibid., 1, 8.

17. John Britton, "Interview with Ella Baker: June 19, 1968," Moorland-Spingarn Collection, Howard University, Washington, D.C., 2, quoted in Catherine M. Orr, "'The Struggle Is Eternal': A Rhetorical Biography of Ella Baker" (master's thesis, University of North Carolina at Chapel Hill, 1991), 26.

18. Grant, *Ella Baker,* 20.

19. Ibid., 12; Cantarow and O'Malley, *Moving the Mountain,* 61.

20. Sue Thrasher and Casey Hayden, "Interview with Ella Baker, April 19, 1977, New York, New York," Southern Oral History Program,

Southern Oral History Collection, University of North Carolina at Chapel Hill, 24.

21. Ibid., 25.

22. Grant, *Ella Baker,* 21.

23. Ibid., 83 passim; Ransby, "Ella J. Baker and the Black Radical Tradition," 58.

24. Grant, *Ella Baker,* 21; Ransby, "Ella J. Baker and the Black Radical Tradition," 71.

25. Grant, *Ella Baker,* 23.

26. Ibid., 23; Cantarow and O'Malley, *Moving the Mountain,* 62; "Interview with Ella Baker," *The Urban Review* 4:3 (May 1970): 20.

27. Cantarow and O'Malley, *Moving the Mountain,* 64.

28. Ibid., 64.

29. Grant, *Ella Baker,* 114.

30. Ibid., 30–36; Cantarow and O'Malley, *Moving the Mountain,* 62–64; Ransby, "Ella J. Baker and the Black Radical Tradition," 71.

31. Grant, *Ella Baker,* 32, 37.

32. Ibid., 37–38; Cantarow and O'Malley, *Moving the Mountain,* 64.

33. Ella Baker and Marvel Cooke, "The Bronx Slave Market," *The Crisis* (November 1935): 330. See Delores S. Williams, *Sisters in the Wilderness: The Challenge of Womanist God-Talk* (Maryknoll, N.Y.: Orbis, 1993), 60ff.

34. Baker and Cooke, "The Bronx Slave Market," 330, 340.

35. Grant, *Ella Baker,* 47.

36. Ella Baker, "Developing Community Leadership," in Gerda Lerner, ed., *Black Women in White America: A Documentary History* (New York: Vintage, 1973), 347.

37. Grant, *Ella Baker,* 49.

38. Cantarow and O'Malley, *Moving the Mountain,* 70, 71.

39. Ibid., 61.

40. See discussion of Gilkes, pp.10–12.

41. Payne, "Ella Baker and Models of Social Change," 887–88; Grant, *Ella Baker,* 44, 68.

42. Payne, "Ella Baker and Models of Social Change," 888; Grant, *Ella Baker,* 81–82.

43. Grant, *Ella Baker,* 89–99.

44. Taylor Branch, *Parting the Waters: America in the King Years, 1954–1963* (New York: Simon & Schuster, 1988), 232–33.

45. Ibid., 264.

46. Ella Baker, "Developing Community Leadership," 351.

47. Lynne Olson, *Freedom's Daughters: Unsung Heroines of the Civil Rights Movement from 1830 to 1970* (New York: Scribner's, 2001), 161.

48. Branch, *Parting the Waters,* 330–31.

49. Payne, "Ella Baker and Models of Social Change," circa 887; Morris, *The Origins of the Civil Rights Movement,* 223; Ransby, "Ella J. Baker and the Black Radical Tradition," 71.

50. Payne, "Ella Baker and Models of Social Change," 887.

51. I consider Baker's humanism to be a blending of her theological belief and her belief in possibilities of human life deriving from experiences of what persons accomplish when they cooperate and organize. For a discussion of theological belief and humanism as sources of vitalities of the Civil Rights Movement, see Rosetta E. Ross, "From Civil Rights to Civic Participation," *Journal of the Interdenominational Theological Center* 28 (fall 2000/spring 2001): esp. 44–46.

52. Grant, *Ella Baker,* 18, 22, 27.

53. Cantarow and O'Malley, *Moving the Mountain,* 60–61.

54. Ibid., 60, emphasis added.

55. Grant, *Ella Baker*, 23.

56. "Interview with Ella Baker," 22.

57. Ella Baker, "Address to Mass Meeting in Hattiesburg, Mississippi," January 21, 1964, quoted in appendix of Catherine M. Orr, "'The Struggle Is Eternal': A Rhetorical Biography of Ella Baker" (master's thesis, University of North Carolina at Chapel Hill, 1991), 78.

58. Ella Baker in Joanne Grant, *Fundi: The Story of Ella Baker* (16 mm., New Day Films, United States, 1981).

59. Baker, "Address to Mass Meeting," 78.

60. Ibid., 79.

61. John Britton, "Interview with Ella Baker: June 19, 1968," Moorland-Spingarn Collection, Howard University, Washington, D.C., quoted in Payne, "Ella Baker and Models of Social Change," 898.

62. Baker, "Address to Mass Meeting," 78–80. Baker quoted from Rom. 13:11-12.

63. Ibid., 80.

64. Ibid., 78.

65. Septima Clark, *Ready from Within: A First Person Narrative,* ed. Cynthia Stokes Brown (Trenton: Africa World Press, 1990), 97.

66. Septima Poinsette Clark, *Echo in My Soul* (New York: Dutton, 1962), 112; Septima Poinsette Clark to Dr. and Mrs. Martin Luther King Jr., October 15, 1964, Septima Clark Papers, Box III, Number 122, Special Collections, The College of Charleston Libraries, Charleston, South Carolina.

67. Cynthia Stokes Brown, "Septima Clark: Educator, Humanitarian, Civil Rights Activist," in Smith, ed., *Notable Black American Women,* 189; Grace Jordan McFadden, "Septima Poinsette Clark," in *Black Women in America,* vol. 1, 249.

68. Clark, *Echo in My Soul,* 14.

69. Clark, *Ready from Within,* 88; Jacquelyn Hall, Interview with Septima P. Clark, July 25, 1976, Southern Oral History Program, University of North Carolina at Chapel Hill, 6, 8.

70. Hall, Interview with Septima P. Clark, 9, emphasis added.

71. Clark, *Echo in My Soul,* 13–14.

72. Clark, *Ready from Within,* 97–98.

73. Hall, Interview with Septima P. Clark, 9; Brown, "Septima Clark," 190.

74. Clark, *Echo in My Soul,* 13.

75. Clark, *Ready from Within,* 89; Brown, "Septima Clark," 190.

76. Clark, *Ready from Within,* 88–89.

77. Hall, Interview with Septima P. Clark, 11.

78. This concern of Mrs. Poinsette to have some autonomy in making determinations about her labor (and by extension, about control of her body) and Mr. Poinsette's refusal to let their daughters work for white families where the men in the homes might seduce or rape the young women represent the early twentieth-century legacy of "surrogacy," which Delores Williams discusses. See discussion on p. 8 above, and see Williams, *Sisters in the Wilderness,* 60ff.

79. Hall, Interview with Septima P. Clark, 11–12; Clark, *Ready from Within,* 89–90.

80. Hall, Interview with Septima P. Clark, 13–14.

81. Ibid., 14.

82. Clark, *Ready from Within,* 93.

83. Ibid., 93, 94; Hall, Interview with Septima P. Clark, 25.

84. Clark, *Ready from Within,* 97.

85. Clark, *Echo in My Soul,* 28.

86. Clark, *Ready from Within,* 90.

87. Clark, *Echo in My Soul,* 29.

88. Clark, *Ready from Within,* 97.

89. Ibid.

90. Clark, *Echo in My Soul,* 27.

91. Ibid., 61–62.

92. Hall, Interview with Septima P. Clark, 10.

93. Clark, *Echo in My Soul,* 22–23.

94. Ibid., 16.

95. Clark, *Ready from Within,* 100.

96. Brown, "Septima Clark," 190; Clark, *Echo in My Soul,* 24, 27.

97. Clark, *Echo in My Soul,* 28.

98. Ibid., 37.

99. Ibid., 69.

100. McFadden, "Septima Poinsette Clark," 249.

101. Clark, *Ready from Within,* 110.

102. Clark, *Echo in My Soul,* 51–52.

103. Clark, *Ready from Within,* 106–7.

104. Clark, *Echo in My Soul,* 59; McFadden, "Septima Poinsette Clark," 249.

105. Clark, *Ready from Within,* 100.

106. Clark, *Echo in My Soul,* 61, 69.

107. Clark, *Ready from Within,* 61–62.

108. Clark, *Echo in My Soul,* 63, 113.

109. Ibid., 67; Hall, Interview with Septima P. Clark, 48–50.

110. Clark, *Echo in My Soul,* 67; McFadden, "Septima Poinsette Clark," 249.

111. Clark, *Echo in My Soul,* 69.

112. Hall, Interview with Septima P. Clark, 47; Clark, *Echo in My Soul,* 68.

113. Clark, *Echo in My Soul,* 69.

114. Hall, Interview with Septima P. Clark, 50–51.

115. Clark, *Echo in My Soul,* 73–75; Hall, Interview with Septima P. Clark, 56; McFadden, "Septima Poinsette Clark," 249.

116. Clark, *Echo in My Soul,* 84, 86; McFadden, "Septima Poinsette Clark," 250. Clark records receiving her master's degree in 1946, while McFadden says she received it in 1945.

117. McFadden, "Septima Poinsette Clark," 250; Clark, *Echo in My Soul,* 76–82, 89.

118. Clark, *Echo in My Soul,* 90–111 passim.

119. Ibid., 95–98.

120. Ibid., 98.

121. Ibid., 100–101, 105–6.

122. Ibid., 112; Branch, *Parting the Waters,* 290, 853–54; Clark, *Ready from Within,* 37.

123. Clark, *Echo in My Soul,* 134.

124. Hall, Interview with Septima P. Clark, 67.

125. Ibid., 67; Clark, *Echo in My Soul,* 119, 121.

126. S.C. Code of Laws, *Statutes at Large* (1956) #741, 1747.

127. Clark, *Echo in My Soul,* 3, 111–18; Hall, Interview with Septima P. Clark, 69. Clark's pension never was reinstated, although the state of South Carolina did acknowledge the injustice to some extent by creating a special annual appropriation of $10,000, which was awarded to Clark until her death.

128. McFadden, "Septima Poinsette Clark," 250–51.

129. Hall, Interview with Septima P. Clark, 80.

130. Ibid., 79.

131. Clark, *Ready from Within,* 48.

132. Septima Poinsette Clark, "Citizenship and the Gospel," *Journal of Black Studies* 10 (June 1980): 465–66.

133. Clark, *Ready from Within,* 136–41; Clark, *Echo in My Soul,* 153–63.

134. Clark, *Echo in My Soul,* 203.

135. Ibid., 150; Eugene Walker, Interview with Septima P. Clark, July 30, 1976, Southern Oral History Program, University of North Carolina at Chapel Hill, 7.

136. Clark, *Ready from Within,* 56, 60; Clark, *Echo in My Soul,* 3, 8–9; Brown, "Septima Clark," 191; Walker, Interview with Septima P. Clark, 2; Branch, *Parting the Waters,* 290.

137. Clark, *Ready from Within,* 61; Walker, Interview with Septima P. Clark, 1; Branch, *Parting the Waters,* 264.

138. Clark, *Ready from Within,* 62–63, 65–68; Hall, Interview with Septima P. Clark, 79.

139. Branch, *Parting the Waters,* 478–82; Clark, *Ready from Within,* 70.

140. Hall, Interview with Septima P. Clark, 48.

141. Clark, *Ready from Within,* 42.

142. Hall, Interview with Septima P. Clark, 92.

143. Clark, *Echo in My Soul,* 118, emphasis added.

144. Ibid., 24, 29, 59, 118, 125, 236.

145. Septima Poinsette Clark, "Why I Believe There Is a God," unpublished speech, Septima Clark Papers, Box I, Number 77, n.d., Special Collections, The College of Charleston Libraries, Charleston, South Carolina, 1.

146. Clark, *Echo in My Soul,* 67.

147. Ibid., 132.

148. Clark, "Why I Believe," 2.

149. Ibid., 3.

150. See Lawrence Levine, *Slave Culture and Slave Consciousness* (New York: Oxford University Press, 1977), 23–38, where he discusses the practice among slaves of adapting Christian Scripture to their lives.

151. Clark, *Echo in My Soul,* 159. One translation of the complete verse from 1 Cor. 5:6 reads: "Your boasting is not a good thing. Do you not know that a little yeast leavens the whole batch of dough?"

152. Ibid., 182. She conflates two verses, 1 Cor. 13:13 and Eph. 4:13, both attributed to the apostle Paul.

153. Clark, "Why I Believe," 3.

154. Clark, *Echo in My Soul,* 114.

155. Ibid., 193.

156. Ibid., x.

157. Clark, "Citizenship and the Gospel," 466; Clark, *Echo in My Soul,* 191, 218.

158. Clark, *Echo in My Soul,* 236.

159. Ibid., 48, 237.

160. Clark, "Citizenship and the Gospel," 464.

161. Ibid., 463.

162. Ibid., 462–63.

163. Clark, *Echo in My Soul,* 174–75; Hall, Interview with Septima P. Clark, 104.

164. Clark, *Ready from Within,* 62, 66; Clark, *Echo in My Soul,* 159; Walker, Interview with Septima P. Clark, 2.

165. Clark, *Ready from Within,* 69.

166. Ibid., 78–79, 82.

167. Ibid., 78–83.

168. Ibid., 77; Brown, "Septima Clark," 193.

169. Ibid., 79; Hall, Interview with Septima P. Clark, 82.

170. Hall, Interview with Septima P. Clark, 84.

171. Clark, *Ready from Within,* 77–78.

172. Septima P. Clark to Dr. M. L. King Jr., December 12, 1963 (letter and report), Box III, Number 122, Special Collections, The College of Charleston Libraries, Charleston, South Carolina, 1; McFadden, "Septima Poinsette Clark," 251.

173. Hall, Interview with Septima P. Clark, 85.

174. See discussion on p. 7. See also Katie Geneva Cannon, *Black Womanist Ethics* (Atlanta: Scholars Press, 1988), esp. 125–42.

Chapter 3: Giving the Movement Life

1. Septima Clark, *Ready from Within: A First Person Narrative,* ed. Cynthia Stokes Brown (Trenton: Africa World Press, 1990), 48.

2. June Jordan, *Fannie Lou Hamer* (New York: Crowell, 1972), 39.

3. Helen C. Camp, "Fannie Lou Townsend Hamer," in Alden Whitman, ed., *American Reformers: An H. W. Wilson Biographical Dictionary* (New York: Wilson, 1985), 391; Jacquelyn Grant, "Fannie Lou Hamer," in Jessie Carney Smith, ed., *Notable Black American Women* (Detroit: Gale Research, 1992), 441; Chana Kai Lee, *For Freedom's Sake: The Life of Fannie Lou Hamer* (Urbana: University of Illinois Press, 1999), 1; Barbara L. Morgan, "Fannie Lou Townsend Hamer," in Gail J. Hardy, ed., *American*

Women Civil Rights Activists: Bibliographies of 68 Leaders, 1825–1992 (Jefferson, N.C.: McFarland, 1993), 176.

4. Fannie Lou Hamer, "Fannie Lou Hamer Speaks Out," *Essence* 1 (October 1971): 54.

5. Lee, *For Freedom's Sake,* 1–2.

6. Hamer, "Fannie Lou Hamer Speaks Out," 54.

7. J. H. O'Dell, "Life in Mississippi: An Interview with Fannie Lou Hamer," *Freedomways* 5 (1965): 232–33. See also Fannie Lou Hamer, "To Praise Our Bridges," in Dorothy Abbott, ed., *Mississippi Writers: Reflections of Childhood and Youth, Volume 2: Nonfiction* (Jackson: University of Mississippi Press, 1986), 324.

8. O'Dell, "Life in Mississippi," 232.

9. Hamer, "Fannie Lou Hamer Speaks Out," 54.

10. Lee, *For Freedom's Sake,* 1.

11. Hamer, "Fannie Lou Hamer Speaks Out," 53.

12. O'Dell, "Life in Mississippi," 232; Phyl Garland, "Builders of a New South," *Ebony* 21 (August 1966): 28.

13. Hamer, "Fannie Lou Hamer Speaks Out," 54; Lee, *For Freedom's Sake,* 11.

14. Robert Wright, Oral Interview with Fannie Lou Hamer, August 9, 1968, Morland-Spingarn Research Center, Howard University, Washington, District of Columbia, 1–2.

15. Jordan, *Fannie Lou Hamer,* 15.

16. Garland, "Builders of a New South," 28; Hamer, "Fannie Lou Hamer Speaks Out," 53.

17. Neil McMillen, "An Oral History with Fannie Lou Hamer," April 14, 1972, 721 James Street, Ruleville, Mississippi; University of Southern Mississippi Center for Oral History and Cultural Heritage (http://www.lib.usm.edu/~spcol/crda/oh/hamertrans.htm), 3.

18. O'Dell, "Life in Mississippi," 232; Camp, "Fannie Lou Townsend Hamer," 391.

19. Garland, "Builders of a New South," 28.

20. Hamer, "Fannie Lou Hamer Speaks Out," 53, 54; O'Dell, "Life in Mississippi," 231–32.

21. Camp, "Fannie Lou Townsend Hamer," 391.

22. O'Dell, "Life in Mississippi," 233–34.

23. Hamer, "Fannie Lou Hamer Speaks Out," 53.

24. Wright, Oral Interview with Fannie Lou Hamer, 4.

25. Hamer, "To Praise Our Bridges," 324; Garland, "Builders of a New South," 29; Lee, *For Freedom's Sake,* 18.

26. Jerry DeMuth, "'Tired of Being Sick and Tired,'" *The Nation* 198 (June 1, 1964): 549; O'Dell, "Life in Mississippi," 232; Lee, *For Freedom's Sake,* 20.

27. Lee, *For Freedom's Sake,* 19; Garland, "Builders of a New South," 28–29.

28. Garland, "Builders of a New South, 29.

29. McMillen, "An Oral History with Fannie Lou Hamer," 4. Also see Chana Kai Lee, "Anger, Memory, and Personal Power: Fannie Lou Hamer and Civil Rights Leadership," in Bettye Collier-Thomas and V. P. Franklin, eds., *Sisters in the Struggle: African American Women in the Civil Rights–Black Power Movement* (New York: New York University Press, 2001), 141.

30. Howell Raines, *My Soul Is Rested: Movement Days in the Deep South Remembered* (New York: Penguin, 1983), 249.

31. Garland, "Builders of a New South," 29.

32. Charles Marsh, *God's Long Summer: Stories of Faith and Civil Rights* (Princeton: Princeton University Press, 1997), 13.

33. McMillen, "An Oral History with Fannie Lou Hamer," 5.

34. Ibid., 6.

35. DeMuth, "'Tired of Being Sick and Tired,'" 550; Raines, *My Soul Is Rested,* 250; Marsh, *God's Long Summer,* 15; see also Camp, "Fannie Lou Townsend Hamer," 391–92.

36. DeMuth, "'Tired of Being Sick and Tired,'" 550.

37. Ibid.; Raines, *My Soul Is Rested,* 251; McMillen, "An Oral History with Fannie Lou Hamer," 7.

38. Marsh, *God's Long Summer,* 17.

39. Raines, *My Soul Is Rested,* 251–52.

40. Lee, *For Freedom's Sake,* 36–37.

41. DeMuth, "'Tired of Being Sick and Tired,'" 550; Raines, *My Soul Is Rested,* 252; Lee, *For Freedom's Sake,* 37; McMillen, "An Oral History with Fannie Lou Hamer," 8, 9.

42. McMillen, "An Oral History with Fannie Lou Hamer," 8.

43. Raines, *My Soul Is Rested,* 252; Hamer, "To Praise Our Bridges," 325.

44. Raines, *My Soul Is Rested,* 252.

45. McMillen, "An Oral Interview with Fannie Lou Hamer," 8.

46. Ibid., 9.

47. Raines, *My Soul Is Rested,* 253–54; DeMuth, "'Tired of Being Sick and Tired,'" 550.

48. DeMuth, "'Tired of Being Sick and Tired,'" 550.

49. Lee, *For Freedom's Sake*, 57.

50. Marsh, *God's Long Summer,* 23; Kay Mills, *This Little Light of Mine: The Life of Fannie Lou Hamer* (New York: Dutton, 1993), 65.

51. DeMuth, "'Tired of Being Sick and Tired,'" 550; Taylor Branch, *Parting the Waters: America in the King Years, 1954–1963* (New York: Simon & Schuster, 1988), 819–25.

52. Raines, *My Soul Is Rested,* 254; Susan Kling, *Fannie Lou Hamer: A Biography* (Chicago: Women for Racial and Economic Equality, 1979), 23.

53. McMillen, "An Oral History with Fannie Lou Hamer," 12.

54. Ibid., 8.

55. O'Dell, "Life in Mississippi," 236.

56. Franklynn Peterson, "Sunflowers Don't Grow in Sunflower County," *Sepia* 19 (February 1970): 13–14.

57. Camp, "Fannie Lou Townsend Hamer," 392.

58. O'Dell, "Life in Mississippi," 236.

59. Taylor Branch, *Pillar of Fire: America in the King Years, 1963–1965* (New York: Simon & Schuster, 1998), 457–71; Eric Black, "Mondale's Retrospective Stirs Up Memories of 1964 Convention," *Minneapolis Star Tribune*, Saturday, February 12, 2000, A4.

60. Mills, *This Little Light of Mine,* 118ff.

61. McMillen, "An Oral History with Fannie Lou Hamer," 13.

62. Franklynn Peterson, "Fannie Lou Hamer: Mother of Black Women's Lib," *Sepia* 21 (December 1972): 24.

63. Ibid., 18.

64. Ibid., 21; Fannie Lou Hamer, "It's in Your Hands," in Gerda Lerner, ed., *Black Women in White America: A Documentary History* (New York: Vintage, 1973), 612; Mills, *This Little Light of Mine,* 257–60; Camp, "Fannie Lou Townsend Hamer," 392.

65. Fannie Lou Hamer, "Foreword" to *Stranger at the Gates: A Summer in Mississippi* by Tracy Sugarman (New York: Hill and Wang, 1967), vii, ix.

66. Wright, Oral Interview, 6; Raines, *My Soul Is Rested,* 249.

67. Marsh, *God's Long Summer*, 25. For relevant discussions by Cannon and Williams, see pp. 8–9. See also Katie Geneva Cannon, "'The Wounds of Jesus': Justification of Goodness in the Face of Manifold Evil," in *Katie's Canon: Womanism and the Soul of the Black Community* (New York: Continuum, 1995), 109–10; idem, "Womanist Interpretation and Preaching in the Black Church" in *Katie's Canon*; and Delores S. Williams, *Sisters in the Wilderness: The Challenge of Womanist God-Talk* (Maryknoll, N.Y.: Orbis, 1993), xiii.

68. Hamer, "Fannie Lou Hamer Speaks Out," 75.

69. Hamer, "Foreword," ix.

70. Wright, Oral Interview with Fannie Lou Hamer, 6.

71. O'Dell, "Life in Mississippi," 235–36. Hamer's scripture references here are Mark 3:24-25 and Luke 11:17.

72. Hamer, "Fannie Lou Hamer Speaks Out," 55; scripture quotes are from Prov. 14:34 and Gal. 6:7, respectively.

73. Marsh, *God's Long Summer,* 32.

74. Hamer, "Foreword," viii.

75. Kling, *Fannie Lou Hamer*, 20.

76. Hamer in documentary film *Freedom on My Mind,* produced and directed by Connie Field and Marilyn Mulford (Berkeley, Calif.: Clarity Educational Productions, 1994), quoted in Marsh, *God's Long Summer,* 25.

77. Jordan, *Fannie Lou Hamer,* 39.

78. Hamer, "Fannie Lou Hamer Speaks Out," 56.

79. McMillen, "An Oral History with Fannie Lou Hamer," 19.

80. O'Dell, "Life in Mississippi," 236, 242.

81. Ibid., 235.

82. Hamer, "To Praise Our Bridges," 326–27.

83. Hamer, "It's in Your Hands," 613.

84. Hamer, "Fannie Lou Hamer Speaks Out," 56.

85. Hamer, "Foreword," viii.

86. Author's interview with Victoria Way DeLee, August 8, 1992, Ridgeville, South Carolina. Tape recording.

87. Author's interview with Victoria Way DeLee, July 4, 1988, Ridgeville, South Carolina. Tape recording.

88. Ibid.; Calvin Trillin, "U.S. Journal: Dorchester County, S.C.—Victoria DeLee—In Her Own Words," *New Yorker* 47 (March 27, 1971): 86.

89. Ibid.

90. Author's interview with DeLee, August 8, 1992.

91. Ibid.

92. Author's interview with DeLee, July 4, 1988; Trillin, "U.S. Journal," 86.

93. Author's interview with DeLee, July 4, 1988; author's interview with Thomas H. Ross, Dorchester, South Carolina, March 11, 1994.

94. Author's interview with DeLee, July 4, 1988; Trillin, "U.S. Journal," 86.

95. See Katie Geneva Cannon, "Resources for a Constructive Ethic: The Life and Work of Zora Neale Hurston," in *Katie's Canon,* 79–80, 84–86.

96. Maya Angelou, *Gather Together in My Name* (Toronto: Bantam, 1974), 78–79.

97. Author's interview with DeLee, July 4, 1988; Trillin, "U.S. Journal," 86.

98. Author's interview with DeLee, August 8, 1992.

99. Ibid.; Trillin, "U.S. Journal," 86.

100. Author's interview with DeLee, August 8, 1992.

101. Trillin, "U.S. Journal," 86.

102. Author's interview with DeLee, August 8, 1992.

103. The full name of the denomination is The House of God (the Church of the Living God, the Pillar and Ground of the Truth, Inc.). The denomination was established circa 1903 by an itinerant preacher, now designated denominational founder, elder, and saint, Mary Magdalena Lewis (later Tate), whose pentecostalism may have been connected with the California Azuza Street revivals about the same time. See "General Assembly of the Church of the Living God," *The Constitution Government and General Decree Book* (Chattanooga: New and Living Way, 1923), and *Seventy-fifth Anniversary Yearbook: The Church of the Living God, the Pillar and Ground of the Truth, Inc., 1903–1978*.

104. Author's interview with DeLee, August 8, 1992.

105. See Cheryl Townsend Gilkes, "The Role of Women in the Sanctified Church," *The Journal of Religious Thought* 43 (spring/summer 1986), for a discussion of the independence and fervor of women community workers of the "sanctified" churches.

106. Author's interview with DeLee, July 4, 1988.

107. Ibid.; Trillin, "U.S. Journal," 86–87.

108. Author's interview with JohnEtta Grant Cauthen, Charleston, South Carolina, April 8, 1994, telephone tape recording; Author's interview with DeLee, July 4, 1988.

109. Author's interview with DeLee, July 4, 1988.

110. Ibid.; Trillin, "U.S. Journal," 86–87.

111. Aldon D. Morris, *Origins of the Civil Rights Movement: Black Communities Organizing for Change* (New York: Free Press, 1984), 26; South Carolina Code of Laws, *Statutes at Large* (1956) #741, 1747, #920, 2182; "Propose Open NAACP Roll: Bill Would Require Group to File List," *The [South Carolina] State,* January 25, 1957.

112. County resident Roosevelt Geddis of Givhans says his initial knowledge of DeLee came through these appeals and meetings: "She started working, most a one-family drive, as far as I can remember. She started coming around to the churches and talking to some people about the civil rights. That's how I remember her. . . . That's how she really got to be known to start with. Her plea was for the people of Dorchester County to get together and start . . . some sort of organization. . . ." Author's interview with Roosevelt Geddis, Dorchester, South Carolina, October 26, 1994. Tape recording.

113. Heidi Sinick, "Dealing for the Poor," *Washington Post,* February 8, 1971, B1.

114. Mike Daniel, "Hollings Says He'll Stop FBI Probe," *Charleston News and Courier,* September 29, 1961, A1.

115. See "S.C. Voter Registration History: 1956 to 1979," in *Reports and Resolutions of South Carolina for Fiscal Year Ending 1979* (Columbia, S.C.: State Budget and Control Board), 447. See also "Report of the Secretary of State to the General Assembly of South Carolina," in *Reports and Resolutions of South Carolina for Fiscal Year Ending June 30, 1959* (Columbia, S.C.: State Budget and Control Board, 1959), 222.

116. United States Commission on Civil Rights, *Political Participation,* 72, 114.

117. Author's interview with DeLee, July 4, 1988.

118. United States Commission on Civil Rights, *Political Participation,* 62–63.

119. For example, Fannie Lou Hamer described this phenomenon in Mississippi as well. Ibid., 61–64.

120. Laughlin MacDonald, "An Aristocracy of Voters: The Disfranchisement of Blacks in South Carolina," *South Carolina Law Review* 37 (summer 1986): 568, 570–72. Enacted in 1950, the South Carolina full-slate law invalidated all ballots on which persons voted for more or less than the number of seats open in a multi-member district.

121. James E. Clyburn, Charleston, South Carolina, to Paul Mathias, Columbia, South Carolina, October 20, 1969, South Carolina Council on Human Relations Files, South Caroliniana Collection, University of South Carolina.

122. "Blacks May Support Write-In," *Charlotte Observer,* July 7, 1970, A6; "Black-Oriented Party Head Vows to Dismantle System," *Charleston News and Courier,* September 5, 1970, B12.

123. "Black-Oriented Party Head Vows to Dismantle System," B12.

124. Robert G. Liming, "Mrs. DeLee Says 'Urged to Run,'" *The [South Carolina] State,* January 31, 1971, D3; "Civil Rights Leader Gets UCP First District Nod," *Charleston News and Courier,* January 31, 1971, D1.

125. Liming, "Mrs. DeLee Says 'Urged to Run,'" D3.

126. "Civil Rights Leader Gets UCP First District Nod," D1.

127. Margaret Berry Bethea, "Alienation and Third Parties: A Study of the United Citizens['] Party in South Carolina," master's thesis, University of South Carolina, Columbia, South Carolina, 1973, 22. Bethea writes: "Although it cannot be said with absolute accuracy that the absence of the UCP would have resulted in a Democratic victory in every county, an analysis of black majority precincts comparing votes cast in 1968 to votes cast in

1971 for the Democratic candidates will suggest that the UCP did" affect the Democratic Party's showing in the race.

128. See "Governor Says S.C. 'To Resist Integration,'" *Richmond News Leader,* November 4, 1955; W. D. Workman Jr., "No Integrated Schools for S.C., Says Report to White House Meet," *Charlotte Observer,* November 17, 1955; and "Hollings Praises Assembly for Segregation Actions," *The [South Carolina] State,* May 28, 1960. See also "Two Attack S.C. Segregation Statute Change," *The [South Carolina] State,* May 5, 1960.

129. "Negroes Are Turned Away at 2 Dorchester Schools," *Charleston News and Courier,* August 27, 1965; Jack Bass, "44 School Districts Open; 41 Have Compliance Plans," *The [South Carolina] State,* August 26, 1964, D1.

130. Office of Education, U.S. Department of Health, Education, and Welfare and U.S. Commission on Civil Rights, "Status of School Desegregation in Southern and Border States," an occasional report, March 1966, Southern Regional Council Files, Atlanta University Center Special Collections.

131. *DeLee v. Dorchester County School District Three,* CA#66-183 (USDC S. Carolina 1966).

132. See, for example, "NAACP Asks Protection for Woman," *The [South Carolina] State,* July 25, 1969, B4.

133. Author's interview with DeLee, July 4, 1988. See also United States Commission on Civil Rights, *Political Participation* (Washington, D.C.: Government Printing Office, 1968), 117.

134. Roosevelt Geddis, Ridgeville, to Richard Detreville, Dorchester, January 13, 1969, South Carolina Council on Human Relations Files, South Caroliniana Collection, University of South Carolina.

135. See *DeLee v. Dorchester County School District Three,* "Motion to Add Parties," December 11, 1967; author's interview with DeLee, July 4, 1988; Mordecai Johnson, Florence, to Selected Persons with S.C. School Cases, October 8, 1969, South Carolina Council on Human Relations Files, The South Caroliniana Collection, University of South Carolina.

136. Mordecai Johnson, Florence, to Selected Persons with S.C. School Cases, October 8, 1969; Attorney Fred Moore, Charleston, to Paul Anthony, Atlanta, March 3, 1970, Southern Regional Council Files, Atlanta University Center Special Collections.

137. Author's interview with DeLee, August 8, 1992.

138. Author's interview with DeLee, July 4, 1988.

139. Ibid.

140. Author's interview with DeLee, August 8, 1992.

141. "Mrs. DeLee Arrested after Crash," *The [South Carolina] State,* May 1, 1971, B1.

142. Barbara S. Williams, "Victoria DeLee Denies Charges Lodged by Police," *Charleston News and Courier*, May 8, 1971, B1.

143. Ibid.

144. Barbara S. Williams, "Victoria DeLee Denies Charges Lodged by Police," B1.

145. Author's interview with DeLee, July 4, 1988.

146. "Civil Rights Leader Gets First District Nod," *Charleston News and Courier*, D1.

147. Author's interview with DeLee, August 8, 1992.

Chapter 4: Clara Muhammad

1. C. Eric Lincoln, *The Black Muslims in America* (Boston: Beacon, 1961), 98.

2. I use the term *Muslim* to refer to NOI members in keeping with their self-identification.

3. In 1975, following Elijah Muhammad's death, Clara and Elijah Muhammad's seventh son, Wallace, succeeded his father as leader of the Nation of Islam. Almost immediately, Wallace began to reform the NOI and move toward orthodox Islam through the Sunni denomination. This shift included reversing or dropping several theological claims of Elijah and Clara Muhammad's Nation of Islam doctrine, including that W. D. Fard, who first proselytized Clara and Elijah, was divine, that persons of European descent are devils, and that becoming a Muslim required racial separation. In 1976, Wallace changed the organization's name to the World Community of Islam in the West (WCIW). Later he took the name Warith Deen Mohammed, and again renamed the community, this time calling it the Muslim American Society (MAS), an appellation under which it now functions. The contemporary Nation of Islam was created when some members broke away from the WCIW and, under the leadership of Louis Farrakhan, a minister who served under Elijah Muhammad, revived Elijah Muhammad's earlier teachings. See discussion in Claude Andrew Clegg III, *An Original Man: The Life and Times of Elijah Muhammad* (New York: St. Martin's, 1997), 276–82.

4. Debra Washington Mubashir, "A 'Back to Climb': Clara Muhammad and Female Social Activism within the Nation of Islam," paper presented at the Upper Midwest Regional Meeting of the American Academy of Religion/Society of Biblical Literature (April 20–21, 2001, Luther Seminary, Saint Paul, Minnesota), 5; Ajile A. Rahman, "She Stood by His Side and at Times in His Stead: The Life and Legacy of Sister Clara Muhammad, First Lady of the Nation of Islam" (Ph.D. dissertation, Clark-Atlanta University, Atlanta, Georgia, 1999), 40; FBI File, Clara Muhammad, Memorandum,

SAC, Chicago (100-32519) to SA . . . , May 4, 1962. Note that in all FBI citations, ellipses represent text that was deleted (blacked out with ink) from the original files.

5. Mubashir, "A 'Back to Climb,'" 5; Clegg, *An Original Man,* 12; Rahman, "She Stood by His Side," 40–41; Taylor Branch, *Pillar of Fire: America in the King Years, 1963–1965* (New York: Simon & Schuster, 1998), 16.

6. The FBI reports Clara Muhammad regularly visiting her father in Georgia and giving special attention to him as he neared the end of his life. Quartus Evans died at age ninety-four in Atlanta, Georgia.

7. Mubashir, "A 'Back to Climb,'" 5; Rahman, "She Stood by His Side," 41.

8. Clegg, *An Original Man,* 12–13; Mubashir, "A 'Back to Climb,'" 6.

9. Clegg, *An Original Man,* 16–17; Mubashir, "A 'Back to Climb,'" 6.

10. Rahman, "She Stood by His Side," 18–19; Clegg, *An Original Man,* 19, 14; Mubashir, "A 'Back to Climb,'" 9–11; Lincoln, *The Black Muslims in America,* 73.

11. Mubashir, "A 'Back to Climb,'" 11.

12. Clegg, *An Original Man*, 23.

13. Lincoln, *The Black Muslims in America,* 14–15. Also see, Clegg, *An Original Man,* 35, and Mubashir, "A 'Back to Climb,'" 13.

14. Lincoln, *The Black Muslims in America,* 50, 250.

15. Clara Muhammad, "An Invitation to 22 Million Black Americans," *Muhammad Speaks* 6 (January 13, 1967): 19 (article copied as part of FBI File Memorandum, SAC, Chicago to . . . Correlation Clerk, March 19, 1968). See discussion of Williams, p. 8.

16. Lincoln, *The Black Muslims in America,* 14.

17. Hakim M. Rashid and Zakiyyah Muhammad, "The Sister Clara Muhammad Schools: Pioneers in the Development of Islamic Education in America," *Journal of Negro Education* 61, no. 2 (1992): 178; Mubashir, "A 'Back to Climb,'" 11, 12.

18. Rashid and Muhammad, "The Sister Clara Muhammad Schools," 178.

19. I. Shalaby, "The Role of the School in Cultural Renewal and Identity Development in the Nation of Islam in America" (Ph.D. dissertation, University of Arizona, 1967; University Microfilms, No. 77-11, 958), 11, quoted in Rashid and Muhammad, 181.

20. Lincoln, *The Black Muslims in America,* 250.

21. In 1975, after the death of his father, Wallace D. Muhammad (a.k.a. Warith D. Mohammed) became leader of the Nation of Islam. During that year he began to move the group toward orthodox Islam through the Sunni

branch and eventually renamed the organization the Muslim American Society. See note 3 above.

22. Mubashir, "A 'Back to Climb,'" 13; Rashid and Muhammad, "The Sister Clara Muhammad Schools," 181.

23. Rahman, "She Stood by His Side," 97.

24. Rashid and Muhammad, "The Sister Clara Muhammad Schools," 179; Clegg, *An Original Man,* 35.

25. Rahman, "She Stood by His Side," 48; S. Maryum Muhammad and B. Shakoor-Abdulla, "A Profile: Our First Pioneer Mrs. Clara Muhammad," *Muslim Journal* (October 1996), quoted in Mubashir, "A 'Back to Climb,'" 12.

26. Rahman, "She Stood by His Side," 97; Clegg, *An Original Man,* 39.

27. Rahman, "She Stood by His Side," 98–99; November 5, 1997 interview with W. Deen Mohammed, quoted in Mubashir, "A 'Back to Climb,'" 16–17; FBI Memorandum, SAC, Chicago (100-32519) to . . . Correlation Clerk, March 19, 1968, 5 passim.

28. FBI Memorandum, SAC, Chicago (100-32519*) to . . . Correlation Clerk, January 5, 1967, subsection "The Courier," 16, 19 passim.

29. *Muhammad Speaks* 6 (May 12, 1967), quoted in FBI document, SAC Chicago (10-35635).

30. Rashid and Muhammad, "The Sister Clara Muhammad Schools," 181–82, 184.

31. FBI Office Memorandum, . . . Correlation Clerk to SAC (100-), June 7, 1956.

32. Clegg, *An Original Man,* 85.

33. Mubashir, "A 'Back to Climb,'" 9, says Clara heard of Fard first, while Clegg, *An Original Man,* 23, says Elijah learned of Fard initially through Elijah's father and then introduced Clara to Fard's teachings.

34. Clegg, *An Original Man,* 40.

35. Ibid., 78–80.

36. Ibid., 82, 84; Rahman, "She Stood by His Side," 65.

37. Clegg, *An Original Man,* 86.

38. Ibid., 85, 86.

39. Ibid., 85; FBI Office Memorandum, . . . Correlation Clerk to SAC (100-), June 7, 1956.

40. Clegg, *An Original Man,* 92–93, 95–97; Rahman, "She Stood by His Side," 66–67.

41. Clegg, *An Original Man,* 96–97.

42. Rahman, "She Stood by His Side," 67; Mubashir, "A 'Back to Climb,'" 15–16.

43. FBI File, Clara Muhammad, Document number 100-32519, 28–29.

44. Clegg, *An Original Man,* 97.

45. Rahman, "She Stood by His Side," 71.

46. Ibid., 24, 46.

47. See Cheryl Townsend Gilkes, "'Together and in Harness': Women's Traditions in the Sanctified Church," *Signs: Journal of Women in Culture and Society* 10, no. 4 (1985), and idem, "The Role of Women in the Sanctified Church," *Journal of Religious Thought* 43 (spring/summer 1986).

48. Rahman, "She Stood by His Side," 24.

49. Mubashir, "A 'Back to Climb,'" 15.

50. Lincoln, *The Black Muslims in America,* 83; Clegg, *An Original Man,* 29; Rahman, "She Stood by His Side," 47.

51. FBI Memorandum, SAC, Chicago (100-32519) to SA, June 8, 1961, 8. Also see, FBI Memorandum, SAC, Chicago (100-32519*) to . . . Correlation Clerk, January 5, 1967, subsection "The Courier," 5, and FBI Memo to SAC, Chicago (100-32519), June 8, 1961. In another example, an FBI report on an article from the Muslim newspaper *Muhammad Speaks* (November 20, 1964) says Clara Muhammad wrote in "a spiritual message to black women of America—'Seek Truth and salvation in Islam under the Divine leadership of the Honorable Elijah Muhammad.'" Moreover, she admonished "black women and . . . all Negroes . . . 'Do Not Be Misled . . . There Is No God But Allah and Muhammad Is His Messenger'"(FBI File, Clara Muhammad, document number 100-32519, 18).

52. FBI File, Clara Muhammad, Memoranda December 5, 1963; April 29, 1963; March 5, 1965.

53. Rahman, "She Stood by His Side," 1.

54. Lincoln, *The Black Muslims in America,* 55.

55. Rahman, "She Stood by His Side," 76; Clegg, *An Original Man,* 188–89; FBI File, Clara Muhammad, File Document, Chicago, Illinois, April 30, 1963, "Security Matter: Nation of Islam"; FBI Memorandum, SAC, Chicago (100-32519) to SA . . . , May 4, 1962.

56. Clara Muhammad, "An Invitation to 22 Million Black Americans," 19 (copied in FBI File Memorandum, SAC, Chicago to . . . Correlation Clerk, March 19, 1968).

57. Ibid.

58. *Muhammad Speaks* 3 (July 17, 1964): 7, in FBI File, Clara Muhammad, Document number 100-32519, 18.

59. Rahman, "She Stood by His Side," 46.

60. Clara Muhammad, "An Invitation to 22 Million Black Americans," 19.

61. Ibid.

62. Rashid and Muhammad, "The Sister Clara Muhammad Schools," 178, 179.

63. Lincoln, *The Black Muslims in America,* 250.

64. Cynthia S'thembile West, "Revisiting Female Activism in the 1960s: The Newark Branch Nation of Islam," *The Black Scholar* 26 (fall/winter 1996): 42, 47.

Chapter 5: "Fire Shut Up in My Bones"

1. Diane Nash, "Inside the Sit-ins and Freedom Rides: Testimony of a Southern Student," in Mathew H. Ahmann, ed., *The New Negro* (Notre Dame, Ind.: Fides, 1961), 49.

2. Ibid., 57.

3. David Halberstam, *The Children* (New York: Random House, 1998), 147; Reavis Mitchell and Jessie Carney Smith, "Diane Nash: Civil Rights Activist, Educator," in Jessie Carney Smith, ed., *Notable Black American Women* (Detroit: Gale Research, 1992), 796.

4. Nash, "Inside the Sit-ins," 49.

5. Lynne Olson, *Freedom's Daughters: The Unsung Heroines of the Civil Rights Movement from 1830 to 1970* (New York: Scribner's, 2001), 153; Halberstam, *The Children,* 145–46. See also Kevin K. Gaines, *Uplifting the Race: Black Leadership, Politics, and Culture in the Twentieth Century* (Chapel Hill: University of North Carolina Press, 1996), 4, 5–9 passim; Evelyn Brooks Higginbotham, *Righteous Discontent: The Women's Movement in the Black Baptist Church, 1880–1920* (Cambridge, Mass.: Harvard University Press, 1993), 19–21, 185ff.

6. Halberstam, *The Children,* 146–48.

7. Ibid.

8. Fred Powledge, *Free at Last? The Civil Rights Movement and the People Who Made It* (Boston: Little, Brown, 1991), 208.

9. Henry Hampton and Steve Fayer, with Sarah Flynn, *Voices of Freedom: An Oral History of the Civil Rights Movement from the 1950s through the 1980s* (New York: Bantam, 1990), 55; Nash, "Inside the Sit-ins," 45.

10. Powledge, *Free at Last?* 208.

11. Hampton and Fayer, *Voices of Freedom,* 55.

12. Juan Williams, *Eyes on the Prize: America's Civil Rights Years, 1954–1965* (New York: Viking, 1987), 123–26; Powledge, *Free at Last?* 231.

13. Powledge, *Free at Last?* 208.

14. Williams, *Eyes on the Prize,* 129.

15. Mitchell and Smith, "Diane Nash," 797; Hampton and Fayer, *Voices of Freedom,* 66–67; Olson, *Freedom's Daughters,* 157–59; Halberstam, *The Children,* 141; Williams, *Eyes on the Prize,* 131–33. Williams says students were fined $150.

16. Olson, *Freedom's Daughters,* 159; Powledge, *Free at Last?* 208–9; Halberstam, *The Children,* 213, 233–34.

17. Powledge, *Free at Last,* 208–9.

18. Williams, *Eyes on the Prize,* 133.

19. Powledge, *Free at Last?* 209.

20. Halberstam, *The Children,* 134–35.

21. Olson, *Freedom's Daughters,* 160; Halberstam, *The Children,* 218–19; Sara Evans, *Personal Politics: The Roots of Women's Liberation in the Civil Rights Movement and the New Left* (New York: Random House, 1979), 40.

22. Clayborne Carson, *In Struggle: SNCC and the Black Awakening of the 1960s* (Cambridge, Mass.: Harvard University Press, 1981), 23–24.

23. Ibid., 23; Belinda Robnett, *How Long? How Long? African American Women in the Struggle for Civil Rights* (New York: Oxford University Press, 1997), 102.

24. Carson, *In Struggle,* 28.

25. Ibid., 32; Robnett, *How Long?* 103; Powledge, *Free at Last?* 246–47; Howard Zinn, *SNCC: The New Abolitionists* (Boston: Beacon, 1965), 38–39; Cynthia Griggs Fleming, *Soon We Will Not Cry: The Liberation of Ruby Doris Smith Robinson* (Lantham, Md.: Rowman and Littlefield, 1998), 73, 76–77.

26. Nash, "Inside the Sit-ins," 46.

27. Halberstam, *The Children,* 268.

28. Olson, *Freedom's Daughters,* 160; Halberstam, *The Children,* 268.

29. Olson, *Freedom's Daughters,* 184.

30. James Farmer, *Lay Bare the Heart: An Autobiography of the Civil Rights Movement* (New York: Plume, 1985), 203.

31. Hampton and Fayer, *Voices of Freedom,* 82.

32. Nash, "Inside the Sit-Ins," 53–54.

33. Farmer, *Lay Bare the Heart,* 203ff.; Olson, *Freedom's Daughters,* 184–99; Zinn, *SNCC,* 44ff.; Halberstam, *The Children,* 270ff.; Diane Nash, "Inside the Sit-ins," 53–55; Hampton and Fayer, *Voices of Freedom,* 82; Taylor Branch, *Parting the Waters: America in the King Years, 1954–1963* (New York: Simon & Schuster, 1988), 430 passim.

34. Nash, "Inside the Sit-Ins," 54–55.

35. Olson, *Freedom's Daughters,* 184–99; Nash, "Inside the Sit-ins," 53–55.

36. Powledge, *Free at Last?* 298–99, 307.

37. Lani Guinier, *The Tyranny of the Majority* (New York: Free Press, 1994), 1–20.

38. Zinn, *SNCC,* 58–59; Jeanne Theoharis, "Diane Nash," in Darlene Clark Hine, ed., *Black Women in America: An Historical Encyclopedia* (New York: Carlson, 1993), 835.

39. Theoharis, "Diane Nash," 835; Halberstam, *The Children,* 477–78; Zinn, *SNCC,* 79.

40. Evans, *Personal Politics,* 39–40; Zinn, *SNCC,* 80; Theoharis, "Diane Nash," 836.

41. Hampton and Fayer, *Voices of Freedom,* 173.

42. Ibid., 173; Powledge, *Free at Last,* 619; Olson, *Freedom's Daughters,* 339–42.

43. Diane Nash Bevel, "Journey to North Vietnam," *Freedomways* (spring 1967): 119.

44. Halberstam, *The Children,* 501, 534–35; Theoharis, "Diane Nash," 836; Olson, *Freedom's Daughters,* 403.

45. Nash, "Inside the Sit-ins," 45, 57, 59.

46. Hampton and Fayer, *Voices of Freedom,* 57–58.

47. Nash, "Inside the Sit-ins," 47–49.

48. Ibid., 44–47.

49. Ibid., 44–45, 49.

50. Williams, *Eyes on the Prize,* 138.

51. Ibid., 52–53, 57.

52. Powledge, *Free at Last?* 232.

53. Nash, "Inside the Sit-ins," 58–59, 60.

54. Ibid., 43.

55. Powledge, *Free at Last?* 233.

56. Nash, "Inside the Sit-ins," 53.

57. Ibid., 45.

58. Powledge, *Free at Last?* 232.

59. Ibid., 44.

60. See Evans, *Personal Politics.*

61. Olson, *Freedom's Daughters,* 160.

62. See discussion on p. 9.

63. Andrew Young, *An Easy Burden: The Civil Rights Movement and the Transformation of America* (New York: HarperCollins, 1996), 342.

64. Robnett, *How Long?* 102.

65. Powledge, *Free at Last?* 646.

66. News Release, October 9, 1967, Student Nonviolent Coordinating Committee, recorded in Jacqueline Jones Royster, "A 'Heartbeat' for Liberation: The Reclamation of Ruby Doris Smith," *Sage: A Scholarly Journal on Black Women,* Student Supplement (1988): 65.

67. Evans, *Personal Politics,* 30, 40–41; Clayborne Carson, *In Struggle,* 70.

68. Robnett, *How Long?* 108–9 passim.

69. Fleming, *Soon We Will Not Cry,* 18, 20; William D. Pierson, "Rubye Doris Robinson: Civil Rights Activist," in Smith, *Notable Black American Women*, 948.

70. Fleming, *Soon We Will Not Cry,* 30, 37.

71. Ibid., 29, 31.

72. Ibid., 1618.

73. Ibid., 27–28; Bernice Johnson Reagon, "Rubye Doris Smith Robinson," in Barbara Sicherman and Carol Hurd Green, eds., *Notable American Women: The Modern Period, A Biographical Dictionary* (Cambridge, Mass.: Belknap, 1980), 585.

74. Josephine Carson, *Silent Voices: The Southern Negro Woman Today* (New York: Delacorte, 1969), 253–54. In the book, Carson identifies Robinson as Sarah.

75. Ibid., 254.

76. Royster, "A 'Heartbeat' for Liberation," 65; Fleming, *Soon We Will Not Cry,* 31; Obituary, Ruby Doris Smith, Special Collections, Atlanta University Center, Robert W. Woodruff Library, Atlanta, Georgia.

77. Fleming, *Soon We Will Not Cry,* 28–29.

78. Ibid., 30–31.

79. Reagon, "Rubye Doris Smith Robinson," 585.

80. Ibid., 585; Fleming, *Soon We Will Not Cry,* 36.

81. Karen Elizabeth Vanlandingham, "In Pursuit of a Changing Dream: Spelman College Students and the Civil Rights Movement, 1955–1962" (master's thesis, Emory University, 1985), 67 passim.

82. "Appendix," in David J. Garrow, ed., *Atlanta, Georgia, 1960–1961: Sit-ins and Student Activism* (New York: Carlson, 1989), 187.

83. Vanlandingham, "In Pursuit of a Changing Dream," 3, 74; Zinn, *SNCC,* 17–18.

84. Fleming, *Soon We Will Not Cry,* 68.

85. Ibid., 53.

86. Vanlandingham, "In Pursuit of a Changing Dream," 75, 77–78; Fleming, *Soon We Will Not Cry,* 53–55.

87. Fleming, *Soon We Will Not Cry,* 56.

88. Ibid., 71–72; Vanlandingham, "In Pursuit of a Changing Dream," 78.

89. Carson, *In Struggle,* 25–27, 30; Fleming, *Soon We Will Not Cry,* 70, 72.

90. Halberstam, *The Children,* 267; Fleming, *Soon We Will Not Cry,* 71, 72; Zinn, *SNCC,* 38.

91. Fleming, *Soon We Will Not Cry,* 73.

92. Ibid., 60.

93. Vincent D. Fort, "The Atlanta Sit-in Movement, 1960–1961: An Oral Study," in Garrow, *Atlanta, Georgia,* 150–51.

94. Phyl Garland, "Builders of a New South," *Ebony* 21 (August 1966): 33; Zinn, *SNCC,* 38–39; Fleming, *Soon We Will Not Cry,* 75.

95. Fleming, *Soon We Will Not Cry,* 75.

96. "Spelman Co-ed Returns Home after 30 Days in S. Carolina Jail," *The Atlanta Inquirer,* March 18, 1961.

97. Fleming, *Soon We Will Not Cry,* 76.

98. Garland, "Builders of a New South," 33.

99. Hampton and Fayer, *Voices of Freedom,* 84; Olson, *Freedom's Daughters,* 185.

100. Mary King, *Freedom Song* (New York: William Morrow and Company, 1987), 317.

101. Zinn, *SNCC,* 42–48.

102. Ibid.

103. Gail J. Hardy, *American Women Civil Rights Activists: Bibliographies of 68 Leaders, 1825–1992* (North Carolina: McFarland, 1993), 327.

104. "Freedom Rider Writes: Scripture Reading, Ballet Fill Inmate Leisure Time," *The Atlanta Inquirer,* Saturday, July 1, 1961; Zinn, *SNCC,* 54–55.

105. Zinn, *SNCC,* 55.

106. Hardy, *American Women Civil Rights Activists,* 327.

107. Reagon, "Rubye Doris Smith Robinson," 585; Fleming, *Soon We Will Not Cry,* 88.

108. Reagon, "Rubye Doris Smith Robinson," 585.

109. Royster, "A 'Heartbeat' for Liberation," 65.

110. Vanlandingham, "In Pursuit of a Changing Dream," 74.

111. Fort, "The Atlanta Sit-in Movement," 148–49; Vanlandingham, "In Pursuit of a Changing Dream," 75, 77.

112. Royster, "A 'Heartbeat' for Liberation," 61.

113. Hardy, *American Women Civil Rights Activists,* 327; Reagon, "Rubye Doris Smith Robinson," 585; Royster, "A 'Heartbeat' for Liberation," 65.

114. James Forman, *The Making of Black Revolutionaries* (Seattle: University of Washington Press, 1985), 373; Reagon, "Rubye Doris Smith Robinson," 586; Evans, *Personal Politics,* 95–96.

115. Reagon, "Rubye Doris Smith Robinson," 586.

116. Ruby Doris Smith to Mr. Phillip Tracy, March 26, 1963, SNCC Correspondence Files, Microfilm SNCC Files.

117. Ruby Doris Smith to Mr. Norman Thomas, February 19, 1963; also see, for example, Ruby Doris Smith to Florence Borgmann, October 28, 1962; SNCC Correspondence Files, Microfilm SNCC Files.

118. Ruby Doris Smith to Mr. John Seigenthaler, editor, *The Tennessean,* November 8, 1962, SNCC Correspondence Files, Microfilm SNCC Files.

119. Ruby Doris Smith to George Goss, SSACC, May 17, 1963, SNCC Correspondence Files, Microfilm SNCC Files.

120. Ruby Doris Smith to Moses Davis, May 5, 1964, SNCC Correspondence Files, Microfilm SNCC Files.

121. Reagon, "Rubye Doris Smith Robinson," 586; Hampton and Fayer, *Voices of Freedom,* 204.

122. Royster, "A 'Heartbeat' for Liberation," 65; Reagon, "Rubye Doris Smith Robinson," 586.

123. Cheryl Greenberg, ed., *A Circle of Trust: Remembering SNCC* (New Brunswick, N.J.: Rutgers University Press, 1998), 143.

124. Robnett, *How Long?* 128.

125. Greenberg, *A Circle of Trust,* 138.

126. Josephine Carson, *Silent Voices,* 253.

127. Forman, *The Making of Black Revolutionaries,* 474–75.

128. Evans, *Personal Politics,* 84–85; Reagon, "Rubye Doris Smith Robinson," 586; Fleming, *Soon We Will Not Cry,* 151.

129. Forman, *The Making of Black Revolutionaries,* 480.

130. Carson, *In Struggle,* 144 passim.

131. Reagon, "Rubye Doris Smith Robinson," 586; Evans, *Personal Politics,* 84–85. See also the discussion of the writing of the paper in Casey Hayden, "Fields of Blue," in *Deep in Our Hearts: Nine White Women in the Freedom Movement* by Constance Curry et al. (Athens: University of Georgia Press, 2000), 365 passim.

132. See discussions by Reagon, "Rubye Doris Smith Robinson," 586, and Fleming, *Soon We Will Not Cry,* 155–57 passim. See also Evans, *Personal Politics,* esp. 40–41 and 83–88, for an important analysis of the dynamics of race and gender and Robinson's role in the emergence of women's consciousness. For assertions that Robinson objected to concerns about the role of women in SNCC, see King, *Freedom Song,* 568–69; Lynne Olson, *Freedom's Daughters,* 371; and Curry et al., *Deep in Our Hearts,* especially the essay by Casey Hayden, 333–75, which discusses women's roles but neglects mention of Robinson's perspectives and actions.

133. Forman, *The Making of Black Revolutionaries,* 457.

134. Garland, "Builders of a New South," 31, emphasis added.

135. Carson, *Silent Voices,* 253.

136. Garland, "Builders of a New South," 33.

137. Reagon, "Rubye Doris Smith Robinson," 586; Carson, *In Struggle,* 203–4; Fleming, *Soon We Will Not Cry,* 161.

138. Forman, *The Making of Black Revolutionaries,* 457.

139. Ibid., 472–73.

140. Carson, *In Struggle,* 234–35.

141. Forman, *The Making of Black Revolutionaries,* 480.

142. Ibid., 475–76.

143. SNCC Executive Committee Meeting Minutes, April 12–14, 1965, Holly Springs, Mississippi; Microfilm SNCC Files.

144. Fleming, *Soon We Will Not Cry,* 159–60.

145. Ibid., 172, 180. See complete discussion on pages 169–81.

146. Josephine Carson, *Silent Voices,* 254–55.

147. Carson, *In Struggle,* 239.

148. Ibid., 229–30; Forman, *The Making of Black Revolutionaries,* 519–20. The characterizations of Robinson here by Carson and Forman present her as a pragmatist in regard to what might happen to the organization she hoped would eventually make a significant difference in the political and racial climate, in spite of her own far-left political leanings. Apparently, this meant for Robinson that the survival and building of SNCC as a vehicle should precede openly espousing inflammatory rhetorical positions, which it was not materially equipped to carry out and for which it had no means to defend itself when surveillance or retaliation from the federal government resulted. This may account for perceptions by some persons in SNCC that Robinson characterized their concerns as "diversionary." See, for example, Mary King's discussion in *Freedom Song,* 454 passim.

149. Fleming, *Soon We Will Not Cry,* 56.

150. Ibid., 75.

151. Ibid., 188–89.

152. Forman, *The Making of Black Revolutionaries,* 420.

153. Ibid., 475.

Chapter 6: Testimony, Witness, and Civic Life

1. Sue Thrasher and Casey Hayden, Interview with Ella Baker, April 19, 1977, New York City, Southern Oral History Program, Southern Oral History Collection, University of North Carolina at Chapel Hill, 25.

2. Author's interview with Victoria Way DeLee, Ridgeville, South Carolina, August 8, 1992, tape recording; Calvin Trillin, "U.S. Journal: Dorchester County, S.C.—Victoria DeLee—In Her Own Words," *New Yorker* 47 (March 27, 1971): 86.

3. Trillin, "U.S. Journal," 86.

4. Ellen Cantarow and Susan O'Malley, *Moving the Mountain: Women Working for Social Change* (Old Westbury, N.Y.: Feminist Press, 1980), 60–61.

5. Septima Poinsette Clark, *Echo in My Soul* (New York: Dutton, 1962), 132.

6. Fannie Lou Hamer, "Sick and Tired of Being Sick and Tired," *Katallagete* (fall 1968): 25.

7. Author's interview with Victoria Way DeLee, August 8, 1992.

8. Diane Nash, "Inside the Sit-ins and Freedom Rides: Testimony of a Southern Student," in Mathew H. Ahmann, ed., *The New Negro* (Notre Dame, Ind.: Fides, 1961), 43.

9. Cynthia Griggs Fleming, *Soon We Will Not Cry: The Liberation of Ruby Doris Smith Robinson* (Lantham, Md.: Rowman and Littlefield, 1998), 56.

10. Clara Muhammad, "An Invitation to 22 Million Black Americans," *Muhammad Speaks* 6 (January 13, 1967): 19 (copied in FBI File Memorandum, SAC, Chicago to . . . Correlation Clerk, March 19, 1968).

11. This characterization of behind-the-scenes work coincides with a description of Baker's work by Barbara Ransby. See Barbara Ransby, "Behind-the-Scenes View of a Behind-the-Scenes Organizer: The Roots of Ella Baker's Political Passions," in Bettye Collier-Thomas and V. P. Franklin, eds., *Sisters in the Struggle: African American Women in the Civil Rights–Black Power Movement* (New York: New York University Press, 2001).

12. Ella Baker in Joanne Grant, director, *Fundi: The Story of Ella Baker* (16mm; New Day Films, United States, 1981).

13. Fannie Lou Hamer, "Foreword" to *Stranger at the Gates: A Summer in Mississippi* by Tracy Sugarman (New York: Hill and Wang, 1966), viii.

14. Nash, "Inside the Sit-ins," 45, 49.

15. Ella Baker, "Developing Community Leadership," in Gerda Lerner, ed., *Black Women in White America: A Documentary History* (New York: Vintage, 1973), 347.

16. Clark, *Echo in My Soul,* 48.

17. Septima Poinsette Clark, "Citizenship and the Gospel," *Journal of Black Studies* 10 (June 1980): 464.

18. Baker, "Developing Community Leadership," 347.

19. Clark, *Echo in My Soul,* 159.

20. Hamer, "Sick and Tired," 25.

21. Fred Powledge, *Free at Last? The Civil Rights Movement and the People Who Made It* (Boston: Little, Brown, 1991), 232.

22. See discussion by Katie Geneva Cannon, "The Emergence of Black Feminist Consciousness," in Letty M. Russell, ed., *Feminist Interpretation of the Bible* (Philadelphia: Westminster, 1985), 30 passim; Katie Geneva Cannon, *Black Womanist Ethics* (Atlanta: Scholars Press, 1988), 4 passim; Delores S. Williams, *Sisters in the Wilderness: The Challenge of Womanist God-Talk* (Maryknoll, N.Y.: Orbis, 1993), 108, 206 passim; and Delores S. Williams, "Womanist Theology: Black Women's Voices," in Leon Howell and Vivian Lindemayer, ed., *Ethics in the Present Tense: Readings Christianity and Crisis, 1966–1991* (New York: Friendship, 1991), 67 passim.

23. Hamer, "Foreword," viii.

24. Ibid., ix.

25. Baker, "Developing Community Leadership," 347.

26. John Britton, "Interview with Ella Baker: June 19, 1968," Moorland-Spingarn Collection, Howard University, Washington, D.C., quoted in Charles Payne, "Ella Baker and Models of Social Change," *Signs: Journal of Women in Culture and Society* 14 (summer 1989): 898.

27. For a discussion of theological belief and humanism as sources of vitalities of the Civil Rights Movement, see Rosetta E. Ross, "From Civil Rights to Civic Participation," *Journal of the Interdenominational Theological Center* 28 (fall 2000/spring 2001), esp. 44–46.

Bibliography

Allen, Zita. *Black Women Leaders of the Civil Rights Movement.* New York: Franklin Watts, 1996.

Angelou, Maya. *Gather Together in My Name.* Toronto: Bantam, 1974.

Baker, Ella. "Address to Mass Meeting in Hattiesburg, Mississippi." January 21, 1964. Full text in appendix to Catherine M. Orr, "'The Struggle Is Eternal': A Rhetorical Biography of Ella Baker." Master's thesis, University of North Carolina at Chapel Hill, 1991.

———. "Developing Community Leadership." In *Black Women in White America: A Documentary History.* Edited by Gerda Lerner. New York: Vintage, 1973.

Baker, Ella, and Marvel Cook. "The Bronx Slave Market." *The Crisis* (November 1935).

Bass, Jack. "44 School Districts Open; 41 Have Compliance Plans." *The [South Carolina] State,* August 26, 1964.

Bethea, Margaret Berry. "Alienation and Third Parties: A Study of the United Citizens' Party in South Carolina." Master's thesis, University of South Carolina, 1973.

Bevel, Diane Nash. "Journey to North Vietnam." *Freedomways* (spring 1967).

Billingsley, Andrew. *Mighty like a River: The Black Church and Social Reform.* New York: Oxford University Press, 1999.

Black, Eric. "Mondale's Retrospective Stirs Up Memories of 1964 Convention." *Minneapolis Star Tribune,* February 12, 2000.

"Black-Oriented Party Head Vows to Dismantle System." *Charleston News and Courier,* September 5, 1970.

"Blacks May Support Write-In." *Charlotte Observer,* July 7, 1970.

Branch, Taylor. *Parting the Waters: America in the King Years, 1954–1963.* New York: Simon & Schuster, 1988.

———. *Pillar of Fire: America in the King Years, 1963–1965.* New York: Simon & Schuster, 1998.

Brooks, Evelyn. "Religion, Politics, and Gender: The Leadership of Nannie Helen Burroughs." *The Journal of Religious Thought* 44:2 (winter/spring 1988).

Brown, Cynthia Stokes. "Septima Clark: Educator, Humanitarian, Civil Rights Activist." In *Notable Black American Women*. Edited by Jessie Carney Smith. Detroit: Gale Research, 1992.

Burroughs, Nannie Helen. *New and Old Paths to Fertile Fields*. Washington, D.C.: Women's Convention Auxiliary to the National Baptist Convention, n.d.

———. "Unload Your Uncle Toms." In *Black Women in White America: A Documentary History*. Edited by Gerda Lerner. New York: Vintage, 1973.

———. *What Do You Think?* Washington, D.C.: n.p., n.d. [circa 1950].

Camp, Helen C. "Fannie Lou Townsend Hamer." In *American Reformers: An H. W. Wilson Biographical Dictionary*. Edited by Alden Whitman. New York: Wilson, 1985.

Cannon, Katie Geneva. *Black Womanist Ethics*. Atlanta: Scholars Press, 1988.

———. "The Emergence of Black Feminist Consciousness." In *Feminist Interpretation of the Bible*. Edited by Letty M. Russell. Philadelphia: Westminster, 1985.

———. *Katie's Canon: Womanism and the Soul of the Black Community*. New York: Continuum, 1995.

———. "Moral Wisdom in the Black Women's Literary Tradition." In *The Annual of the Society of Christian Ethics*. Edited by Larry L. Rasmussen. Vancouver: The Society of Christian Ethics, 1984.

———. "Resources for a Constructive Ethic in the Life and Work of Zora Neale Hurston." *Journal of Feminist Studies in Religion* 1 (spring 1985).

Cantarow, Ellen, and Susan O'Malley. *Moving the Mountain: Women Working for Social Change*. Old Westbury, N.Y.: Feminist Press, 1980.

Carson, Clayborne. *In Struggle: SNCC and the Black Awakening of the 1960s*. Cambridge, Mass.: Harvard University Press, 1981.

Carson, Josephine. *Silent Voices: The Southern Negro Woman Today*. New York: Delacorte, 1969.

"Civil Rights Leader Gets UCP First District Nod." *Charleston News and Courier*, January 31, 1971.

Clark, Septima Poinsette. "The Bible and the Ballot." Septima Clark Papers, Box I, Number 21, n.d., Special Collections, the College of Charleston Libraries, Charleston, South Carolina.

———. "The Christian as a Patriot." Septima Clark Papers, Box I, Number 25, n.d., Special Collections, the College of Charleston Libraries, Charleston, South Carolina.

———. "Citizenship and the Gospel." *Journal of Black Studies* 10:4 (June 1980).

———. *Echo in My Soul.* New York: Dutton, 1962.

———. *Ready from Within: A First Person Narrative.* Edited by Cynthia Stokes Brown. Trenton: Africa World Press, 1990.

———. "The Vocation of Black Scholarship: Identifying the Enemy." Handwritten manuscript. Septima Clark Papers, Box I, Number 74, n.d., Special Collections, College of Charleston Libraries, Charleston, South Carolina.

———. "What Religion Does." Typewritten note cards for a speech. Septima Clark Papers, Box I, Number 76, n.d., Special Collections, College of Charleston Libraries, Charleston, South Carolina.

———. "Why I Believe There Is a God." Unpublished speech. Septima Clark Papers, Box I, Number 77, n.d., Special Collections, College of Charleston Libraries, Charleston, South Carolina.

Clegg, Andrew, III. *An Original Man: The Life and Times of Elijah Muhammad.* New York: St. Martin's, 1997.

Coleman, Will. *Tribal Talk: Black Theology, Hermeneutics, and African/American Ways of "Telling the Story."* University Park: Pennsylvania State University Press, 2000.

Collier-Thomas, Bettye, and V. P. Franklin, editors. *Sisters in the Struggle: African American Women in the Civil Rights–Black Power Movement.* New York: New York University Press, 2001.

Curry, Constance, et al. *Deep in Our Hearts: Nine White Women in the Freedom Movement.* Athens: University of Georgia Press, 2000.

Dallard, Shyrlee. *Ella Baker: A Leader behind the Scenes.* Englewood Cliffs, N.J.: Silver Burdette, 1990.

Daniel, Mike. "Hollings Says He'll Stop FBI Probe." *Charleston News and Courier,* September 29, 1961.

Davis, Vanessa Lynn. "Midwifery and Grassroots Politics: Ella Jo Baker and Her Philosophy of Community Development." Master's thesis, Vanderbilt University, Nashville, Tennessee, 1992.

DeLee v. Dorchester County School District Three, CA#66-183 (USDC S. Carolina 1966).

DeMuth, Jerry. "'Tired of Being Sick and Tired.'" *The Nation* 198:1 (June 1, 1964).

Earl, Riggins R., Jr. *Dark Symbols, Obscure Signs: God, Self and Community in the Slave Mind.* New York: Orbis, 1993.

Easter, Opal V. *Nannie Helen Burroughs.* New York: Garland, 1995.

Elliott, Aprele. "Ella Baker: Free Agent in the Civil Rights Movement." *Journal of Black Studies* 26:5 (May 1966).

Elliott, Joan Curl. “Ella Baker.” In *Notable Black American Women*. Edited by Jessie Carney Smith. Detroit: Gale Research, 1992.

Evans, Sara. *Personal Politics: The Roots of Women's Liberation in the Civil Rights Movement and the New Left*. New York: Random House, 1979.

Farmer, James. *Lay Bare the Heart: An Autobiography of the Civil Rights Movement*. New York: Plume, 1985.

FBI File, Clara Muhammad. FOIPA No. 432856.

Fleming, Cynthia Griggs. *Soon We Will Not Cry: The Liberation of Ruby Doris Smith Robinson*. Lantham, Md.: Rowman and Littlefield, 1998.

Fletcher, Juanita. “Nannie Helen Burroughs.” In *Notable American Women, The Modern Period: A Biographical Dictionary.* Edited by Barbara Sicherman and Carol Hurd Green. Cambridge, Mass.: Belknap, 1980.

Forman, James. *The Making of Black Revolutionaries*. Seattle: University of Washington Press, 1985.

Fort, Vincent D. “The Atlanta Sit-in Movement, 1960–1961: An Oral Study.” In *Atlanta, Georgia, 1960–1961: Sit-ins and Student Activism*. Edited by David J. Garrow. New York: Carlson, 1989.

Fraser, Gerald. Obituary, *New York Times,* December 17, 1986.

“Freedom Rider Writes: Scripture Reading, Ballet Fill Inmate Leisure Time.” *The Atlanta Inquirer,* July 1, 1961.

Gaines, Kevin K. *Uplifting the Race: Black Leadership, Politics, and Culture in the Twentieth Century*. Chapel Hill: University of North Carolina Press, 1996.

Garland, Phyl. “Builders of a New South.” *Ebony* 21 (August 1966).

Garrow, David, J. *Bearing the Cross: Martin Luther King, Jr. and the Southern Christian Leadership Conference*. New York: Vintage, 1988.

———, editor. *Atlanta, Georgia, 1960–1961: Sit-ins and Student Activism*. New York: Carlson, 1989.

General Assembly of the Church of the Living God. *The Constitution Government and General Decree Book*. Chattanooga: New and Living Way Publishers, 1923.

Genovese, Eugene. *Roll, Jordan, Roll: The World the Slaves Made*. New York: Pantheon, 1974.

Gilbert, Olive, and Frances W. Titus. *The Narrative of Sojourner Truth*. New York: Arno, 1968, 1878.

Gilkes, Cheryl Townsend. “Building in Many Places: Multiple Commitments and Ideologies in Black Women's Community Work.” In *Women and the Politics of Empowerment*. Edited by Ann Bookman and Sandra Morgan. Philadelphia: Temple University Press, 1988.

———. "Going Up for the Oppressed: The Career Mobility of Black Women Community Workers." *Journal of Social Issues* 39 (fall 1983).

———. "'If It Wasn't for the Women . . .': African American Women, Community Work, and Social Change." In *Women of Color in U.S. Society.* Edited by Maxine Baca Zinn and Bonnie Thornton Dill. Philadelphia: Temple University Press, 1994.

———. "The Role of Women in the Sanctified Church." *Journal of Religious Thought* 43:1 (spring/summer 1986).

———. "The Roles of Church and Community Mothers: Ambivalent American Sexism or Fragmented African Familyhood." *Journal of Feminist Studies in Religion* 2 (spring 1986).

———. "Successful Rebellious Professionals: The Black Woman's Professional Identity and Community Commitment." *Psychology of Women Quarterly* 6 (spring 1982).

———. "'Together and in Harness': Women's Traditions in the Sanctified Church." *Signs: Journal of Women in Culture and Society* 10:4 (1985).

"Governor Says S.C. 'To Resist Integration.'" *Richmond News Leader*, November 4, 1955.

Grant, Jacquelyn. "Black Theology and the Black Woman." In *Black Theology: A Documentary History.* Edited by Gayraud S. Wilmore and James H. Cone. Maryknoll, N.Y.: Orbis, 1979.

———. "Fannie Lou Hamer." In *Notable Black American Women.* Edited by Jessie Carney Smith. Detroit: Gale Research, 1992.

———. *White Women's Christ and Black Women's Jesus*. Atlanta: Scholars Press, 1989.

———. "Womanist Theology: Black Women's Experience; as a Source for Doing Theology." In *Black Theology: A Documentary History, Volume 2: 1980–1992.* Edited by James H. Cone and Gayraud S. Wilmore. Maryknoll, N.Y.: Orbis, 1993.

Grant, Joanne. *Ella Baker: Freedom Bound*. New York: Wiley and Sons, 1998.

———, director. *Fundi: The Story of Ella Baker*. 16mm. New Day Films, United States, 1981.

Greenberg, Cheryl, editor. *A Circle of Trust: Remembering SNCC*. New Brunswick, N.J.: Rutgers University Press, 1998.

Guinier, Lani. *The Tyranny of the Majority: Fundamental Fairness in Representative Democracy*. New York: Free Press, 1994.

Halberstam, David. *The Children*. New York: Random House, 1998.

Hamer, Fannie Lou. "Fannie Lou Hamer Speaks Out." *Essence* 1:6 (October 1971).

———. "Foreword." *Stranger at the Gates: A Summer in Mississippi* by Tracy Sugarman. New York: Hill and Wang, 1967.

———. "It's in Your Hands." *Black Women in White America: A Documentary History.* Edited by Gerda Lerner. New York: Vintage, 1973.

———. "Sick and Tired of Being Sick and Tired." *Katallagete* (fall 1968).

———. "To Praise Our Bridges." *Mississippi Writers: Reflections of Childhood and Youth, Volume 2: Nonfiction.* Edited by Dorothy Abbott. Jackson: University of Mississippi Press, 1986.

Hampton, Henry, and Steve Fayer, with Sarah Flynn. *Voices of Freedom: An Oral History of the Civil Rights Movement from the 1950s through the 1980s.* New York: Bantam, 1990.

Hardy, Gail J. *American Women Civil Rights Activists: Bibliographies of 68 Leaders, 1825–1992.* Jefferson, N.C.: McFarland, 1993.

Hayden, Casey. "Fields of Blue." In *Deep in Our Hearts: Nine White Women in the Freedom Movement* by Constance Curry et al. Athens: University of Georgia Press, 2000.

Higginbotham, Evelyn Brooks. *Righteous Discontent: The Women's Movement in the Black Baptist Church, 1880–1920.* Cambridge, Mass.: Harvard University Press, 1993.

"Hollings Praises Assembly for Segregation Actions." *The [South Carolina] State,* May 28, 1960.

Hoyt, Thomas, Jr. "Testimony." *Practicing Our Faith: A Way of Life for a Searching People.* Edited by Dorothy C. Bass. San Francisco: Jossey-Bass, 1997.

"Interview with Ella Baker." *The Urban Review* 4:3 (May 1970).

Johnson, Clifton H., editor. *God Struck Me Dead: Voices of Ex-Slaves.* Cleveland: Pilgrim, 1993.

Jordan, June. *Fannie Lou Hamer.* New York: Crowell, 1972.

King, Mary. *Freedom Song: A Personal Story of the 1960s Civil Rights Movement.* New York: Morrow, 1987.

Kling, Susan. *Fannie Lou Hamer: A Biography.* Chicago: Women for Racial and Economic Equality, 1979.

Ladner, Joyce A. "'Black Women as Do-ers': The Social Responsibility of Black Women." *Sage: A Scholarly Journal on Black Women* 4:1 (summer 1989).

Lee, Chana Kai. "Anger, Memory, and Personal Power: Fannie Lou Hamer and Civil Rights Leadership." In *Sisters in the Struggle: African American Women in the Civil Rights–Black Power Movement.* Edited by Bettye Collier-Thomas and V. P. Franklin. New York: New York University Press, 2001.

———. *For Freedom's Sake: The Life of Fannie Lou Hamer*. Urbana: University of Illinois Press, 1999.

Levine, Lawrence. *Slave Culture and Slave Consciousness*. New York: Oxford University Press, 1977.

Liming, Robert G. "Mrs. DeLee Says 'Urged to Run.'" *The [South Carolina] State,* January 31, 1971.

Lincoln, C. Eric. *The Black Muslims in America*. Boston: Beacon, 1961.

Lincoln, C. Eric, and Larry Mamiya. *The Black Church in the African American Experience*. Durham: Duke University Press, 1990.

MacDonald, Laughlin. "An Aristocracy of Voters: The Disfranchisement of Blacks in South Carolina." *South Carolina Law Review* 37 (summer 1986).

McFadden, Grace Jordan, director. *Oral Recollections of Septima Poinsette Clark*. Columbia: University of South Carolina Instructional Services, 1980. Video recording.

———. "Septima P. Clark and the Struggle for Human Rights." In *Women in the Civil Rights Movement: Trailblazers and Torchbearers, 1941–1965*. Edited by Vicki L. Crawford, Jacqueline Anne Rouse, and Barbara Woods. New York: Carlson, 1990.

———. "Septima Poinsette Clark." In *Black Women in America: An Historical Encyclopedia,* volume 2. Edited by Darlene Clark Hine. New York: Carlson, 1993.

Marsh, Charles. *God's Long Summer: Stories of Faith and Civil Rights*. Princeton: Princeton University Press, 1997.

Mills, Kay. *This Little Light of Mine: The Life of Fannie Lou Hamer*. New York: Dutton, 1993.

Mitchell, Reavis, and Jessie Carney Smith. "Diane Nash: Civil Rights Activist, Educator." In *Notable Black American Women*. Edited by Jessie Carney Smith. Detroit: Gale Research, 1992.

Morgan, Barbara L. "Fannie Lou Townsend Hamer." In *American Women Civil Rights Activists: Bibliographies of 68 Leaders, 1825–1992*. Jefferson, N.C.: McFarland, 1995.

Morris, Aldon. *The Origins of the Civil Rights Movement: Black Communities Organizing for Change*. New York: Free Press, 1984.

"Mrs. DeLee Arrested after Crash." *The [South Carolina] State,* May 1, 1971.

Mubashir, Debra Washington. "A 'Back to Climb': Clara Muhammad and Female Social Activism within the Nation of Islam." Paper presented at the Upper Midwest Regional Meeting of the American Academy of Religion/Society of Biblical Literature, April 20–21, 2001, Luther Seminary, Saint Paul, Minnesota.

Mueller, Carol. "Ella Baker and the Origins of 'Participatory Democracy.'" In *Women in the Civil Rights Movement: Trailblazers and Torchbearers, 1941–1965*. Edited by Vicki L. Crawford, Jacqueline Anne Rouse, Barbara Woods. New York: Carlson, 1990.

Muhammad, Clara. "An Invitation to 22 Million Black Americans." *Muhammad Speaks* 6:17 (January 13, 1967).

"NAACP Asks Protection for Woman." *The [South Carolina] State,* July 25, 1969, B4.

Nash, Diane. "Inside the Sit-ins and Freedom Rides: Testimony of a Southern Student." In *The New Negro*. Edited by Mathew H. Ahmann. Notre Dame, Ind.: Fides, 1961.

"Negroes Are Turned Away at 2 Dorchester Schools." *Charleston News and Courier,* August 27, 1965.

O'Dell, J. H. "Life in Mississippi: An Interview with Fannie Lou Hamer." *Freedomways* 5 (1965).

Office of Education, U.S. Department of Health, Education, and Welfare, and U.S. Commission on Civil Rights. "Status of School Desegregation in Southern and Border States." An occasional report, March 1966, Southern Regional Council Files, Atlanta University Center Special Collections.

Olson, Lynn. *Freedom's Daughters: The Unsung Heroines of the Civil Rights Movement from 1830 to 1970*. New York: Scribner's, 2001.

Orr, Catherine M. "'The Struggle is Eternal': A Rhetorical Biography of Ella Baker." Master's thesis, University of North Carolina at Chapel Hill, 1991.

Painter, Nell Irvin. "Sojourner Truth." In *Black Women in America: An Historical Encyclopedia,* volume 2. Edited by Darlene Clark Hine. New York: Carlson, 1993.

———. *Sojourner Truth: A Life, A Symbol*. New York: Norton, 1996.

Paris, Peter. *The Social Teaching of the Black Churches*. Philadelphia: Fortress, 1985.

Payne, Charles. "Ella Baker and Models of Social Change" *Signs: Journal of Women in Culture and Society* 14:4 (summer 1989).

Peterson, Franklynn. "Fannie Lou Hamer: Mother of Black Women's Lib." *Sepia* 21 (December 1972).

———. "Sunflowers Don't Grow in Sunflower County." *Sepia* 19 (February 1970).

Pierson, William D. "Ruby Doris Robinson: Civil Rights Activist." In *Notable Black American Women*. Edited by Jessie Carney Smith. Detroit: Gale Research, 1992.

Powledge, Fred. *Free at Last? The Civil Rights Movement and the People Who Made It*. Boston: Little, Brown, 1991.

"Propose Open NAACP Roll: Bill Would Require Group to File List." *The [South Carolina] State,* January 25, 1957.

Raboteau, Albert J. *Canaan Land: A Religious History of African Americans*. New York: Oxford University Press, 1999.

———. *Slave Religion: The "Invisible Institution" in the Antebellum South*. Oxford: Oxford University Press, 1978.

Rahman, Ajile A. "She Stood by His Side and at Times in His Stead: The Life and Legacy of Sister Clara Muhammad, First Lady of the Nation of Islam." Ph.D. dissertation, Graduate School of Arts and Sciences, Clark-Atlanta University, Atlanta, Georgia, 1999.

Raines, Howell. *My Soul Is Rested: Movement Days in the Deep South Remembered*. New York: Penguin, 1983.

Ransby, Barbara. "Ella J. Baker and the Black Radical Tradition." Ph.D. dissertation, University of Michigan, Ann Arbor, 1996.

———. "Ella Josephine Baker." In *Black Women in America: An Historical Encyclopedia,* volume 2. Edited by Darlene Clark Hine. New York: Carlson, 1993.

Rashid, Hakim M., and Zakiyyah Muhammad. "The Sister Clara Muhammad Schools: Pioneers in the Development of Islamic Education in America." *Journal of Negro Education* 61:2 (1992).

Reagon, Bernice Johnson. "Rubye Doris Smith Robinson." In *Notable American Women: The Modern Period, A Biographical Dictionary*. Edited by Barbara Sicherman and Carol Hurd Green. Cambridge, Mass.: Belknap, 1980.

"Report of the Secretary of State to the General Assembly of South Carolina." In *Reports and Resolutions of South Carolina for Fiscal Year Ending June 30, 1959*. Columbia, S.C.: State Budget and Control Board, 1959.

Riggs, Marcia. *Awake, Arise, and Act: A Womanist Call for Black Liberation*. Cleveland: Pilgrim, 1994.

Robnett, Belinda. *How Long? How Long? African American Women in the Struggle for Civil Rights*. New York: Oxford University Press, 1997.

Ross, Rosetta E. "From Civil Rights to Civic Participation." *Journal of the Interdenominational Theological Center* 28:1, 2 (fall 2000/spring 2001).

Royster, Jacqueline Jones. "A 'Heartbeat' for Liberation: The Reclamation of Ruby Doris Smith." *Sage: A Scholarly Journal on Black Women,* Student Supplement (1988).

Seventy-fifth Anniversary Yearbook: The Church of the Living God, the Pillar and Ground of the Truth, Inc., 1903–1978. N.p.: n.d.

Sinick, Heidi. "Dealing for the Poor." *Washington Post,* February 8, 1971, B1.

SNCC [Student Nonviolent Coordinating Committee] Executive Committee Meeting Minutes, April 12–14, 1965, Holly Springs, Mississippi. Student Nonviolent Coordinating Committee Files. Microfilm.

South Carolina Code of Laws. *Statutes at Large* (1956) #741, 1747, #920, 2182.

"S[outh] C[arolina] Voter Registration History: 1956 to 1979." In *Reports and Resolutions of South Carolina for Fiscal Year Ending 1979.* Columbia, S.C.: State Budget and Control Board, n.d..

"Spelman Co-ed Returns Home after 30 Days in S. Carolina Jail." *Atlanta Inquirer,* March 18, 1961.

Stanton, Elizabeth Cady, Susan B. Anthony, and Matilda Joslyn Gage, editors. *History of Woman Suffrage*, volume 1. New York: Fowler and Wells, 1881.

Sterling, Dorothy. *We Are Your Sisters: Black Women in the Nineteenth Century*. New York: Norton, 1984.

Theoharis, Jeanne. "Diane Nash." In *Black Women in America: An Historical Encyclopedia.* Edited by Darlene Clark Hine. New York: Carlson, 1993.

Trillin, Calvin. "U.S. Journal: Dorchester County, S.C.—Victoria DeLee in Her Own Words." *New Yorker* 47 (March 27, 1971).

"Two Attack S.C. Segregation Statute Change." *The [South Carolina] State,* May 5, 1960.

United States Commission on Civil Rights. *Political Participation: A Study of Participation by Negroes in Electoral and Political Processes in Ten Southern States since the Passage of the Voting Rights Act of 1965.* Washington, D.C.: Government Printing Office, 1968.

Vanlandingham, Karen Elizabeth. "In Pursuit of a Changing Dream: Spelman College Students and the Civil Rights Movement, 1955–1962." Master's thesis, Emory University, 1985.

Walker, Alice. *In Search of Our Mothers' Gardens: Womanist Prose.* San Diego: Harvest, 1983.

West, Cornel. *Prophesy Deliverance! An Afro-American Revolutionary Christianity*. Philadelphia: Westminster, 1982.

West, Cynthia S'thembile. "Revisiting Female Activism in the 1960s: The Newark Branch Nation of Islam." *The Black Scholar* 26:3–4 (fall/winter 1996).

Williams, Barbara S. "Victoria DeLee Denies Charges Lodged by Police." *Charleston News and Courier,* May 8, 1971, B1.

Williams, Delores S. *Sisters in the Wilderness: The Challenge of Womanist God-Talk*. New York: Orbis, 1993.

———. S.v. "Theology, Womanist." In *Dictionary of Feminist Theologies.* Edited by Letty M. Russell and J. Shannon Clarkson. Louisville: Westminster John Knox, 1996.

———. "Womanist Theology: Black Women's Voices." In *Ethics in the Present Tense: Readings in Christianity and Crisis, 1966–1991.* Edited by Leon Howell and Vivian Lindemayer. New York: Friendship, 1991.

Williams, Juan. *Eyes on the Prize: America's Civil Rights Years, 1954–1965.* New York: Viking, 1987.

Wilmore, Gayraud. *Black Religion and Black Radicalism: An Interpretation of the Religious History of Afro-American People.* New York: Orbis, 1986.

Workman, W. D., Jr. "No Integrated Schools for S.C., Says Report to White House Meet." *Charlotte Observer,* November 17, 1955.

Young, Andrew. *An Easy Burden: The Civil Rights Movement and the Transformation of America.* New York: HarperCollins, 1996.

Zinn, Howard. *SNCC: The New Abolitionists.* Boston: Beacon, 1964.

Index